Chinese Citizenship

This book makes a novel contribution to the study of citizenship by examining how individuals at the margins of Chinese society deal with state efforts to transform them into model citizens.

Based on extensive original research, this book examines how such individuals experienced the rights and responsibilities of Chinese citizenship in the late 1990s and early 2000s. Arguing that social and cultural citizenship have had a greater impact on people's lives than civil and political citizenship, the seven case studies in this book present intimate portraits of the conflicted identities of marginalized individuals, such as farmers, criminals, ethnic minorities, the urban poor, rural migrant children in the cities, mainland migrants in Hong Kong and Chinese youth studying abroad, as they struggle to negotiate the perilous dilemmas presented by globalization and neoliberalism. By examining the perspectives of marginal groups, this book highlights the conflicts and tensions embedded in the concept of Chinese citizenship itself.

Drawing on a diverse array of theories and methods from anthropology, sociology, education, geography, political science, cultural studies and development studies, *Chinese Citizenship* presents fresh perspectives and highlights the often devastating consequences that citizenship distinctions can have on Chinese lives.

Vanessa L. Fong is an Assistant Professor in the Graduate School of Education at Harvard University. Her publications include *Only Hope: Coming of Age under China's One-Child Policy* (Stanford University Press, 2004), *Women in Republican China* (co-edited with Hua R. Lan, M.E. Sharpe, 1999), and articles on identity, nationalism, globalization, gender and population in China.

Rachel Murphy is a research fellow in the Contemporary Chinese Studies Programme and Pembroke College, University of Oxford. Her publications include *How Migrant Labour is Changing Rural China* (Cambridge University Press, 2002) and articles on rural development, entrepreneurship, education, gender and population in China.

Routledge Studies on the Chinese Economy

Series Editor
Peter Nolan, University of Cambridge

Founding Series Editors
Peter Nolan, University of Cambridge and
Dong Fureng, Beijing University

The aim of this series is to publish original, high-quality, research-level work by both new and established scholars in the West and the East, on all aspects of the Chinese economy, including studies of business and economic history.

1 **The Growth of Market Relations in Post-reform Rural China**
A Micro-Analysis of Peasants, Migrants and Peasant Entrepreneurs
Hiroshi Sato

2 **The Chinese Coal Industry: An Economic History**
Elspeth Thomson

3 **Sustaining China's Economic Growth in the Twenty-First Century**
Edited by Shujie Yao & Xiaming Liu

4 **China's Poor Regions: Rural-urban migration, poverty, economic reform and urbanisation**
Mei Zhang

5 **China's Large Enterprises and the Challenge of Late Industrialization**
Dylan Sutherland

6 **China's Economic Growth**
Yanrui Wu

7 **The Employment Impact of China's World Trade Organisation Accession**
A.S. Bhalla and S. Qiu

8 **Catch-Up and Competitiveness in China**
The Case of Large Firms in the Oil Industry
Jin Zhang

9 **Corporate Governance in China**
Jian Chen

10 **The Theory of the Firm and Chinese Enterprise Reform**
The Case of China International Trust and Investment Corporation
Qin Xiao

11 **Globalisation, Transition and Development in China**
The Case of the Coal Industry
Huaichuan Rui

12 **China Along the Yellow River**
Reflections on Rural Society
Cao Jinqing, translated by Nicky Harman and Huang Ruhua

13 **Economic Growth, Income Distribution and Poverty Reduction in Contemporary China**
Shujie Yao

14 **China's Economic Relations with the West and Japan, 1949–79**
Grain, Trade and Diplomacy
Chad J. Mitcham

15 **China's Industrial Policy and the Global Business Revolution**
The Case of the Domestic Appliance Industry
Ling Liu

16 **Managers and Mandarins in Contemporary China**
The Building of an International Business Alliance
Jie Tang

17 The Chinese Model of Modern
Development
Edited by Tian Yu Cao

18 Chinese Citizenship
Views from the Margins
*Edited by Vanessa L. Fong and
Rachel Murphy*

19 Unemployment, Inequality and Poverty
in Urban China
Edited by Shi Li and Hiroshi Sato

20 Globalisation, Competition and Growth
in China
Edited by Jian Chen and Shujie Yao

21 The Chinese Communist Party in
Reform
*Edited by Kjeld Erik Brodsgaard and
Zheng Yongnian*

Chinese Citizenship
Views from the margins

**Edited by Vanessa L. Fong
and Rachel Murphy**

Routledge
Taylor & Francis Group

LONDON AND NEW YORK

First published 2006
by Routledge
2 Park Square, Milton Park, Abingdon, Oxon OX14 4RN

Simultaneously published in the USA and Canada
by Routledge
270 Madison Ave, New York, NY 10016

Transferred to Digital Printing 2006

Routledge is an imprint of the Taylor & Francis Group

© 2006 selection and editorial matter, Vanessa L. Fong and Rachel
Murphy; individual chapters, the contributors

Typeset in Sabon by Graphicraft Limited, Hong Kong
Printed and bound in Great Britain by Biddles Ltd,
King's Lynn, Norfolk

British Library Cataloguing in Publication Data
A catalogue record for this book is available from the British Library

Library of Congress Cataloging in Publication Data
  Chinese citizenship : views from the margins / edited by Vanessa
L. Fong and Rachel Murphy.
     p. cm. — (Routledge studies in the Chinese economy)
  Includes bibliographical references and index.
  ISBN 0-415-37145-7
     1. Marginality, Social—China. 2. Citizenship—China. 3.
  Citizenship—Study and teaching—China. 4. People with social
  disabilities—Government policy—China. I. Fong, Vanessa L.,
  1974– II. Murphy, Rachel, 1971– III. Series.
HN740.Z9M263 2005
323.6′0951—dc22
2005006724

ISBN 10: 0–415–37145–7
ISBN 13: 9–78–0–415–37145–2

Contents

Acknowledgements   ix
Tables   x
Contributors   xi

1 Introduction: Chinese experiences of citizenship at the
   margins
   RACHEL MURPHY AND VANESSA L. FONG   1

2 Citizenship education in rural China: the dispositional
   and technical training of cadres and farmers
   RACHEL MURPHY   9

3 The urban Chinese educational system and the
   marginality of migrant children
   LU WANG   27

4 Choosing between ethnic and Chinese citizenship:
   the educational trajectories of Tibetan minority
   children in northwestern China
   LIN YI   41

5 *Legal Report*: citizenship education through a television
   documentary
   YINGCHI CHU   68

6 "Civilizing" Shanghai: government efforts to cultivate
   citizenship among impoverished residents
   TIANSHU PAN   96

viii   *Contents*

7   Teaching "responsibility": social workers' efforts to
    turn Chinese immigrants into ideal Hong Kong citizens
    NICOLE NEWENDORP   123

8   Chinese youth between the margins of China and the
    First World
    VANESSA L. FONG   151

    Bibliography   174
    Index   189

Acknowledgements

We, the co-editors, would like to thank each other for the rewards of collaborative works. The editing process was an equal partnership, and the order in which our names appear is due only to the randomness of alphabetical order.

We would like to thank our contributors for their commitment to this project. It has been our immense good luck to cooperate with these talented and dedicated researchers whose enthusiasm, industriousness and goodwill made this volume possible.

We are grateful to the Centre for Research in the Arts Social Sciences and Humanities (CRASSH) at the University of Cambridge for sponsoring the conference on which this volume is based and for awarding a visiting fellowship to Vanessa Fong so that she could collaborate with Rachel Murphy in arranging the conference and this publication. We are deeply indebted to Professor John Morrill, Professor Ian Donaldson, Ms Mary-Rose Cheadle and Ms Virginia Pierce at CRASSH for all their support and hard work in making this project possible. We are grateful to the scholars at CRASSH and especially to Professors Geoffrey Hawthorn and Tim Wright for their early support of the intellectual basis of this project. We also wish to express our thanks to the British Academy and the British Council for their financial support so that international scholars could participate in the conference.

We wish to thank conference participants, especially Fu Weili, Ya-Pei Kuo, Pik-ki Leung, Eddy U, Elizabeth Van der Ven, and Yin Shihong, for their insightful contributions to the discussion and the development of the themes that are explored in the papers.

Whilst the editing of the book and the writing of the introduction was underway, Rachel Murphy was a research fellow in contemporary Chinese Studies Programme at Oxford University, and is grateful to the programme for support. Vanessa Fong is grateful to her colleagues, students, friends and staff at Harvard, where she is an assistant professor in the Graduate School of Education.

Finally, we are grateful to Professor Mark Selden for invaluable and detailed feedback on the proposal and the introduction. We wish also to thank the anonymous reviewer at Routledge and our editor, Peter Sowden, for his time and support in ushering this book through to publication.

Tables

3.1	Sex of participating children	28
3.2	Places of origin of participating children	28
3.3	Migrant children's comments	32
3.4	Average monthly life expenses for migrant households (Yuan)	33
3.5	Increase of enrolment of Huangzhuang Primary School (1998–2002)	36
3.6	Teachers of Xinghua Primary School, Beijing	38
4.1	Ethnic minority population in Huangnan TAP, 2002	45
4.2	Illiteracy rate, college and university graduate rate, and high school and high specialized school graduate rate in Qinghai and Huangnan, 2000	46
4.3	Ethnic population and government officials in Huangnan, 2002	48

Contributors

Chu Yingchi is Chair of Chinese Studies and lecturer in the Media Studies Programme at Murdoch University, Perth, Western Australia. Her research field is Chinese and Asian cinema. Dr Chu is the author of *Hong Kong Cinema: Colonizer, Motherland and Self* (RoutledgeCurzon 2003) and articles on citizenship, children and media in China. Her current research focuses on documentary film in China.

Fong, Vanessa L. is an Assistant Professor in the Graduate School of Education at Harvard University. Her research focuses on a cohort of youth who were born at the start of China's One Child Policy in 1979. She is in the early phases of a longitudinal project that follows members of this cohort throughout the course of their lives. She received her PhD in Anthropology from Harvard University in 2002, is also the author of *Only Hope: Coming of Age under China's One-Child Policy* (Stanford University Press 2004) and co-editor with Hua R. Lan of *Women in Republican China* (M.E. Sharpe 1999).

Murphy, Rachel is a Research Fellow in the Contemporary Chinese Studies Programme and Pembroke College, University of Oxford. She obtained her PhD in the Faculty of Social and Political Sciences at the University of Cambridge, where she subsequently held a British Academy Post-Doctoral Research Fellowship. Her publications include *How Migrant Labor is Changing Rural China* (Cambridge University Press 2002) and several articles on rural-urban interactions, entrepreneurship, human development, gender and population in China.

Newendorp, Nicole is a Lecturer in Social Studies, Committee on Degrees in Social Studies, Harvard University. She received her PhD in Anthropology in June 2004 from Harvard. She is currently working on a manuscript entitled *Uneasy Reunions: Chinese Women, Immigration, and Citizenship in Post-1997 Hong Kong*. She continues to focus her research interests on how women and families experience migration and citizenship, particularly in situations of politically-enforced familial separation.

Pan Tianshu is a Visiting Assistant Professor at the School of Foreign Service at Georgetown University. His research has focused on urban culture and planning, food rationing and consumption practices under state socialism, welfare reform during the post-reform era, the professionalization of China's social services, and neighborhood gentrification in late socialist Shanghai. Prior to earning a PhD in Anthropology at Harvard University, Dr. Pan served as an officer for the international programs at Fudan University and a volunteer for a rural development program in Shanghai's Nanhui County.

Wang Lu is Associate Professor at the Institute of International and Comparative Education, the School of Education, Beijing Normal University, the Peoples' Republic of China. She obtained her PhD in social sciences at Sussex University and subsequently worked as a research fellow at the Institute of Development Studies, Sussex, UK. She has researched and published widely on education provisioning and schools in China.

Yi Lin is currently a PhD candidate based in the Department of Sociology at the University of Bristol. He is completing his thesis on *Schooling, Social Mobility and Cultural Difference in Multiethnic Northwestern China*. Lin Yi was a lecturer in Chinese literature and language in Guangdong University of Foreign Studies and the University of Rome, 'La Sapienza'.

1 Introduction: Chinese experiences of citizenship at the margins

Rachel Murphy and Vanessa L. Fong

What does citizenship mean for those at the margins of Chinese society? What can such individuals do to maximize their access to citizenship rights? How do agents of the Chinese state deal with such individuals? Must a minority teenager abandon his ethnic identity in seeking the advantages of assimilation by the cultural majority? Must a family that migrated from the countryside pay the outrageous fees required to place a rural child in an urban public school? Must a farmer abandon local traditions in order to develop a modern agribusiness? Must a Chinese woman marry a man with First World citizenship? Must impoverished migrants from mainland China do volunteer work in Hong Kong? Must neighborhood committee cadres become professional social workers? Must an official value law over morality? How can such strategies help individuals achieve upward mobility? What are the conflicts between such strategies and the efforts of state agents to build and maintain the Chinese state's citizenship categories?

This volume deals with vexing questions like these by examining the interplay between the Chinese state and the individuals at the margins of Chinese society. Much of the literature on citizenship in China (Goldman and Perry 2002; Harrison 2000; Solinger 1999) and elsewhere (Kymlicka and Norman 2000; Shafir and Peled 2002; Smith 1999; Torpey 2000) has focused on the national identities and legal rights and responsibilities associated with dominant state definitions of legal, civil, and political citizenship. Some scholars have also presented nuanced studies of the Chinese state's strategies for the construction of citizenship (Anagnost 1995; Bakken 2000). Missing in this literature, however, is an exploration of the agency and experiences of marginal actors who create, resist, or have to live with the consequences of those state strategies. This book is such an exploration. Our volume sheds new light on the relationship between marginal Chinese individuals, the Chinese state, and the capitalist world system.

Citizenship is commonly defined as inclusion in a shared community that confers a set of rights and responsibilities (Marshall 1950; Turner 1986). Scholars often draw distinctions between the legal, civil, political, social and cultural dimensions of citizenship. Legal citizenship refers to the legal rights and responsibilities associated with how one is classified by documents such as passports and residency cards. Civil citizenship refers to rights which are protected by the legal system (such as the right to own property, enforce contracts through the courts, and enjoy freedom from government constraints on privacy, association, speech, and beliefs), as well as to the responsibility to behave in ways that respect the civil rights of others. Political citizenship refers to rights and responsibilities to participate in the political activities of the nation-state such as the right to stand for office, to vote in elections, or to participate in mass movements. Social citizenship refers to rights to socioeconomic protections such as subsidized education, welfare benefits, health and retirement benefits, and living wages, as well as responsibilities to work for the greater good of society. Cultural citizenship refers to the right to belong to a broader community in ways that are felt by the individual and recognized by others, as well as to the responsibility to protect the dignity of that community.

A recurring theme in this volume relates to how individuals at the margins of Chinese society try to gain greater access to social rights and the most prestigious kinds of cultural citizenship, even as the Chinese state demands that they fulfill citizenship responsibilities while ignoring their demands for social rights and cultural belonging. A view common among citizenship scholars is that "Civil and political rights set the rules of the game, social rights represent the outcome of the game" (Mishra 1981). Our volume challenges this perspective by exploring how acquisition of or exclusion from social and cultural citizenship can change the rules as well as the outcome of the game. While the legal, civil, and political dimensions of citizenship are often governed by laws and systems that seem difficult for an individual to transform directly, the relaxation of social controls and the deepening of market reforms in China have enabled marginal individuals and groups to pursue social and cultural rights that transcend their legal, civil, and political citizenship. At the same time, it is also increasingly possible for exclusion from social and cultural citizenship to have devastating consequences, even for those with full legal, civil, and political citizenship.

Our volume deals with individuals at the margins of Chinese society. Some, such as the poor farmers described by Rachel Murphy, the victims and criminals portrayed in the television programs analyzed by Yingchi Chu, and the unemployed Shanghai residents described by Tianshu Pan, are marginal because they do not fit dominant state ideals of citizenship. In their cases, marginality deprives them of the rights and responsibilities of the only kind of citizenship available to them. Others, such as rural migrants described by Lu Wang, the minorities described by Lin Yi, the mainland migrants described by Nicole Newendorp, and the transnational Chinese youth described by Vanessa Fong, are marginal because they move between different citizenship categories. In these cases, marginality is a mixed blessing that allows them to access the rights and dodge the responsibilities of multiple citizenship categories, even as it hinders their efforts to attain full citizenship in any one category.

Marginality is always relative. The rural cadres described by Murphy had powerful positions at the center of their rural county, but were still marginal in a broader Chinese society dominated by affluent urban residents. The shadowy world of semi-legal migrant schools in Beijing and Xiamen described by Lu Wang was created by relatively wealthy rural migrants who were nevertheless subject to capricious state crackdowns. The legal documentary examined by Yingchi Chu was made by the mainstream Chinese media for a mainstream audience, but derived much of its popularity from its sensational focus on the legal dilemmas of marginal criminals and outcasts. The Tibetan teachers described by Lin Yi enjoyed relative prestige and job security in labor markets where ethnic minorities were systematically disadvantaged, but they remained marginal in a Han-dominated Chinese society. Many of the transnational Chinese youth described by Fong were children of elite families at the center of Chinese society, but they became marginal as they prolonged their sojourns abroad. The "granny cadres" described by Pan were agents of the state, but they could also be seen as marginal players in a state structure dominated by higher officials. As Pan pointed out, the threat of being marginalized as a "troublemaker" always hung over the heads of idealistic lower-level residents committee cadres like Feng Ting, who had tried to expand her slum-dweller charges' social rights by asking, "Didn't Chairman Mao say that every one has the right to eat a bowl of rice?"

Marginality is often defined by legal, civil, and political citizenship categories, which produce as well as reflect inequalities. Some of the starkest inequalities in China were created by the household registration system, which grants urban citizens social rights that are denied to rural citizens including the millions who live and work in cities but are denied the wide range of rights associated with urban registration (Murphy 2002; Solinger 1999; Zhang 2001). The children interviewed by Lu Wang recounted how their lack of urban registration papers meant that they were constantly turned away from urban public schools, while facing harassment by urban residents who called them "outsider dogs." Chinese citizens who were not of the majority Han ethnicity often found that their minority cultural citizenship deprived them of certain rights even as it enhanced their access to other rights (Litzinger 2000; Mueggler 1998; Schein 2000). Despite affirmative action policies that gave ethnic minorities priority for many schooling and employment opportunities, Tibetans interviewed by Lin Yi still feared that they would be excluded from most such opportunities if they did not develop fluency in the language and culture of the Chinese state, often at the expense of maintaining their Tibetan cultural citizenship. Yet even those with inferior legal, civil, and political citizenship inscribed on their registration papers could transcend the rigidities of their documentation by joining the national and transnational elite in the much more flexible realms of social and cultural citizenship. As a wealthy 24-year-old female rural migrant told Li Zhang in Beijing, "Look at those arrogant Beijing *xiaojie* [ladies] – they work in state-owned units but make little money. . . . How can they be so proud? Just for the piece of *hukou* paper? . . . Don't they realize that today's society belongs to those of us who have money?" (Zhang 2001:44). Though such cases were rare (and still problematic, as Zhang's ethnography showed), they inspired disadvantaged migrants like those studied by Fong, Wang, and Yi in this volume with the hope of making their legal, civil, and political disadvantages matter less by improving their lot in the social and cultural realm.

Hierarchies in social and cultural citizenship were so powerful that they could produce dramatic inequalities between people with identical legal, civil, and political citizenship statuses. Though they were civil and political citizens of Shanghai, one of China's most elite cities, the slum-dwellers described by Pan still lacked the prestige, privacy, and comfortable lifestyles enjoyed by their neighbors in upscale areas. The Hong Kong social workers studied by Newendorp considered poor immigrants from mainland China unworthy of the high living standards taken for granted by wealthier Hong Kong natives, even though the immigrants held the same legal, civil, and political citizenship status as the natives. A former Chinese college instructor who became a cook and small business owner in Australia told Fong that, despite his hard-won Australian legal citizenship, he often felt "more miserable than the rural migrants in Chinese cities, because at least they could speak the same language as the people around them."

Citizenship classifications and the inequalities they produce are not immutable. Rather, they are constantly renewed, maintained, lost, or transformed in processes of individual and social struggle. It is possible for someone classified as a rural, ethnic minority citizen of mainland China at birth to transform into an urban, culturally Han, First World citizen. Though difficult to achieve, upward mobility through transformations in citizenship status was common enough to fuel the hopes of many individuals on the margins of Chinese society. Despite the hardships they experienced, the rural migrant children studied by Lu Wang were likely to have greater access to schooling, jobs, and consumption than their counterparts who remained in the countryside. A Hong Kong social worker told Newendorp about feeling inspired by an illiterate, impoverished, rural widow who had immigrated from mainland China and then learned to read both English and Chinese, and even did volunteer work in the kitchen of a retirement home. Lin Yi found that some Tibetans who developed fluency in the culture and language of the Han majority attained higher education, elite jobs, and even opportunities to go abroad. The transnational Chinese youth in Fong's study who won college degrees or permanent residency rights in First World countries gained opportunities for wealth and status far beyond what they could have attained with Chinese citizenship alone.

The agency of marginal individuals seeking self-transformation could also lead to broader social transformations. In the villages visited by Murphy, some farmers who learned modern technology and engaged in the market economy were able to transform themselves from 'peasants' into 'rural entrepreneurs' or even village cadres. In the schools studied by Wang, some migrant teachers endeavored to improve the educational quality of the lessons, opening up possibilities for expanding migrant children's access to social and cultural rights, much as the migrant-run markets and housing compounds did for migrants studied by Li Zhang in Beijing (2001). Mainland migrants who did volunteer work in Hong Kong expanded newer arrivals' access to the rights associated with Hong Kong citizenship while demonstrating that immigrants could be responsible Hong Kong citizens. Well-educated Tibetans who gained high positions in the Chinese state helped to elevate the prestige of Tibetan culture and present it as a tradition of "extensive knowledge and profound scholarship" that deserved the respect of the Han majority. The First World wealth and prestige attained by the more successful emigrant Chinese youth in Fong's chapter fueled the transnational yearnings of those who remained in China.

Many neoliberal democratic states have focused on strengthening the legal, civil, and political dimensions of citizenship that would allow individuals to act as free agents in a global economy (Caldeira 2000; Holston 1999). While Chinese leaders have been eager to integrate China into the global economy, they have also tried to maintain what Aihwa Ong called the "pastoral" state–society relationship (1999). Rooted both in imperial Chinese Confucian models and in socialist models of social transformation, this pastoral approach demands that the state take an active role in transforming backward citizens into modern citizens. Under the autarkic Maoist state (1949–1976) the pastoral model was expressed in the form of class struggle and socialist education campaigns – by transforming one's ideological consciousness, the individual became entitled to share in the collective welfare provisioning of socialism. Under the post-Mao policies of globalization and neoliberalism, the pastoral model changed form: as the state withdrew from direct involvement in providing the material entitlements of social citizenship, its role became one of creating the conditions in which individuals were able to provide for their own well-being.

Even while they promoted discourses that stigmatized poor, rural, ethnic minority, and Third World citizenship statuses, Chinese policymakers also encouraged educators, television producers, and social workers to lead those with such stigmatized statuses toward wealthy, urban, Han, and First World social and cultural citizenship. We found that individuals with such stigmatized statuses were highly ambivalent about the Chinese state's supposedly pastoral care. On the one hand, they embraced the state's valorization of citizenship statuses associated with modernity. On the other hand, however, they were dismayed by how this valorization devalued their own citizenship statuses, and they were disappointed in the often inadequate social and economic support that came with the state's exhortations. This dismay was expressed by the farmers Murphy met in Rivercounty who were perturbed that state efforts to improve their 'quality' were largely confined to ideological education rather than useful interventions such as infrastructural investment, and by the new arrivals in Newendorp's community center who expressed skepticism about lifestyle advice from the social workers they turned to for practical material assistance.

Some scholars have contrasted passive and active notions of citizenship. They point out that in pastoral states, citizenship has commonly been understood as rights conferred by benevolent authorities on loyal and passive subjects (Anagnost 1997; Ong 1999), while in liberal democracies, citizenship has been seen as based on rights obtained and protected through active struggle (Barbalet 1988; Bendix 1964; Tilly 1999; Turner 1986). Jim Scott (Scott 1985, 1999) and Elizabeth Perry and Mark Selden (Perry and Selden 2000), on the other hand, have argued that struggle can occur in all kinds of societies, including those that are not liberal democracies. The chapters in this volume highlight how struggles over citizenship are common even in a pastoral state like China.

In our examination of the cultural dimensions of citizenship, we follow Aihwa Ong (Ong 1999, 2003), who in turn was inspired by the work of Michel Foucault (Foucault 1977, 1980) in her examination of the dialectical process between "being made" and "self-making" (Ong 1996:738) among Asians in the United States. Our volume shows how this process works for citizens of the People's Republic of China who try to claim or escape labels such as "urban," "rural," "minority," "Chinese," "foreign," "high-quality," or "low quality." We shed light on the flip side of Ong's examination of cultural citizenship among immigrants in the First World, by exploring cultural citizenship in the context of the modernization discourses that dominate Third World societies like China. Our exploration shows that cultural citizenship results not only from struggles between individuals and the state, but also from individuals' engagement with local and global discourses and economic systems that are not necessarily controlled by any state. We also expand on Ong's discussion by highlighting the significance of social citizenship as a product of and pathway to cultural citizenship. While cultural citizenship is vital to the construction of social citizenship, it is the latter that is most fervently desired by and painfully elusive to the migrants, farmers, and impoverished citizens at the margins of Chinese society.

During the final two decades of the twentieth century, Chinese society was transformed by Chinese leaders' decision to adopt neoliberal policies that eroded the social welfare net, by increasing migration from rural areas to urban areas as well as from China to First World societies, and by the incorporation of China into global flows of knowledge, capital, commodities, and people. Dorothy Solinger (1999) showed how markets created spaces which migrants used "to creep around the back of the state" to claim the social and civil rights that were denied to them by their rural household registration. Studies of global capitalism (Hooper 2000; Orlove

1997; Watson 1997) have revealed that individuals established membership in global communities through transnational consumption practices. Michael Keane (Keane 2001) argued that consumerism underpinned the social citizenship contract that the Chinese state established with its citizens: the right to buy goods in exchange for hard work and conformity with national policies. Such developments have created new, increasingly flexible relationships between individuals and states that do not fit neatly into the state-dominated formulations of citizenship common in the existing literature. Combined with increasingly flexible and mobile concepts of citizenship and the state, the decline of state control has led to the flourishing of social life at the margins of Chinese society. The essays in this volume highlight the complexities, dilemmas, and possibilities of citizenship in the context of marginality.

As globalization processes intensified at the dawn of the twenty-first century, discourses about the need to "catch up" to First World societies became even more powerful in shaping images of the nation and citizenship. China was seen as backward in comparison to First World societies. Within China, a hierarchy of social groups emerged that were differentially positioned in relation to modernity. People internalized their positioning within the hierarchy in two ways. First, through everyday encounters with institutions, places, lifestyles, consumer goods, officials, experts, procedures, and representations, the valuations associated with different kinds of citizenship became inscribed into peoples' self-understanding. Second, people aspired to become social and cultural citizens of communities that were more strongly identified with modernity: rural citizens tried to become part of urban modernity; Chinese citizens tried to become part of First World modernity; and minority citizens tried to become part of Han modernity.

Chinese leaders tried to combine the pastoralism associated with Confucian and socialist models of governance and the neoliberalism associated with First World models of governance by maintaining social stability through limits on civil and political rights, freeing up the marketplace, attracting foreign business, and promoting certain state-valorized personal qualities as keys to individual upward mobility and the attainment of dominant ideals of social and cultural citizenship. Agents of the state such as media producers, social workers, and educational officials tried to transform marginal individuals into responsible, patriotic, civilized, industrious, high-quality, law-abiding, well-educated citizens, even as they expressed grave doubts about marginal individuals' ability to attain these qualities. State leaders hoped that such qualities could help China become more competitive in the capitalist world system. In addition, by focusing on personal transformation as the key to citizenship rights, state leaders could blame their inability to guarantee social rights such as education and satisfactory living conditions on individual failings and dispositional inadequacies.

In the context of the transformation of the Chinese economy and state-society relations, the cultural model of personal transformation was powerful enough to have been internalized by many Chinese citizens. Yet these citizens were not just passive reproducers of state discourses; on the contrary, they resisted some aspects of those discourses, while using others to their own advantage. The farmers described by Murphy employed the state's language of 'low quality' and lack of skills to refuse to plant state-designated crops. The new immigrants in the community center visited by Newendorp understood that they were classified as welfare subjects, and they used aspects of this subject positioning in their struggle for access to benefits and information. Some of the Tibetan students interviewed by Lin Yi were able to use official rhetoric about the uniqueness of Tibetan culture to assert the dignity of their religious rituals despite the hostility of Han Chinese teachers towards their visibly observant practices. Our volume explores the agency of such marginal individuals as they use, resist, or accept elements of the state in their negotiations of everyday life. We examine how such individuals sought upward mobility, sometimes by trying to move toward the center of state power in China or elsewhere, and other times by capitalizing on the flexibility afforded by their marginality.

Social and political scientists have increasingly recognized that capturing the complexity and flexibility of citizenship practices necessitates moving beyond a simplistic state/society dichotomy. A point of departure for developing a more nuanced approach to citizenship involves recognizing that the state is intertwined with society rather than separate from it (Shue 1988). This is because the state is not a monolith but a fragmented ensemble of individuals in an array of organizations, including schools, courts, social work offices, police stations, customs, agricultural extension depots, village and township governments, municipal governments, television stations (Gupta 1995; Migdal 2001). Even though in China, as in many countries, the state is retreating from claims that it could guarantee social rights, a vast army of state agents continues to struggle with their own fears of increasing marginality as well as with dilemmas between their responsibilities to the state and their responsibilities to individuals at the margins of society. Television producers have to decide how to portray state laws that seem to contradict social morality; officials wonder how to deal with transnational citizens who may be dissidents as well as investors; social workers fret over how to deal with the gap between social welfare resources and the needs of the poor and powerless. The essays in our volume highlight the humanity of these individuals who create, manage, and deny the rights and responsibilities of citizenship.

2 Citizenship education in rural China

The dispositional and technical training of cadres and farmers

Rachel Murphy

... the spatial metaphor of the panopticon ... must be amended to suggest that its working is contingent upon the hypervisibility of the apparatus of power and its operations on the social body. The tower at the center is not entirely a darkened space inhabited by an invisible gaze but an illuminated stage from which the party calls, 'Look at me! I make myself real to you. Your return gaze completes me and realizes my power.'

(Ann Anagnost, 1997)

This chapter examines how the Chinese state tried to use citizenship education to maintain its authority in the face of the livelihood challenges arising from the new market economy. Drawing on research I conducted in 2000 in Rivercounty, a poor and marginal rural area in the southeastern province of Jiangxi, I show how the Chinese state tried to deal with the pressures of global market integration and the imperatives of neoliberalism by subjecting farmers to citizenship education projects that emphasized responsibilities rather than rights. One project involved equipping local cadres with the knowledge and attitudes that would make them willing and able to work benevolently and honestly to promote modernization on behalf of rural people (Thøgersen 2003). Another project involved inculcating in farmers the rational, modern and scientific qualities that were necessary for them to be law-abiding citizens who would promote prosperity within their communities. Despite their ostensibly empowering promises, these kinds of citizenship education served to preserve the top-down structure of rural society and maintain the position of farmers as perpetually marginalized subjects of development.

For both cadres and farmers, the content of the pedagogy incorporated 'moral/dispositional' and 'technical/economic' components: the 'two transformations' (*liang ge zhuanbian*) of the mind and economy (Qin and Chen 2000; Yang and Wu 2000). Cadres were supposed to reform their work-style by rectifying their arrogance, laziness and corruption, and by obtaining modern knowledge in market economics, agricultural technology and law by taking courses at the Rivercounty Technical Vocational College. Farmers were supposed to reform their generic ignorance, irrationality, narrow-mindedness and feudal patriarchal outlook, and receive knowledge about cash crops, planting techniques, legal commercial contracts and market forces. Both kinds of citizenship education reflected state attempts to legitimize a pastoral approach to rural governance that exhorted farmers to fulfil citizenship responsibilities while denying them civil and political rights and failing to deliver on many of the social rights they were promised.

The first section introduces the background against which citizenship education took place, outlining the neoliberal shift in socioeconomic policies and their incompatibility with existing governing structures. The second section examines how pedagogic activities in Rivercounty enabled cadres to acquire and display their moral and modernizing credentials. It then considers the ways in which the cadres performed their role as tutors and how their pedagogic activities encoded the label of 'backward' in their evaluations of farmers' behavior. The third section explores the pedagogic activities directed at farmers, showing that modern knowledge and policies were always 'sent down' to them and that their ambivalence and even resistance to state interventions were used as evidence of their low quality (*suzhi*) and the continuing need for top-down pedagogy (Gupta 1998, 11).[1]

Neoliberal transition and a rigid bureaucracy

The neoliberal transition in rural China shifted responsibilities from the state center to the rural margins. First the dismantling of the communes and the subcontracting of plots to households in the early 1980s transferred control over income from collectives to farming households. Although this enhanced the incentives for villagers to produce, it also undermined collective schemes to pay for education and to pool risk in meeting health care costs (Oi 1992). Second, fiscal decentralization intensified pressure on local governments to augment the total revenue within their administrative jurisdictions. Previously all revenue was ceded to the centre with a portion reallocated down through the state system as a budgetary allocation. In addition to a national tax contribution, counties and their subordinate townships became responsible for raising most of their revenue for expenditure on overheads, administrators' salaries, social security and public works (Oi 1992; Wong 1992). In 1996, further decentralization requiring county and township governments to 'eat in separate kitchens' meant that townships were no longer able to rely on the county to help with funding, so they raised this money from the farmers through 'special agricultural taxes' on cash crops and livestock (Peng 1996; Wu 2003, 49; Zuo 1997).

There were also fundamental changes in how China's grain was priced. In 1995 the state raised the price of grain and assumed a monopoly over its purchase and marketing with the assumption that as sole trader it would be able to charge higher prices and so improve rural incomes. This strategy led to an oversupply of grain and the state granaries were unable to sell a huge proportion of their reserves. Recognizing the policy mistake, in the latter half of 1999 the state was forced to abandon the price subsidies and its monopoly on grain purchase and distribution (Tao 2004). At the same time, China's increasing integration into global markets throughout the 1990s culminated in a decision to enter the World Trade Organization. This meant that China's farmers became increasingly vulnerable to market fluctuations and competition from cheaper and superior imports (Blum 2002; Liu 2000; Unger 2002, 228). The initial impact was a steep fall in farmers' cash incomes. Although in 2002/3 strategic reduction in acreage under grain cultivation led to rises in grain prices, farmers were now exposed to both policy fluctuations and the vagaries of global markets.

Rather than directly providing welfare buffers, the role of the state increasingly became one of educating individuals at its margins to cultivate the personal and technical attributes that would enable them to secure their livelihoods (Ong 2002). This change in how the government promoted the wellbeing of its citizens was articulated through a new social contract that emphasized the responsibilities of social and cultural citizenship. Like the citizenship education offered by Hong Kong social workers to mainland migrants in Nicole Newendorp's study (this volume), rural citizenship education exhorted individuals to improve their dispositions and technical competence in ways prescribed by the state. Those who did so would be eligible for social rights to *xiaokang,* a 'comfortable standard of living' (Keane 2001). Farmers and cadres accepted the contract because it appealed to their own material aspirations, and resonated with the culturally embedded belief that benevolent government and individual industriousness were important for enabling prosperity.

Although the new social contract increased the burdens of socioeconomic risk and responsibility to local governments and to individuals, it did not deliver most of the increased social, civil, and political rights promised implicitly in the accompanying discourse of empowerment and modernization. This was because the legacy of vertical planning remained intact.

County, township and village cadres within the vertical planning system were preoccupied with reaching top-down targets for raising tax revenue, increasing local GDP, meeting social development targets and implementing state policies such as birth planning. Reaching or surpassing the targets directly affected personal advancement, with strong performers standing a better chance of being assigned to a good location and institution and to a higher level on their next posting (see also Cao 2004; Edin 2000). Although unlike their superiors, village cadres were not career bureaucrats, they too prioritized quota completion because they regularly hosted township inspection teams and were rewarded with good relations with higher level officials and salary bonuses. Meanwhile, cadres at all levels who failed to reach targets risked public criticism.

Cadres in agricultural counties such as Rivercounty responded to the imperative to increase GDP and revenue by keeping the planning of production in their own hands. This involved using the tools bequeathed by the socialist planning era. In particular, in finding and implementing new economic projects, the cadres used the bureaucracy as a source of information and technology; convened mobilization meetings; adapted the Maoist method of visits to learn information and ideas from advanced work units and regions; and publicly praised and criticized individuals (Oi 1999, 123–7; Unger 2002).[2]

During the 1980s, Rivercounty cadres visited counties in other prefectures and provinces that had excelled in tobacco cultivation. These visits enabled them to obtain information about growing and curing techniques as well as marketing outlets. Following their return to Rivercounty the officials coordinated mobilization and demonstration meetings at the township and village levels and township level praise meetings were held to publicize the examples of farmers who had achieved outstanding yields. Tobacco has been a popular 'pillar'[3] in poor agricultural counties such as Rivercounty because the government enjoys a monopoly on sales and can levy a 'special agricultural tax' that is much heavier than for other cash crops (Peng 1996). In Rivercounty at the end of 2000 tobacco contributed between 40–50 percent of the fiscal revenue (Rivercounty Bureau of Statistics). In late 1999, following the fall in grain prices, local cadres became extra active in developing other products to replace the early rice crop and to supplement the role of tobacco as a pillar.

As elsewhere in China, the top-down system of government placed immense pressure on rural cadres in Rivercounty whilst affording them much power within their localities. This circumstance led cadres to use coercive and corrupt practices when carrying out their work, especially when managing agricultural production. Officials frequently forced farmers to plant tobacco, and imposed fines or uprooted offending crops in cases of disobedience. Moreover, government purchasing agents at the township and county levels commonly appropriated part of the price of the tobacco crop, and the county tobacco company purchasing agents evaluated the leaves of their friends at a higher grade, a practice which depressed the prices paid to other farmers (interviews with farmers 2000; Yuan 2000). The upper levels of the Party-state responded to these local level 'work-style' problems by organizing cadre rectification classes and cadre study groups.

The purpose of citizenship education for cadres and farmers was to reduce the political and economic costs of using coercion to implement policies. It was supposed to give cadres a sense of purpose to their work, which would make them behave in a manner that would win the respect and trust of the masses. It was supposed to make Party-state cadres visible to the rural masses as agents of development (Anagnost 1997). It was supposed to make the cadres and farmers regulate their behavior voluntarily in ways that conformed to the overall drift of Party-state policies, this latter aim being expressed through the common saying, "if people understand (*liaojie*) then they will self-consciously (*zijue*) behave in the appropriate manner."

Citizenship education for cadres

In Rivercounty as elsewhere in rural China, the task of coordinating citizenship education for cadres fell under the jurisdiction of the Organization Bureau, the most powerful organ within the Party-state apparatus, which is responsible for managing internal party discipline, Party recruitment, personnel deployment, and cadres' relations with the masses. Citizenship education was both moral/dispositional and technical. Dispositional pedagogy took the form of ideological campaigns and work-style and political study classes run by the local branch of the Party school. Technical pedagogy involved classes in agriculture, the market economy and law coordinated by the Rivercounty Vocational College.

From the end of 1999 to early 2001, the moral/dispositional education of Jiangxi cadres focused on the 'three stresses' (*sanjiang*) campaign: 'study' (*xuexi*), 'politics' (*zhengzhi*) and 'a healthy atmosphere' (*zhengqi*). The purported aim was to 'collectively educate' (*jizhong jiaoyu*) cadres to improve their 'quality' (*suzhi*) and enable them to improve their own work-style. The education occurred in small study groups in which cadres at the levels of the prefecture, county and township discussed theoretical documents such as Jiang Zemin's 'three represents'[4] and real life official corruption cases such as those of Hu Changqing and Cheng Kejie. The cadres also wrote self-reflexive essays on their morality, ability, industriousness and enthusiasm (*de*, *neng*, *qin* and *ji*) and solicited criticism from their peers. These groups were known as 'democratic life groups' (*minzu shenghuo hui*).

Like the Socialist Education Movement of the early sixties (Meisner 1977, 288–304), the pedagogy for cadres in Rivercounty was managed by external work teams sent from the higher levels. In the case of *sanjiang*, the self-examination essays by county and township cadres were inspected by members from these teams – section level cadres (*kezhang*) who descended from the provincial level. These inspectors either passed the self-examinations by signing them, or else they requested that pieces be re-written. These work teams were the means by which the centralized party apparatus exercised surveillance over lower level party cadres. This was a method of intervention consistent with the role of the Party as the sole and superior arbiter of correctness, improvement and progress.[5] It was also a method of intervention which attributed policy failures to the weakness of lower level cadres, thereby deflecting blame from neoliberalism, imprudent central state policies and the Party-state's monopoly on power.

Through the co-ordination of the work teams, the *sanjiang* campaign used not only self-criticism essays but also internal democracy to enable the masses to guide the cadres. At each level, even down to that of the village, 'opinion boxes' were circulated so that villagers and village cadres could lodge anonymously petitions against their superiors and make appeals for particular kinds of change. These opinion boxes were handed over to the external *sanjiang* inspection teams. Notably, many petitions were lodged against the Rivercounty Party Secretary who was perceived to be the instigator of an ambitious scheme to move the county seat from one side of the river to the other, a project that entailed building a new town and resettling the residents. Aside from the logistical inconveniences of constructing a new county seat, the project was widely unpopular because it was financed entirely with local funds and would exacerbate the tax burden on farmers.

Other petitions focused on government failings that compromised rural livelihoods and well-being. Typical examples included the practice of moving money from poorer village schools to richer ones to create local prestige schools, failures to repair roads, and the excessive tax burden on farmers. Three thousand petitions were submitted in Rivercounty – ten times the number in any other Jiangxi county. The large number of submissions reflected local unrest, but was due also to the fact that the Jiangxi Provincial Party Secretary who was stationed in Rivercounty during the campaign actively encouraged widespread participation.

After the initial phase of *sanjiang*, the township and county cadres were given three months to address problems in their localities. The provincial inspection team then returned in a follow-up activity referred to as 'looking back on *sanjiang*' (*sanjiang huitou kan*). During the period of looking back, media reports gave much publicity to cases where local officials had been responsive to the needs of local farmers. Similar to the 'show-casing' strategies of local Shanghai officials described by Tianshu Pan (this volume), projects in Rivercounty included various 'real' contributions of the cadres to the economic well-being of farmers such as newly-laid roads, electricity connections, and technical agricultural training demonstrations. The *sanjiang* suggestions also resulted in cadres being allocated new top-down work goals: in addition to failure to meet birth planning quotas, failure to maintain social stability and to reduce the peasant burden would lead to the failure in the entire career appraisal of a senior cadre. Farmers for their part were issued with 'taxes and fees clarity cards' which they could show to any official trying to extort more than was officially permitted – though hardly any farmers that I encountered were able to produce their cards and most could not recall getting them!

Sanjiang education made use of a historically constituted repertoire of terms and techniques, in particular, those based on the revolutionary idiom of closeness between the cadres and the masses. This resonates with what Ann Anagnost has referred to as a 're-memorization' or the (re)narration of the past – the nation's propensity for continually looking backwards in order to face the future in ways that claim an impossible continuity and shared cultural essence (1997, 2). In print and television media and in official speeches about *sanjiang*, the cadres of Jiangxi were portrayed as being engaged in 'a continuing revolutionary tradition of education' – a process that involved entering villages and rural households (*zhu cun ru hu*), listening to the masses (*tingqu qunzhong*), doing 'real' things to solve their problems and serving as exemplars for subordinate cadres (*Jiangxi ribao*, 1 September 2000; *Jingganshan bao*, 30ᵗʰ August 2000). They were praised for continuing the proud revolutionary spirit of the *Jingangshan* mountain base area, as demonstrated by their determination to struggle, practice self-discipline, endure hardship, penetrate the grassroots, and 'boldly criticize people and events where necessary' (*Jingganshan bao*, 29ᵗʰ August 2000). The publicity material even went as far as talking about creating new age 'soviet base' cadres.

Sanjiang education aimed to quell widespread discontentment in the Rivercounty countryside in four ways. Most obviously, it provided an outlet for people to voice their frustrations, whilst also using the instruments of the 'mass line' and democratic centralism to ensure that unrest was vented within the parameters of the Party-state system. *Sanjiang* made Party-state cadres visible as caring agents of development: '*sanjiang* democratic work teams' were televised entering villages, listening to the concerns of farmers and doing real things on their behalf (*wei qunzhong ban shishi*). The campaign had the further advantage of facilitating the removal and reloca-tion of unpopular county and township leaders whilst avoiding political upheaval or systemic instability. Most notably the Rivercounty Party Secretary was transferred to the same post in another county. This kind of personnel rectification was identified as being essential for 'winning the trust of the masses' and improving relations with them (*Jingganshan bao*, 29ᵗʰ August 2000). Finally, by highlighting problems and making cadres address them, *sanjiang* may have actually led to some work-style improvements!

Yet, in focusing on the disposition and morality of cadres, the *sanjiang* pedagogy overlooked and paradoxically reinforced structural aspects of the Party-state apparatus that underpinned 'work-style problems'. Cadres at each level were still tied to quota completion, a circumstance that led to coercion. At the same time, cadres still enjoyed tremendous power, which when combined with the increased latitude afforded by the market economy and the absence of an external supervisory mechanism, facilitated dishon-esty. Manifestations of the dishonesty included fudging economic achieve-ments, for example taking out loans to deliver on inflated tax targets, as well as rent-seeking and corruption, especially creaming off money from large modernizing construction projects. *Sanjiang* reinforced the structural incentives for coercion and dishonesty. This is because the campaign was run through and within the vertical structure of the Party-state: targets and red letter directives were 'sent down' with instructions for convening meet-ings, writing essays, inspecting the work of subordinates, and doing 'real things' for the masses. *Sanjiang* achievements were therefore produced through the same bureaucratic rationalities and showcasing imperatives as those used in implementing agricultural production and fertility limitation policies.

Citizenship education designed to enhance the technical competence of Rivercounty cadres were coordinated by the Organization Bureau in conjunction with the Agricultural Bureau and the Science and Technology Bureau. In 1997 at the level of the province in Jiangxi, these institutions began arranging for township cadres, village party members and other rural cadres to attend training classes in modern knowledge. According to one report, the township and village cadres who participated in these classes would 'lead the farmers to prosperity through reliance on technology . . . and through training in market economy knowledge, they would open a new road to prosperity, [o]ne example being tobacco cultivation in Rivercounty.' More recently the Rivercounty Party Organization Bureau stipulated that at least one cadre in each village must take a three-year part time course run through the County Technical School. The curriculum covered rural economic management, horticulture and crop cultivation techniques and resulted in the award of a certificate from the Provincial Ministry of Education. By late 2000, cadres had already been participating in the course for six months. Ideally, once trained, they would serve as effective instructors of technical innovation and agricultural diversification.

In Rivercounty the process of making township and village cadres into agents of agricultural diversification and progress was screened on the county television station. Township leaders were shown attending lessons and sitting exams on 'expert' subjects such as agricultural technology, the market economy and law while village cadres were shown receiving instruction in farming techniques and new policies.

Expert and economic forms of knowledge were further emphasized in the forum of the 'open village elections' (*haixuan*), these being the first elections where villagers voted from a candidate list that they themselves proposed rather than from a top-down list. Although these open elections might be interpreted as creating a space for new and liberal forms of political citizenship, arguably they served primarily to expand local capacity for self-regulation in ways that would advance economic development under Party-state mentorship. Policy documents and a general acceptance of the moral discourse of development informed the content of the election speeches, with the candidates for village head elaborating on their credentials for and commitment to implementing the new agricultural diversification policies. Meanwhile the election pledges of all the candidates promised to promote high quality crop varieties, improve agricultural extension and work with township cadres to find marketing outlets. Take for example the following extract from a televised election speech by Mr. Zhu Xiaohua of Jiangkou village:

> If everybody elects me to be village head, then during my time in office I will use all my efforts to develop various aspects of the economy, lead everybody from poverty to prosperity and charge towards *xiaokang*, and gradually change the backward situation of the economy in our village . . . I will use three years of hard work to gradually realize Jiangkou village's special agricultural production plan of 'plant paddy

in the fields; plant cash crops, raise pigs and chickens at home; plant trees, bamboo and fruit on the hills.' . . . [I will] promote excellent varieties . . . Next year, the guaranteed price for the early rice will be removed and prices will be set according to quality. So we will energetically promote good varieties of cash crops like rape, water melons, and sugar cane.

(25 October 1999)

Citizenship education for cadres in Rivercounty privileged a certain kind of citizenship that aimed to enhance the willingness and competence of cadres to govern benevolently *for* the people rather than to facilitate government *by* them. The civil and political rights of the masses remained limited. Although the *sanjiang* and technical pedagogies aimed to inculcate in cadres a sense of commitment to a wider historical and patriotic purpose and to endow them with the knowledge and authority to supervise modernization, the scope of such citizenship education did not extend to changing the work-style of cadres in ways that would encourage them to help the farmers govern for themselves. Nor did it extend to diversifying the content of village self-governance beyond attaining targets for agricultural output, taxes and fertility limitation. To be sure, rural people used the window of opportunity provided by *sanjiang* to lobby for social rights to material entitlements. But both their demands and the ways in which these demands were dealt with (through the public 'doing of real and good things') were enactments of the same old pastoral relationship between the cadres and the masses, based on social rights rather than civil and political rights.

Citizenship education for farmers

Moral/dispositional and technical/economic pedagogies

Citizenship education for farmers included both moral/dispositional and technical/economic components. The moral aspects were directed towards an image of a 'generic peasant' (Appardurai 1988): the Jiangxi 'country cousin' (*laobiao*) – lazy, irrational, complacent, ignorant and backward. Transforming this generic disposition was seen as necessary for increasing the receptiveness of farmers to technical knowledge, market information and ideas about progressive forms of agriculture. Ideally, once absorbed, this technical pedagogy would enhance both the farmers' inclination and capacity to advance state agricultural policies. The tools used to carry out the moral/dispositional aspects of education included media prescriptions for modern and civilized behavior, wall slogans and sending down village work teams.

Newspaper reports and the 'political education' segment of the Rivercounty television news featured stories about farmers who had prospered because they had changed their feudal and narrow outlook. One example was of brides who had followed the new 'social winds on marriage', namely bringing prosperity to their homes by insisting on economically productive dowry gifts such as seedlings, piglets, bean curd makers and sewing machines. Another example was that of poor and conservative farmers who became receptive to the 'thought work' of caring cadres, and who subsequently engaged successfully in the scientific cultivation of the pillar crop.

Slogans on village walls urged farmers to 'work hard towards prosperity,' 'create civilized households and charge towards *xiaokang* (a comfortable standard of living),' and 'diversify agricultural production and prosper.' Other physical symbols of state pedagogy included 'three unity plaques' mounted on the doors of households that 'practice birth planning,' 'prosper through hard work and science' and 'maintain happy and civilized relationships.'

Work teams comprising county and township cadres descended periodically to the villages to carry out the 'three send downs to the countryside' (*san ge xiaxiang*): technology, law and culture. The teams criticized unhealthy and wasteful practices such as gambling; disseminated printed materials about law and market contracts; distributed books about agricultural production techniques to village offices; taught farmers about the dangers of superstitions and religion and the advantages of science; and encouraged individuals to fulfill their family duties such as providing and caring for the elderly (Rivercounty Television News, 31 October 2000). Specific purpose work teams also entered the villages. As examples, legal teams convened local public hearings so that the farmers could learn about law and reasonableness – *dang chang kaiting*. Films were sent down to the villages once a year, with the deliberate and formal policy of always coupling an entertaining film with a patriotic one (Taped interview, manager of Rivercounty Film Company, 28 September 2000). And at Spring Festival, performing troupes were dispatched, with their repertoire including not only folk songs and historical favorites, but also songs about *xiaokang* – a comfortable standard of living.

> Race towards *xiaokang*, race towards *xiaokang*, *xiaokang* life moves always upwards
> By the 21st century, everywhere in the countryside is transformed.
> The young have advocates, the old have support, old people with the five guarantees[6] have support.
> The five evils[7] have been wiped out, new people, new events, new winds.
> Completely popularize mechanization, the farmers' lives improve.
> Cement floors, red bricks, farmers live in stylish little houses.
> There is electric lighting upstairs and downstairs and telephones have entered the village . . .
> The road goes to the door of every house and motorbikes race by.

Everyone gets education; everyone enters the school room . . .
The cherries are good to eat and the tree is difficult to break. Happiness
won't fall from the sky, aim for the target then work realistically, the
flower of Xiaokang is fully open, fully open!!
(Taped Interview, Village Performing Troupe, December 2000)[8]

The tools for carrying out the technical aspects of pedagogy included
exemplary demonstration methods as well as more formalized forms of
education such as agricultural lessons in schools.

Technical education was the means by which cadres guided farmers'
'choices' about crop production, so it formed an intrinsic part of the governing *for* rather than *by* the people (Cao 2004; Wu 2003). In policy documents, the farmers were to be given the freedom to choose how to diversify
their crop production in response to falling grain prices with the role of
cadres being one of facilitating innovation by providing information, technical support, and services. However, in practice, plans for restructuring
were devised by the county and township cadres and then implemented in
the usual top-down manner (Qin 2000, 21). As is clear in the words of the
Rivercounty head responsible for agriculture, a diligent and seasoned cadre
in his sixties, the township cadres spent considerable time instructing the
farmers in cultivation:

> The main problem is the *suzhi* (quality) of the farmers, and that is why
> Mao said that education is the main task in the countryside. I have
> been to Taiwan and the *suzhi* of the farmers there is much higher. It is
> difficult to persuade the farmers here to diversify from paddy rice. We
> have to keep going down to the countryside to instruct the farmers in
> the next task. When I saw you in XK village that time we were telling
> the farmers to plant grass for all the cows.
> (Interview, 11 October 2000)

The Party Secretary of Baqiu Township, a confident and articulate man
in his late forties, explained the necessity of government *for* the people in a
similar way:

> As a local official, I have to ensure that the rural masses are settled and
> that society is stable so my responsibilities are onerous. But the greatest
> pleasure in my present situation is helping the country cousins to
> prosper. I want to change their outlook and aspirations and achieve
> something tangible for ordinary people. These words are easy to say
> but difficult to achieve . . . It is very difficult to change their old views
> and customs and this includes their traditional method of tilling and
> their cultivation customs; they are very hard to change.

He went on to detail how this education work was carried out.

The main work method is to open a meeting at each level: a big cadre meeting in the township; a village committee meeting, a Party members gathering. Then township cadres go into the villages and into country cousins homes to do publicity work ... Our cadres explain the facts, doing the sums for the farmers, telling them the input-output ratio of paddy rice and of cash crops such as tobacco. With this kind of persuasion, education and guidance we hope to win agreement with their hearts and words.

(Taped interview, 19 October 2000)

Other pedagogic activities in Rivercounty were more explicitly paternalistic. One example was the household linkage system whereby a cadre was assigned responsibility for helping a group of between five to ten households to 'charge towards *xiaokang*': providing them with technical help and guidance in agricultural production and doing thought work on them. This was generally regarded by villagers to be well-intentioned but insubstantial. Another example involved cadres doing thought work on poor farmers, persuading them to produce the pillar crop or another cash crop by means of a sponsorship system. The cadre would guarantee that if a farmer cultivated the crop according to his instructions, he would be compensated should the venture fail. In media accounts of such successes, the greater the initial ignorance or distrust on the part of the farmer, the greater the subsequent success and the more potent the demonstrated capacity of the Party-state to deliver a good standard of living through education and caring. It must be noted, however, that although the sponsorship method was much hailed on television news, its promises were rarely delivered in real life.

At the instigation of the Organization Bureau, in Rivercounty, as in many other parts of Jiangxi, the township governments were required to establish agricultural demonstration depots (*nongye shifan jidi*). These depots experimented with new varieties of rice, crops and livestock. Ideally they shifted the risk of experimentation from farmers to the township government; provided examples of success for emulation; and distributed seeds, resources and technical support. The depots were first set up in the relatively wealthy northern coastal province of Shandong where they enjoyed considerable success. Then in the latter half of 1997 the central committee instructed all rural localities to create similar depots. Cadres from throughout Jiangxi visited Shandong and then returned to set up their own versions. The depots were to foster agricultural development whilst helping state institutions claim legitimacy by making their developmental efforts visible. As one cadre explained:

The main purpose is to generate social and political benefits. Economic benefits are important but we are emphasizing the social benefits. The aim is to create a good impression among the masses.

(Interview, township cadre, 5 October 2000)

Although some of the depots in richer townships along main transport routes were able to sustain operations, most of them went bankrupt and existed in name only. The township depots that I visited in 2000 were commonly brick sheds and tobacco plots with a sign saying 'agricultural demonstration depot.' The depots failed because they were supposed to operate as businesses and yet were a product of an administrative order, a throwback to the very same planned economy that they were designed to lead the peasants away from. The township cadres managing the depots knew that they would, within a few years, be assigned to a new locality, so did not wish to invest much time and effort into them. And although a key objective for establishing the depots was to reduce the tax burden on the masses by providing employment and income for underemployed township staff, many staff members lacked the motivation or expertise to generate profit, especially as they would receive the same wage regardless.

Citizenship education for farmers in Rivercounty served visually to (re)produce the image of the state as the guarantor of rights, especially social rights, whilst at the same time making individuals responsible for attaining those rights. Although interventions to help farmers escape poverty and become self reliant by encouraging them to improve their *suzhi* (*suzhi fupin*) were well-intentioned, focusing on dispositions and knowledge enabled more fundamental systemic problems to be glossed over. In the case of Rivercounty the state response to the fallout from imprudent state grain policies and the pressures of global market integration was not to allow greater civil and political rights for rural producers but to devise new production plans and to execute them through the vertical state apparatus. A top-down bureaucratic rationality drowned out the concerns of the farmers and hindered the scope for them to devise their own strategies such as forming information and co-operative networks based on kinship.

Farmers' responses

Despite the insubstantial content of many pedagogic activities directed at the farmers, the performance and language of these activities nevertheless contributed to a conceptual mapping of modernization across spatial and administrative hierarchies in which villages were at the 'bottom' and their inhabitants were classified as 'backward' (see Pigg 1992; Xin 2000). Similar to the self-perception of the Tibetan students interviewed by Lin Yi and the migrant children who spoke with Lu Wang (this volume), many farmers in Rivercounty internalized the valuations embodied in this mapping of modernization and attributed their hardship to their own *suzhi* deficiencies (Murphy 2004).

But this is not to say that the farmers were entirely passive in the face of quotas, policy failings, market insecurities and repeated waves of pedagogy. Many scholars have documented how 'subaltern' people devise small tactics and strategies to resist the socio-political order: sometimes known as 'alternative citizenship practices' (Ku 2003; Scott 1985). This resistance has been shown often to involve appropriating or reworking aspects of official mainstream discourse (de Certeau 1988). For instance, many farmers used the excuse of low *suzhi* to resist the production quotas allocated to them. They would say to township cadres: 'we don't grow X crop because our *suzhi* is low.' As one farmer, a sad and tired looking woman in her fifties explained to me:

> We don't plant such crops because we don't have the skills. We've tried tobacco but our family doesn't have any contacts. It has to be sold at the tobacco purchasing dept and as we aren't familiar with that person we cannot get a good price for our tobacco and when we see this we feel very angry, but there is nothing we can do except stifle our anger and not plant tobacco. We would prefer not to complete our tobacco quota and let the government be fined. Anyway we don't have the skills.
>
> (Taped interview, October 2000)

Such instances of resistance by farmers to top-down instructions were habitually interpreted by cadres as further evidence that the country cousins were unfit to manage their own agricultural production, let alone contribute to devising responses to the challenges of falling grain prices, global market competition and the imperatives of agricultural diversification.

Although the discourse of *suzhi* was so entrenched that farmers generally accepted that their socioeconomic disadvantage derived from deficiencies in their attributes, some farmers nevertheless questioned the systemic factors for their disadvantage. Part of the questioning arose because of the incongruence between the highly publicized claims that the state made for its modernizing achievements and the farmers' own observations and experiences of cadres and institutions. Drawing on concepts and symbols used in citizenship education, some farmers argued for the freedoms (in agricultural production and marketing) that were espoused in neoliberal discourse but denied by a rigid vertical political structure, and for the socioeconomic entitlements promised in developmental discourse but denied by both bureaucratic abuses and state retreat from welfare provisioning. As discussed already, the *sanjiang* campaign provided a key forum for many farmers to demand their social, political, and civil rights.

Farmers would also resist by using humor to question the *suzhi* of cadres and their pedagogic performances. As an example, when cadres were televised visiting rural homes and sending warmth to farmers (*song wennuan*) by giving money for school fees to hardship households and food to households with sick members, farmers would quip that when they wanted to build houses or obtain help they had to 'send warmth' to the cadres. As a further example, following a news bulletin about how Rivercounty cadres were now convening 'civilized meetings' where attendees would arrive on time, study the documents seriously, and refrain from drinking and smoking, farmers joked with a rhyming ditty that included the lines 'holding a meeting is to get drunk, summing up is to eat ones' fill.'

Citizenship education for cadres and farmers in Rivercounty shows how, as in the old Maoist days, the relationship between state and society was constructed to privilege social aspects of citizenship and sidestep political ones. The pedagogy for farmers dramatized 'development' as a moral discourse – one that created a particular type of subject, valorized particular kinds of knowledge for particular groups, and ordered these groups in relation to their distance from modernity and civilization. In the case of Rivercounty, the farmers were not involved in deciding what was good for them. There was no egalitarian process of problem solving. Rather the upper levels prescribed how the farmers had to be changed, with the redemption of poor farmers being possible only through their acceptance of the guidance and teachings of the Party. Farmers, however, were not entirely accepting of models of citizenship premised on assumptions about their *suzhi* inadequacies and the need to accept the instructions of a benevolent and caring state. Indeed, some farmers' perceptions of the gap between modernization rhetoric and reality caused them to focus on the inadequacies in state provisioning and actions as the reason for their difficulties in obtaining the rights associated with social citizenship.

Conclusion

In Rivercounty at the end of 2000 both lower level cadres and farmers were subject to citizenship education that included moral/dispositional and economic/technical components. These components overlapped considerably. Rather like the 'prosperity gospel' of some Christian evangelical groups, the pedagogic discourse in Rivercounty portrayed a good material life as proof of a civilized disposition, moral integrity and correct apprehension of Party doctrine. Accordingly, redemption and subsequent prosperity were constructed as being delivered to farmers through cadres.

But even though the dispositional and technical components of citizenship education played complementary roles, they also played discrete roles. The dispositional/moral pedagogies served as a band-aid for the symptoms arising from flaws in the Party-state governance structures, such as poor policies, corruption and bullying. They substituted for more fundamental changes in political and economic structures to enable government *by* the people instead of *for* them.[9] In particular, they deflected attention from the ways in which rural peoples' position at the margins of Chinese society contributed to their 'peasant traits' of distrust, conservatism and ignorance. Although village elections were certainly a positive step in the direction of systemic change, it is unclear the extent to which a small, contained and directed pocket of political participation within a rigid vertical hierarchy would be able to ameliorate those systemically-induced aspects of poor governance that so outraged farmers.

The technical/economic component of the pedagogy affirmed and legitimated the vertical power structure and its top-down method of directing modernization. This aspect of the pedagogy portrayed the rural cadres as professional elites, and encouraged them to see themselves as standing apart from and above the masses. Meanwhile the farmers were constructed as the most marginal group, distant from and in need of modernity, with the value of their local social networks and innovations often being overlooked and even stifled. This is not to deny that some top-down technological interventions (such as the introduction of high yielding varieties of grain) greatly enhanced farmers' access to social rights. Nor is it to deny that farmers needed resources and information to be made available to them. But the process of formulating production plans and the direction of knowledge flow were always top-down, keeping the farmers at the margins of Chinese society and assuming that they had nothing to contribute to problem-solving. Despite state appeals for farmers to be entrepreneurial and innovative, the scope for actually achieving this was constrained by the rigid political framework and inefficient fiscal system.

The dispositional/moral and the economic/technical facets of citizenship education together constructed a particular kind of paternal or 'pastoral' relationship between the cadres and the rural masses. But the inconsistencies between the ideals of a caring and pastoral government on the one hand and the farmers' simultaneous experiences of the top-down planning system and market vulnerabilities on the other were becoming increasingly visible. Most pertinently, although the state's pedagogic discourse denounced corruption and coercion, appealed to farmers to innovate in the market place, and promised a better standard of living, the farmers remained at the margins of Chinese society, and continued to experience abuse, official interference in production and increasing economic insecurities.

At the time of fieldwork, tensions were mounting because of the incompatibility between rigid political structures on the one hand and the challenges of neoliberalism and global market integration to rural livelihoods on the other. It was unclear how long the discursive construction of a pastoral relationship between the cadres and the farmers would be able to provide reinforcement to cover over the many points of strain.

Postscript

I returned to Rivercounty in August 2004. At this time the grain shortage caused by the 2000 policy of replacing early rice with cash crops had led to an increase in the purchase price for grain. Meanwhile, official concern about food security caused central state planners to demand that farmers prioritize grain production. The government distributed subsidies to farmers with the sum that each received being calculated according to their area of land under grain cultivation. The government also issued production targets to each locality. The task of lower level cadres became one of 'stimulating the enthusiasm of the farmers' for rice production and ensuring that they applied fertilizer and pesticide at appropriate times and used high quality seed varieties.

The media widely praised exemplar villages and townships where the enthusiasm of farmers and the work of cadres had contributed to bumper grain yields. The media also hailed the increased grain prices, the grain production subsidies and the technical assistance for rice growing as evidence of the Party's care and concern for the rural populace.

The language about the need to 'diversify agricultural production' that prevailed in 2000 was retained, but by 2004 the meaning of this slogan had changed. In 2004 agricultural diversification was not to occur as a substitute for early rice production. It was ideally to assume the form of more specialized and larger-scale production bases promoted through re-vamped and commercialized agricultural extension depots. Despite the difference in the state's production priorities in 2000 and 2004, the top-down mobilization methods of the cadres and the requirement that they carry out work on the disposition (the enthusiasm) and technical competence of the farmers continued.

Also in 2004 as part of a nationwide attempt at reforming the rural fiscal system, counties in Jiangxi province began preparing to 'convert fees to tax'. This reform involved abolishing the village and township tax levied at 5% of per capita income and abolishing miscellaneous informal levies and fees, replacing them with a fixed-rate tax. The aim was to relieve the burden on farmers by preventing local governments and village committees from imposing arbitrary charges and by increasing supervision over the deployment of the collected revenue. In marginal agricultural counties such as Rivercounty, this reform led to a severe shortage in funds for public and administrative expenditure so cadres were forced to reintroduce the informal levies and fees, a situation referred to as 'the rebounding of the farmers' burden' (*nongmin fudan fantan*). In 2004 this rebounded farmers' burden seemed likely to persist because the fiscal reforms were not accompanied by fundamental systemic changes such as the removal of structural bias against the countryside, the institutionalization of sustained and substantial monetary redistribution by the central state, the streamlining of rural bureaucracy or the political empowerment of farmers. On a more positive note, however, these efforts at fiscal reform indicated that the new Hu-Wen leadership recognized that systemic changes more substantial than pedagogy were needed to help farmers better their lives.

References

This article draws on articles from the local newspaper, *Jingangshan bao* (Jinggang mountain news) 01 September–15 December 2000, as well as local government reports and circulars from Rivercounty.

Notes

The field research and writing for this paper was supported by funding from a British Academy Post-Doctoral Research Fellowship, Jesus College at University of Cambridge, the Simon Population Trust and the Contemporary Chinese Studies Programme at University of Oxford.

1 Gupta argues that underdevelopment is a form of identity.
2 Both Oi and Unger point out the continuation of Maoist governing structures in the era of the market economy. Oi's work in richer industrializing rural areas sees them as a source of change. Unger offers a slightly different perspective. Whilst he acknowledges that some remnants of the Mao-style governing provide livelihood guarantees for farmers, he sees the continuation of these structures as ultimately causing problems for farmers in poor areas and preventing further reform.
3 'Pillar' is the term used by Blecher and Shue (2001) to refer to economic projects backed as winners by local governments in China.
4 The 'Three Represents' (*san ge daibiao*) are 1) the development trends of advanced productive forces, 2) the orientations of an advanced culture and 3) the fundamental interests of the majority of the people in China.
5 The rationale, techniques and the form of the *sanjiang* campaign inevitably invite comparisons with those of the Socialist Education Movement (1960–62). Both movements aimed to improve the work-style of party cadres, counter the widespread corruption that pervaded rural party organs, raise the consciousness of the masses and combat the growing separation between the leaders and the masses. Both movements gave the masses the opportunity to express their views, make criticism of errors and expose bad people and deeds. Both movements too involved the deployment of external central party work teams to the grassroots.
6 Food, shelter, clothes, medical care and funeral expenses.
7 Stealing, fighting, drugs, prostitution and gambling.
8 This interview was conducted in Wanzai county, Jiangxi province. However, similar songs are sung in Rivercounty.
9 Examples of such fundamental changes might include establishing external institutions for supervising cadres, involving farmers in a consultative democracy and allowing development programs to be devised at the community level rather than through top-down quotas.

3 The urban Chinese educational system and the marginality of migrant children

Lu Wang

This chapter explores how the urban educational system served to frustrate rural migrant children's efforts to obtain the kinds of education that they associated with the privileges of urban citizenship. Because they lacked urban citizenship, migrant children were prevented by legal, social, and cultural barriers from enrolling in urban public schools, suffered discrimination and exclusion in these schools, and lacked adequate support to adapt to the new environment. Urban citizenship was legally inscribed in household registration (*hukou*) and identification documents, and entailed access to social rights such as economic security, health and education. For migrant children, an education that could enable them to compete with urban children for professional work opportunities was the key to preparing them for greater integration and acquiring the cultural capital that could eventually win them cultural belonging and urban social rights. Because they worried the expansion of citizens eligible for urban social rights, however, state officials made little effort to remove educational obstacles that would preserve the marginality of migrant children in urban areas.

Research methods

Focusing on children studying in private schools set up by migrants themselves, I randomly selected 61 children from four such schools in Beijing and 48 children from four such schools in Xiamen. The private migrant schools in Beijing were recommended to me by friends, acquaintances, and colleagues in Beijing. The private migrant schools in Xiamen were recommended by the Xiamen Education Bureau. My research assistant and I conducted child-focused group discussions and interviews with children from these schools. We used semi-structured interview questions, and tape-recorded and transcribed the discussion and the interviews. Among the 61 children in Beijing, there were 29 boys and 32 girls, and among the 48 children in Xiamen, 25 were boys and 23 were girls. Eight out of 61 children in Beijing had attended urban public schools and later transferred to migrant schools.

Table 3.1 Sex of participating children

Cities	Male	Female	Total
Beijing	29	32	61
Xiamen	25	23	48
Total	54	55	109

Table 3.2 Places of origin of participating children

Beijing		Xiamen	
Place of origin	Total	Place of origin	Total
Anhui	11	Fujian	34
Hebei	11	Guangdong	1
Heilongjiang	5	Hubei	2
Henan	10	Hunan	1
Hubei	8	Jiangsu	1
Fujian	2	Jiangxi	3
Jiangsu	2	Liaoning	1
Jilin	4	Sicuan	5
Inner Mongolia	1		
Shandong	1		
Shanxi	1		
Shannxi	1		
Sichuan	3		
Zhejiang	1		
Total	61	Total	48

The participating Beijing children came from 14 different provinces and, of these, Anhui, Heibei and Henan were the most common. In the case of Xiamen sample, nearly 70% of the children came from within Fujian Province (See Table 3.2).

Contexts of case study cities

In 1995, there were 80 million migrants throughout China, including two or three million school age children; by 2000, the total number of migrants increased to 100,000,000, while the number of migrant children reached 7–10 million (Zhou, 2000:3). Beijing and Xiamen were both prosperous cities that drew large numbers of rural migrants.

The capital and political, economic and cultural center of the nation, Beijing had always been one of the major destination cities for migration. Migrant population made up one third of the total population of Beijing. There were about 3 million migrants in 1997, which was ten times more than in 1978 (Office of Census of migrants, 1997). Concerned that the rapid growth of the migrant population would have a negative impact on the image of the capital and put pressure on limited social resources, the Beijing municipal government tried to keep the number of migrants, especially those who took along their entire families, under control. Policymakers feared that better educational opportunities for migrant children would encourage more migrants to bring their entire families with them, and this attitude prevented them from making better educational opportunities available to migrant children. Beijing's government did not make many efforts to legalize or regulate the private migrant schools that sprang up in response to migrant families' demand for education.

A coastal city in the southern part of China, Xiamen was an island in the Taiwan straits. Administratively, it belonged to Fujian Province, which was located in the southeast part of China. It was officially defined as a special economic zone by the central government in the early 1980s. Because of the favorable policies associated with its status as a special economic zone, the economy of Xiamen City developed rapidly. In addition, its pleasant environment and good living conditions had attracted increasing numbers of rural migrants. The proportion of the migrant population was equal or even greater than that of local residents. Between 1984 and 1997, the migrant population grew from 39,000 to 380,000 (Mi & Ding, 1998:41). In Kaiyuan District, where my research was conducted, local residents numbered 290,000, while migrants numbered 230,000 (Government of Kaiyuan District, 2000). In 2000, there were about 30,000 migrant children between ages 6 and 14 in Xiamen, and half of these children were in Kaiyuan District.

Unlike Beijing's government, Xiamen's government issued its own "Temporary Methods of Education for Migrant Children" in 2000 (Xiamen Municipal Government, 2000). This document pronounced that the government would recognize migrant schools officially when they met the requirements, so that they could acquire legal status for operation, and become integrated into the management system of local education authorities. Section 3 of the "Methods" spelled out detailed requirements and conditions for opening a private school tailored for migrant children. It laid down accreditation requirements for space, conditions and facilities, finances, qualifications of school principals and teachers, teaching and learning, and management. The local school inspection had set up inspection and evaluation systems for these schools in order to supervise their quality.

Life at the margins of urban society

Although rural citizens could move to urban areas, getting formal approval to register in medium-sized or large city was still largely beyond their reach (Kam Wing Chan, 1999:52). *Hukou* transfers had historically been reserved for state-initiated projects that needed to bring in laborers. It was extremely difficult for most rural citizens to gain urban citizenship. In the post-Mao era, a new form of transfer has involved the sale of urban citizenship documents. Smaller cities began to sell permanent registration certificates in the late 1980s and the practice was introduced in the big cities in the early 1990s. The price seemed to depend very much on a spatial hierarchy of cities in China. Beijing, Shanghai and other great cities, considered the most desirable places to live, became the most difficult to gain residency in. After them came the medium sized cities, large towns, county towns and small county towns. At the bottom of the hierarchy were the villages (Delia Davin, 1999:45). A permit cost 3,500–6,000 yuan in a small city in Jiangsu Province in 1993, but it could cost as much as 20,000–30,000 yuan in the Pearl River Delta. A *hukou* in a suburb of Beijing cost 30,000 yuan, and a *hukou* in Beijing city proper cost as much as 50,000 yuan, or 100,000 yuan if it was paid by an employer (Delia Davin, 1999:45).

Though the largest cities rarely gave out *hukou*, the registration system in small and medium sized cities in southern areas of China, such as Xiamen, underwent some reform. Migrants who had the capability to buy an apartment in the destination cities could obtain one permanent *hukou* (red sealed household registration, *hongyin hukou*) as well as two or three pre-permanent *hukou* (blue sealed household registration, *lanyin hukou*, that would automatically turn into permanent *hukou* after five years) for family members. Migrants who could afford to bring their children to the destination cities have normally stayed there for years. However, only a small number of migrants had enough wealth to purchase apartments. About 30,000, or 7.8%, of 380,000 migrants had a blue household registration in 1997 (Mi & Ding, 1998:41). They often had to make painful choices about which child to support and to buy household registration for, as it was difficult to pay for all their children to study in Xiamen.

Migrants suffered a "wanted but not welcome syndrome (economically wanted migrants labor which is, culturally and politically, not welcome" (Veit Bader, 1997:10). As Bader wrote "Immigrant workers are welcomed by employers and resented by resident workers; immigrant entrepreneurs are viewed as undesirable business competitors or welcomed as providers of unusual goods and services at low prices. Immigrants as customers of goods and services may be welcomed as buyers and taxpayers as well as resented as extra clients crowding public services" (1997:9). At the same time, however, rural migrants were feared, both as potential bearers of criminality and as potential competitors for the social rights associated with urban citizenship. Rural migrants were also loathed because of the kinds of stereotypes Rachel Murphy (this volume) described as pervasive in official constructions of farmers as backward and stupid. The migrant children I studied spoke of painful personal experiences of exclusion they experienced due to their lack of urban citizenship. Local children called them, "wild children" (*ye haizi*), "*waidi gou*" (dogs from outside), and "little bastard" (*xiao zaizi*). As a 10-year-old migrant boy in Beijing said:

Once we were playing somewhere, they (local kids) screamed to us "Where did these wild children come from? Go away!" Last time we were playing in the fun fair (youle chang), they shouted to us (local children) "Get out of the way, we are playing here!" and then they cursed us waidi dogs. We cursed them as Beijing dogs.

As the following interview excerpts with migrant children in Beijing suggest, household registration was a crucial factor in determining cultural as well as legal citizenship.

Q: How can you become a Beijing person? Is speaking very good Beijing accent help you to become a Beijing person?
A: No. You should be born in Beijing, having household registration and houses here.

(Liu Xiaohua, female, age 14)

You will not be bullied or insulted verbally once you become a Beijing person.

(Wang Dong, male, age 11)

I hope to get Beijing household registration because I can then become a real person of the capital of the motherland.

(Guo Nana, female, age 15)

As in Vanessa Fong's study of transnational Chinese youth (this volume), and Nicole Newendorp's study of mainland New Arrivals in Hong Kong, the rural migrants I studied longed for acceptance in their new homes, but were constantly reminded that they were unwelcome and inferior to local citizens. Migrant children said that such exclusion made them feel "very uncomfortable", "angry", "lacking in a sense of security" and "annoyed". Though they praised the prosperity and advanced development of their new urban homes, migrant children lamented that their new neighbors were "not friendly", "bullying", "detesting", and "isolating". Table 3.3 lists migrant children's comments about Xiamen and Xiamen people.

Obstacles to migrant children's enrolment in urban public schools

Students lacking local registration could only enroll in local public schools as *jiedu* students (students from outside community, borrowing a place to study). A recent study (Beijing Committee for Mingmeng Party, 2000) showed that *jiedu* students had to pay the following three types of fees in addition to the regular fees that all students paid:

- *jiedu fei* (fee for study in a school where you are not a local resident): 480 yuan/term per head according to the regulations of Beijing municipality.

Table 3.3 Migrant children's comments

About Xiamen city	About Xiamen People
• More developed economically • Environment is better • Life is richer (*fengfu*) • Beautiful scenery • Green mountains and pretty water (*shanqin shuixiu*) • Huge supermarket and department store • Has many interesting places	• Some people are more conservative and can tell between local and *waidi* (outside) people • They use local dialects to swear at me • They are not as honest as we are • They are not friendly • They bully *waidi* people on the grounds that they are local • They call us *xiangbalao* (people from rural areas) • They are spoiled • They are annoyed by us and detest (*xianqi*) us • They are more fussy/picky • They isolate me • Xiamen people are not very good

Source: Personal interview by Lu Wang (27th Feb.–6th March 2002).

- *ze xiao fei* (fee for selection of school): 1,000 yuan/term per head.
- *zan zhu fei* (fee for supporting the school): In principle, this should not exceed the standard of fee for selecting schools, but the actual amount is based on the negotiation between the school and the parents. In 2000 70% of the schools requested this fee. The highest fees were 20,000–30,000 yuan, while the average fee was 1,908 yuan.

Few migrant parents were able to pay such high fees. A study of the household backgrounds of 500 pupils in migrant schools (Zhao, 2000b:14) indicated that most parents were small family stall owners and casual workers. In most cases, their monthly household income was between 800–1,500 yuan. Per capita income was between 200–350 yuan per month, which was around the local poverty line (Wang & Cook, 2000). A study in Shanghai showed that the migrant households' expenses were around 100–600 yuan per month. The general average was 524 yuan per household. The Engle coefficient[1] was as high as 63.7% for them when expenses were broken down, as 288 yuan out of 523 yuan would be spent on the consumption of food each month. The next two biggest expenses were savings and money sent home, and housing. Only 2.9% of the expenses were directed towards children's education (Zhang *et al.*, 1998:255).

Because of their families' poverty, most migrant children could not afford public schools. Among the 61 students in my Beijing survey, 8 used to study in urban public schools but later transferred to migrant schools. The high cost of urban public education was one of the major reasons for them to transfer out of the urban schools. When I asked a 12-year-old migrant boy in Beijing if he would prefer to study in an urban public school, he replied:

Yes. But (we have) no money, prices are too high. I studied there before, (I paid) about a thousand yuan one year. Now it went up to

Table 3.4 Average monthly life expenses for migrant households (Yuan)

Items	Average amount	% in total
Daily drink and food	287.53	54.91
Saving and sending home	72.33	13.81
Housing	63.19	12.07
Cigarettes and wine for men	40.92	7.81
Clothing and make ups for women	17.73	3.39
Water, electricity and gas	15.31	2.92
Children's education	15.18	2.90
Entertainment	7.91	1.51
Transportation	3.54	0.68
Total	523.65	100.00

Source: Zhang et al., 1998:256.

> 2,000 or 3,000 yuan. . . . We pay more than them (local children). We have to pay jiedu fee as wandi ren (people from outside Beijing). We paid 480 yuan jiedu fee in advance and later it went up to 600 yuan. Beijing children don't have to pay this fee.

Before transferring to Huangzhuang school, a private Beijing migrant school, Zhang Yasong (a 12-year-old migrant girl) had studied in a public school for two years. In describing the reasons for her transfer, she said that she had to pay about 1,000 yuan just to enter the public school. In addition she had to pay another 1,000 yuan for all kinds of other fees. But she only paid 400 to 500 yuan each term for everything in Huangzhuang. Hanxu, a 13-year-old migrant boy who went to a public school before transferring to Zhenghua (a private migrant school in Beijing), said that

> The tuition and fees were too high for my family. Just myself will consume a few thousand yuan a year. This time you paid 70–80 yuan for the vaccine and next time you had to pay for something else. Every time there is a parent meeting, fee is collected for something.

At one Beijing public school where I conducted interviews, a migrant child had to pay 150 yuan for lunch per month. A child who did not eat at school had to pay 30 yuan per month just to stay in the classroom during lunch hours. Moreover a migrant child had to pay 30 yuan for the school uniform for warm weather, and 80 yuan for the school uniform for the cold weather. Children at this school complained that they had to buy too many sets of school uniforms. As Gao Yadan, a nine-year-old Xiamen migrant girl, said, "We have too many school uniforms but we still have to buy the new ones each term. You are not allowed not to buy it. The old ones are still in good condition before we buy the new ones."

The dual household registration system that divided rural and urban residents was a means of limiting the number of people who could claim the social rights associated with urban social citizenship. As Yang (1996:65) argued, "it divides urban and rural residents into two sectors in entitlements, opportunities and risks."

While all primary school children registered in a primary school's district were automatically admitted, this was not the case for migrant children, who had to take difficult entrance examinations to gain admittance even to primary schools. One Xiamen primary school principal said that 80 migrant children applied to enter his school in August of 2001, but only 15 were admitted. Another Xiamen primary school principal said that more than 100 migrant children applied for her school last year, but only 20 were admitted.

Many children in private schools had been rejected from public schools. As the following excerpt from an interview with a 10-year-old migrant boy in a Xiamen private school shows, such rejection could be humiliating.

> Q: What do you feel are the differences between your school and public schools?
> A: Public schools look down upon people from outside Xiamen for we are poor.
> Q: Do you want to go to public schools?
> A: Yes. How we not think of it?
> Q: Did you ever try to take entrance examinations for public schools?
> A: It is no use to take exams. We have to pay another 500 yuan in addition to 800 yuan. Having come to Xiamen, I will study hard, not let those local people look down upon us. I will improve the reputation (zenguang) of outside people. They think that outside people are not good in their studies. In fact there are some outside people who can study well. I will perform well and let all of local people know that we outside people are not poor and easy to be bullied as they think.

Public schools and even some state-recognized private migrant schools also refused to admit students from families that had violated fertility control policies. Xiguo, a private migrant primary school in Xiamen, refused to admit children from families with more than two children. Kaihe, another private migrant primary school in Xiamen, required that each student show three certificates in order to gain admission to his school: a) one-child certificate; b) family planning medical examination certificate; and c) provisional residential certificate.

Discrimination in public schools

Migrant children knew that urban public schools were superior to private migrant schools. They said that "We can learn more knowledge in the public schools because they have the strengths of better teaching quality" (Xiaomei, female, age 12, Beijing), "their school can develop our intelligence, and they organize many activities such as summer camp" (Li Jia, female, age 14, Beijing), and "there are more extra-curriculum activities there and quality of teaching is also good" (Liu Fang, female, age 13, Beijing). Some also saw public school as a means of social integration. As Yang Song, an 11-year-old migrant boy in Xiamen, said, "It is better for us to study in the same school with local children so that we can better understand each other."

Yet, like the minority students studied by Lin Yi (this volume), the rural migrant students I studied felt uncomfortable with mainstream schools that made them feel unwelcome. As the following excerpt from an interview with Hu Peng (a 14-year-old migrant boy in Beijing) suggests, such discomfort could motivate even a relatively wealthy migrant child to transfer to private migrant schools.

> Lu Wang: Why didn't your father send you to public school?
> Hu Peng: It is not because it is too expensive. My father sent me to the public school. But I only stayed for a few weeks and couldn't carry on staying there.
> Lu Wang: Why couldn't you stay on?
> Hu Peng: The things are that when the teacher asks questions in the class, even if I put up my hand, the teacher would not call me. The teacher would play with them and was not interested in playing with us.
> Lu Wang: You only stayed for a few weeks. Would things be different if you had stayed longer?
> Hu Peng: It will be the same if you stay on. The teachers and the classmates do not speak to you.

The fact that migrant children were categorized as *jiedu* students "created a boundary marker that could be used to exclude or marginalize other groups. It could be used to create 'us – them' situation" (Neil Thompson, 2003:16). When describing her experience in the public school, Zhang Yafang (a 12-year-old migrant girl in Beijing) said, "The classmates often cursed at us. Once when we had physical education, a Beijing classmate started swearing at me. They called us waidi bangzi (gang of outsiders)." Wang Qiang (a 15-year-old migrant boy in Beijing) said, "I feel we are not part of them (urban children), that is to say our hearts and soul could not meet together."

Private migrant schools and the reproduction of migrant marginality

Since the mid-1990s, many private migrant schools have emerged to meet rising demand from migrant families that could not afford to or did not want to send their children to urban public schools. In Beijing, there were over 100 private migrant schools in 1999, and this number increased to 150 in 2000 and over 300 in 2001. Duan Chenrong estimated that, as of 1999, there were 50,000 migrant children (about one third of all the migrant children in Beijing) studying in this type of school (Duan, 2000:3). Migrant schools first appeared in Shanghai in 1992. Out of the 95,000 migrant children present in Guangzhou in 1999, 40,000 were studying in private migrant schools (Zhou, 2000:7).

Ms. Zhang, the principal of Xinghua Primary School for Migrant Children, was herself a migrant from Hebei Province. She used to be a public teacher in a rural primary school. She and her children went to Beijing to join her husband, who had migrated to Beijing a few years earlier. Realizing that it would be hard for their children to go to school in Beijing, she started to teach them herself. She lived in a migrant area in Fentai district, and her neighbors were all migrants. They all had difficulties trying to get their children enrolled at local public schools. When they heard that she was a teacher and taught her own children, they sent their children to her classes and soon she found her own home was too small to teach so many students. In 1998, she decided to set up her own school, which she called Xinhua Primary School. She rented an unwanted courtyard that used to be a township government building. She hired a few teachers from her hometown. Like others who started migrant schools in Beijing, she couldn't get official permission to open her school. It was often closed down following inspection by Fentai district officials, but after each closing she moved the school to another place to continue. When they instructed her to close the school, the local officials did not make effective arrangements for the children to go to other schools. But the enrollments in this school continued, even though it was not welcomed by the local government. There were around 80 pupils in 2000 and it increased to around 500 in the second term of 2000–01 and 800 in the fall of 2001. The following table shows the rapid annual growth of the enrolment of another migrant school, Huangzhuang School, in Beijing.

Because Beijing's municipal government preferred to outlaw rather than regulate private migrant schools, most such schools in Beijing had extremely poor facilities and human resources. Xiamen had some better-quality

Table 3.5 Increase of enrolment of Huangzhuang Primary School (1998–2002)

School year	First term	Second term	Growth rate (%)
1998–99	100	300	
1999–00	500	700	57.1
2000–01	1,200	1,500	53.3
2001–02	1,500	2,100	28.6
Annual average increase rate			46.3

Source: Fieldwork 2001.

private migrant schools that operated legally and were regulated by Xiamen's educational officials, but also many low-quality, illegal private migrant schools that lacked the resources to qualify for official recognition. The better private migrant schools charged high fees and were run by business people who had other enterprises and were thus able to put more investment into the schools. The worst private migrant schools were run by migrants or people who earn their living from opening such schools targeted for the needs of migrating parents with low income. Motivated by a desire for profit, these schools were normally poor in school premises and conditions, paying a very low salary to teachers who were mostly unqualified migrants who were likely to leave for better opportunities after a short period of time. They rented a few dilapidated rooms and used poor-quality desks and chairs that had been discarded by local public schools, given by various donors, or brought by students themselves. Without state intervention, market rules dominated the development and operation of migrant schools. With the demand getting higher and higher, entrepreneurs amongst migrants realized that it was a rather profitable business. They competed with public schools by offering low entrance fees and costs. They invested as little as possible in teaching facilities and equipment, hired as few teachers as possible, and paid as low salary as possible to teachers. The relationship between the principals and teachers were like those between bosses and employees (Zhao, 2000b:8), and teachers were not treated as professionals. School owners aimed at making maximum profit from a very small initial investment. The owner of a migrant school could easily make 20,000 yuan in profit each year.

Like the owners and clients of migrant markets and housing compounds described by Li Zhang (2002), students, teacher, and owners of illegal private migrant schools lived in constant fear of adverse, unpredictable government action. For instance, in 2001, Beijing's Fengtai District closed over 50 private migrant schools, leaving only six intact. Most of the migrant schools that had been closed by the government eventually re-opened, returning back to their illegal, unregulated conditions. But the educational disruptions caused by the constantly looming threat and occasional reality of forcible school closures exacerbated the marginality of these schools.

Like migrants themselves, private migrant schools operated between the margins of rural and urban areas. The conditions at private migrant schools were not only worse than those at urban public schools, but also worse than some of the better public schools in the migrants' rural hometowns. Private migrant school facilities were very unpleasant, and often surrounded by piles of rubbish. The classrooms were small and dark, with broken windows and falling ceilings. Desks and chairs did not match. Almost no space or equipment was provided for play or sports. Migrant children referred to state urban schools as "proper schools" (*zhenggui xuexiao*), implying that their schools were not proper. "Sometimes the ceiling in the back of the classroom is falling in this school," a nine-year-old boy in

Beijing said about his private migrant school. "So we have our hearts in our mouths. It is quite dangerous." "The chairs are not identical to each other," a 12-year-old migrant girl said about another private migrant school in Beijing. "Some are round ones. Some have nails coming out which hurt our bottom. Some are too low and some too high."

National requirements specified that teachers at public primary schools had to have received professional teacher training at the secondary level. These requirements, however, were not enforced even at legally recognized private migrant schools. Most of the teachers at legally recognized private migrant schools in Xiamen were not educated for the teaching profession. The local school inspectors also reported that some of the teachers were extremely unfamiliar with teaching and learning processes including preparation, delivering lessons or correcting homework. The actual performance of the teachers was very inconsistent with the qualifications they presented.

Teacher preparation was even worse at illegal private migrant schools. For instance, none of the teachers in Xinghua School in Beijing had any teacher training, and two of them only had junior secondary school education (See Table 3.6).

The motivation of the teachers was also low because they were very poorly paid. The monthly average salary for the teachers of Xinghua School in Beijing was only between 250–333 yuan, 600–700 yuan for Zhenhua School in Beijing and 600–1,000 yuan for Huangzhuang School in Beijing. The salary was not regulated for the teachers in migrant schools, and the salary level was determined by the principals. As a result the teaching force in migrant schools was very unstable. Most of them took it as a temporary job when they first came to the city. They left soon after they found another job that paid more. The principal of Jingming Primary School, a private migrant school in Xiamen, said that a third of the teachers had left between fall term of 2001 and spring term of 2002.

Although teachers in legally recognized private migrant schools in Xiamen had some opportunities to participate in the in-service teacher training organized by the state, they lacked the social rights of public school teachers, such as living allowances, housing allowance, medical security, retirement payment, and preferable policies for the education of their children (Xiao, 1997). According to the principal of Songyue School in

Table 3.6 Teachers of Xinghua Primary School, Beijing

Qualification	Number (%)	Annual wages
Junior secondary school	2 (20%)	3,000
Senior high school	6 (60%)	4,000
Secondary professional school	2 (20%)	4,000
Total	10	

Xiamen, the salary of the teachers in her school was less than half of the average salary of public school teachers. Many children said that the quality of teachers in the private migrant schools they attended was not even as good as that of teachers in their old rural public schools. They felt that the teachers were not committed and responsible. A 12-year-old migrant boy in Beijing said about his private migrant school teacher:

> He is so fierce and horrible. He curses our mothers and calls us 'fools'. His quality is so low. We feel very bad when he swears at us. He calls us the brainless, says 'all there is in your head is water,' and slams exercise books in our faces. Sometimes we cannot understand him, he blames us, saying that we have pig's heads. Every time he is fierce to us, we just want to cry. When he loses, his temper we dare not move. We forget everything we know when he shouts at us,

Private migrant schools taught most of the subjects taught in public schools, including Chinese, Math., Writing, Physical Education, English, Fine Arts, Moral Education, and Social studies. But often one teacher had to teach many subjects, including those for which he or she was minimally qualified. Some students pointed out that the school did not want to spend money on employing more teachers. Without specialized teachers and necessary facilities, minor subjects such as PE, Music, Fine Arts were not often taught in migrant schools. Children were unhappy about the lack of variety in their curriculum.

I went into a private migrant school classroom in Beijing on a Thursday afternoon in 2002. The first lesson in the afternoon should have been math, according to the official timetable the principal had given me. But the teacher was not there. When asked "What are you doing at the moment?" students said that they did not know what to do. When I asked, "Where is the teacher?" the next question, the answer was: "He is sleeping."

Conclusion

Private migrant schools provided a valuable alternative for migrant children who found urban public schools too expensive, too far away, and too unwelcoming. As Duan (2000:3) wrote, "Migrants setting up schools for migrant children was a reasonable and inevitable development under the current constraints on educational resources in urban areas." From an economic perspective, Zhou argued that private migrant schools could create more educational opportunities at lower costs. Zhou also supported this type of school from a demographic perspective. He argued "Migrants are not stable in their residential areas. It was relatively easy for the simple schools (or teaching classes) set up by the migrants to move with the movement of these people. It was more convenient for their children to get access to schooling at a commuting distance" (1998:23). Yet the poor quality of private migrant schools made it difficult for the migrant children they enrolled to use education as a means to break through barriers to attain urban citizenship. Rather than helping them attain the full urban citizenship that they desired, private migrant schools ensured that most migrant children would not get enough education to gain the higher education and professional work that could help them win urban citizenship. The responsibility that the government therefore faces is one of working to ensure that migrant children receive the educational opportunities that will enable them to acquire the social and cultural resources that they need to live full lives.

Note

1 Engle coefficient means the proportion of expenses on food in the total expenses. This coefficient is used internationally to indicate the consumption level of people and as an indicator for the standard of living in different countries. For example, the standards used by the Organization of Food of the UN to indicate the standards of living are above 60% is poverty, 50–60% is Wenbao, 40–50% is Xiaokang and below 40% is Fuyu.

4 Choosing between ethnic and Chinese citizenship

The educational trajectories of Tibetan minority children in northwestern China

Lin Yi

Introduction

This chapter draws on fieldwork in a Tibetan administrative region to explore how minority children's efforts to attain social mobility through education were complicated by the Chinese state agenda of integrating them into the Han nation-state. This complication can be understood as a tension between their desires for full social citizenship in the form of rights to employment, education and opportunity, and the requirement that they also adopt Han cultural citizenship – that they acquire the knowledge and language for "belonging" to mainstream society. As my field study shows, by focusing on integration and equipping students to become part of the Han-dominated mainstream, Chinese state educational policies devalued Tibetan culture and language. This situation prevented Tibetan students from acquiring the kinds of cultural capital that would enable them to "progress", and caused many to become academic underachievers. Meanwhile, successful Tibetan students were also disadvantaged by schools' devaluation of their minority cultural citizenship: as has been observed of minority students more generally, they could have done "significantly better and enjoy[ed] their education much more were the barriers to their success eliminated or reduced" (Gibson 1988:167).

Understanding the impact of education on the social mobility and citizenship aspirations of minority people necessitates understanding the concerns that shape minority education policies and practices. Perhaps the most salient feature of China's minority education policy is that it is shaped by a fear that ethnic and religious allegiances may undermine the capacity of minority people to be loyal political and cultural citizens of the Chinese nation-state. This applies particularly to Western China,[1] where Muslim and Tibetan areas are thought to harbor "violent and terrorist forces, religiously extreme forces and ethnic divisive forces" (*Renmin Ribao Shelun* 2001).

A desire to dilute knowledge bases that threaten to produce alternative forms of cultural citizenship has caused educational planners to separate out religion from popular education (*guomin jiaoyu*). One way in which this separation has occurred involves Party functionaries educating the masses in general, and students in particular, about atheism, materialism and scientism and encouraging them to consciously resist feudal superstition, cult and ethnic secession (JBB and GMB 1999; Guowuyuan 2002; Jiaoyu Bu 2002; D. Li 2002; *Renmin Ribao Shelun* 2001). The only religion-related content in textbooks is an introduction to the origin of religion which portrays religion as a backward element in society that will ultimately wither away (*Lishi* 2001:116).[2] Even though the constitution guarantees citizens freedom of religious belief,[3] this freedom is circumscribed by the several "must-nots", including proscriptions against proselytizing, instruction or the practice of religion in school (Jiaoyu Bu 1983). The direct result of this policy is the marginalization of religion in both the classroom and the wider society.

Caution on the part of Han pedagogues towards alternative and marginal bases of knowledge for cultural citizenship also means that minority education is characterized by chauvinistic approaches towards minority language, history and other cultural aspects of the curriculum. Requests for official permission to teach minority language and literature are assessed according to the perceived threat they pose to the wider national form of cultural citizenship. So when officials permitted Tibetan language and literature to be introduced into the curriculum of some Tibetan minority schools (*minzu xuexiao*), it was within the context of Han instruction in the core subjects with the wider emphasis being on encouraging Tibetan students to master Chinese to facilitate their integration into the mainstream (see, for example, Ma 2001:231–249; Teng and Wang 2001:311–312).

With regard to the history component of the curriculum, minority history barely exists except when being represented in the contexts of social evolution and national unity. With regard to social evolution, all ethnic groups are ordered from a primitive to an advanced stage, with Han at the top and bearing an obvious responsibility for 'civilizing' the less civilized minorities (Harrell 1995; ZJXS 2000:148–149; *Zhongguo Lishi* 1995:187–189). The history curriculum also devotes much space to mapping out the historical process by which different ethnic groups have closely interacted with one another, and as a result contributed to the emergence of a Chinese nation that has a unified national culture and identity. The Han are said to be the nucleus of this unity (*ningju hexin*) (Fei 1989).[4]

Instruction in other aspects of minority cultures in the curriculum is even more limited. On the whole, publicity and education in minority cultures, wherever there is any, is not a systematic instruction or introduction; instead, minority cultures are frequently equated with colourful dress, beautiful dance and song, special dwellings, exotic food, or language and script (Teng et al. 1997). This representation of minority cultures is fragmented and tokenized.

A final issue affecting minority education policy has been that the "troublesome" or "disloyal" minorities are concentrated in the economically least developed regions of Western China (Hu and Wen 2002; Tang 2003). These regions typically have rural populations and rural-urban inequalities that are above the national average[5] and harsh, inhospitable physical environments (Shen 1995; Zhou 1957:237). The disadvantages that face ethnic minorities have been described by Han officials as the "three backwardnesses" (*sange luohou*) of economic productivity, cultural and educational level and living standards (D. Li 2002). The Party-state has increasingly designated a role for education in "developing" the West and integrating it with the rest of China. Much of this policy has invoked the familiar developmental discourse of "catching up"; it has been widely assumed by both the mainstream Han and the members of minorities themselves that, if they did not want to be "phased out" (*taotai*), they had to catch up to the mainstream Han.

The following sections draw on fieldwork conducted 2002–2003 in Tongren County in Huangnan Tibetan Autonomous Prefecture in Qinghai province to examine the cultural citizenship choices and constraints facing Tibetan people. Section One provides a geographical and historical background to ethnicity and education in the field-site of Huangnan Tibetan Autonomous Prefecture, Qinghai province. The next section examines how the government at its different levels created opportunities for the social mobility of Tibetans. Section Three explores the positive attitude of Tibetans towards schooling and their hopes for social mobility. Section Four examines educational policy and practice in two different schools: a mainstream or "ordinary" school (*putong xuexiao*) and a minority school. Section Five considers how parents justified their decisions to send their children to either ordinary or minority schools. Section Six examines students' evaluations of their own schooling type versus the alternative form of schooling. The final section discusses the predicament that Tibetan parents and students faced in school choice, which was rooted in their ambivalence towards the value of their culture – an effect of its subordination to the dominant discourse of advanced culture (*xianjin wenhua*). The conclusion reflects on whether or not inclusive education for Tibetans is possible and whether or not fully inclusive social citizenship – social and economic rights, and equal opportunities – can be achieved whilst at the same time preserving Tibetan cultural integrity. These empirical sections flesh out tensions between Tibetans' aspirations for personal advancement in an era of economic change, counterbalanced against their competing desires to sustain the integrity of their culture and identity – tensions which exemplify their marginal position in the Chinese nation-state.

Fieldwork

Huangnan Prefecture is in Qinghai province, bordering Gansu province. Qinghai province has the third highest proportion of minorities (45.97 percent) among over 30 provinces and regions in China (GRPB and GTRSKT 2002). For several centuries, the east of Qinghai and the neighboring parts in Gansu were inhabited by several different ethnic groups, rather than by just one or two. The region was therefore historically a hub of communication between various ethnic groups who have identified respectively with Tibetan Buddhism (the Tibetan, Mongolian and Tu), Islam (the Hui, Salar, Bonan and Dongxiang)[6] and Confucianism/atheism (mainly the Han). So for minorities, this area was always a frontier where they encountered mainstream culture as well as other minority cultures. Furthermore, Huangnan Prefecture is also an area of agricultural, pastoral and urban populations. This feature of the fieldwork site enabled me to consider the educational experiences and choices of students from both rural and urban backgrounds.

Fieldwork was conducted for this project between February and May 2003. The main source materials were government documents, questionnaires and interviews with school people (students, teachers, etc.) and parents. I received 81 student questionnaires from a mainstream school, and of these respondents, 12 were Tibetan, 33 were other minorities and 36 were Han. I interviewed 50 of the students in person and this included 11 Tibetan students. I received a further 41 valid questionnaires from a Tibetan minority school.[7] I also interviewed several Tibetan parents and their socio-economic backgrounds of the parents included government officials, public servants, manual workers, self-employed business people or farmers. Interviews were conducted in a range of settings including schools, offices, urban dwellings and farmhouses.

Huangnan Tibetan autonomous prefecture: an overview

Huangnan Prefecture is located in the southeast of Qinghai Province. It adjoins two Muslim autonomous counties in northeast Qinghai, and is surrounded by the three Tibetan autonomous prefectures in Qinghai and Gansu provinces in the northwest, southeast and southwest. Huangnan consists of four counties; two of these are largely agricultural (Jianzha and Tongren), while the other two are pastoral (Zeku and Henan). In 2002 the minority population accounted for 92.19 percent of the total, and the breakdown of the ethnic minority population was as follows: 65.94 percent Tibetan, 13.65 percent Mongolian, 8.01 percent Muslim, 4.55 percent Tu and 0.04 percent others (HZT 2003a, 2003b). The Tibetan people were distributed mainly in Tongren and Zeku counties (39.80 percent and 37.09 percent), and to a lesser extent, Jianzha (22.76 percent).[8] In 2002 the ethnic population in Tongren, the seat of the prefectural government, was

Table 4.1 Ethnic minority population in Huangnan TAP, 2002

Area	TP	MP(P)	TP(P)	MP(P)	MuP(P)	TuP(P)	OP(P)
Prefecture	212,504	195,897 (92.19)	140,126 (65.94)	29,013 (13.65)	17,011 (8.01)	9,672 (4.55)	75 (0.04)
Tongren	77,165	69,442 (90)	55,602 (72.06)	129	4,285 (5.55)	9,385 (12.16)	41
Jianzha	49,672	44,151 (88.89)	31,873	46	12,075	131	26
Zeku	54,761	52,545 (95.95)	52,161	15	303	58	8
Henan	30,906	29,759 (96.29)	490	28,823	348	98	–

Key
TP = Total Population
MP(P) = Ethnic Minority Population (and Percentage)
TP(P) = Tibetan Population (and Percentage)
MP(P) = Mongolian Population (and Percentage)
MuP(P) = Muslim Population (and Percentage)
TuP(P) = Tu Population (and Percentage)
OP(P) = Other Ethnic Minority Population (and Percentage)

72.06 percent Tibetan, 5.55 percent Muslim, 10 percent Han and 12.16 percent Tu (HZT, 2003b) (see Table 4.1).

According to the Census, in 2000 the rural populace accounted for 72.16 percent of the population in Tongren County and 78.29 percent of the whole of Huangnan Prefecture. The Han and Muslims of Tongren County mostly resided in Longwu *Zhen* (Longwu Township), so they were urban dwellers. By contrast, most of the Tibetans were rural, engaged in agriculture and some animal husbandry.

At the time of fieldwork, Huangnan Prefecture was one of the three worst performers for education in Qinghai province, having an illiteracy rate of 30.30 percent – the other two poor performing prefectures were Guoluo (34.81 percent) and Yushu (43.77 percent). Together these three prefectures form the *Qingnan Diqu* (South Qinghai Area), the least developed area in Qinghai as measured by economic and educational indicators. At the other end of the educational spectrum, Huangnan had a lower proportion of the college and university graduates (2.39 percent), as well as high school and high specialized school graduates (6.84 percent) than the provincial level (3.3 percent and 10.43 percent) (see Table 4.2).[9]

Since 1990 there were 13 high schools in Huangnan Prefecture. Four of them were located in Longwu Township, the seat of the prefectural and Tongren county governments. Two were ordinary schools: the *Huangnanzhou Zhongxue* (Huangnan Prefecture High School), the oldest school in the prefecture with a history of more than 40 years, and the *Tongrenxian Zhongxue* (Tongren County High School). The other two

Table 4.2 Illiteracy rate, college and university graduate rate, and high school and high specialized school graduate rate in Qinghai and Huangnan, 2000

Area	TP	IR2000	CUGR	HSGR
Province	5,181,560	18.03	3.3	10.43
Huangnan	225,462	30.30	2.39	6.84
Tongren	80,856	23.04	3.33	9.58
Jianzha	48,971	27.72	2.44	6.14
Zeku	57,334	39.97	0.73	3.08
Henan	33,707	38.31	1.23	3.88
Yushu	268,825	43.77	0.76	3.85
Guoluo	140,397	34.81	1.33	5.76

Key
TP = Total Population
IR = Illiteracy Rate (%)
CUGR = College and University Graduates Rate (%)
HSGR = High School and High Specialized School Graduates Rate (%)

were minority schools: the *Huangnanzhou Minzu Gaozhong* (Huangnan Prefecture Minority Senior High School) established in 1990, and the *Tongrenxian Minzu Zhongxue* (Tongren County Minority High School). Since minority education in Huangnan Prefecture refers primarily to the education of Tibetans or Tibetan speakers (Mongolians or Tu), it was not surprising that Tibetan students comprised the majority of the student body in the two minority schools. Han students traditionally dominated Huangnan Prefecture High School, the prestigious school of the prefecture. Muslim students made up the largest part of the student body in Tongren County High School (half of the students). This ethnic composition of the student body in the two schools reflected residential patterns in Longwu Township as well as the government policy of "attending the neighborhood school" (*jiujin ruxue*).

Historically, Longwu Township was called Longwu *Jie Qu* (Longwu Street District). The town emerged to meet the daily needs of the monks of Longwu monastery (Longwu *si*) and its dependants. It formally became a market town at the end of the 19th century when the reincarnation of Buddha in Longwu monastery permitted the business people from Gansu, Xunhua[10] and the vicinities to engage in trade in the Longwu area. After the Longwu market area came into being, the Tibetans, the locally dominant ethnic group, called it "jiakeri", which means "the Han city". Half of these business people were Muslims and they eventually became the main residents of the Longwu market area. From 1954 onwards, a new city area was built up to the west of the Longwu market area. This new settlement became the seat of both the prefectural and county government administrations (HZZBW 1999; TXBW 2001; HZT 1999, 2002, 2003a, 2003b).

On account of this history, Longwu Township was divided into two parts: *xianshang* (the county part), previously the Longwu market area, and *zhoushang* (the prefecture part), which was the new town center. The new town center was home to both prefectural and county administrative sectors in Longwu and commercial and entertainment blocks. In accordance with the "attending the neighborhood school" policy, Huangnan High School, which was located in the prefecture part, mainly recruited students from the new prefecture part of town. As is also noted by Wang regarding migrant children (this volume), this schooling policy meant that residential and socio-economic forms of inequality became reinforced within the school setting. In the case of Huangnan High School, most students were the children of government officials, public servants, teachers and factory workers and/or from Han background. By contrast, Tongren County High School, which was situated in the county part, mainly recruited students from the old part of town. The students included Muslim children as well as those from some other ethnic backgrounds whose families were usually engaged in business.

The two minority schools recruited predominantly Tibetan students, with most from the agricultural or pastoral areas in the prefecture and from Tongren. In the mid 1990s, a donation from Shao Yifu, a Hong Kong businessman enabled another minority junior high school to be set up next to Huangnan High School, named the *Yifu Minzu Zhongxue* (Yifu Minority Junior High School) which recruited Tibetan or Tibetan-speaking students. In September 2002, Tongren County High School merged with Huangnan Prefecture High School because of the decline in student numbers owing to demographic transition.[11] Hence Longwu Township retained four high schools but the ethnic make-up of the student body in secondary education changed considerably over the course of twelve years.

Opportunities for social mobility

State policy in Huangnan Prefecture gave Tibetan graduates priority access to top leadership positions in government.[12] The Tibetans were specifically selected, cultivated and employed as cadres[13] at all levels of administration and in all kinds of scientific and technological positions within the autonomous government organs (*zizhi zhengfu jiguan*). They were similarly favored by the recruitment practices of state work units, and also received preferential treatment for enrolment in local schools, minority colleges or universities (*minzu xueyuan, minzu daxue*) within the province as well as nationwide.[14]

As early as 1955, just two years after Huangnan Prefecture was established, Tibetans became the majority ethnic group among cadres in Huangnan Autonomous Prefecture (HZZBW 1999). Although the Han represented a higher proportion of cadres, Tibetans nevertheless formed the dominant group in terms of absolute numbers. The proportion of Tibetan cadres was especially high when compared to the proportion of cadres from other ethnic minority groups (see Table 4.3).

Table 4.3 Ethnic population and government officials in Huangnan, 2002[15]

	Han	Muslim	Tibetan	Mongolian	Tu	Others
EP %	7.81	8.01	65.94	13.65	4.55	0.04
OPC %	38.28	4.62	44.88	6.93	4.95	0.33
OP %	32.86	2.86	45.71	10	7.14	1.43

Key
EP = Ethnic Population
OP = Government Officials at Prefectural Level
OPC = Government Officials at both Prefectural and County Levels

In addition to privileging Tibetan people within the government, the local government also established a number of Tibetan-oriented key prefectural organizations and institutions for ethnic minority studies covering subjects such as Tibetology (*Zangxue*), ethnic folk art, and ethnic medicine (ibid.). The Longwu Township area was host to establishments such as the Regong Art Gallery (*Regong Yishu Guan*),[16] the Prefectural Ethnic Song and Dance Ensemble (*Zhou Minzu Gewu Tuan*), and the Prefectural Tibetan Medical Hospital (*Zhou Zang Yiyuan*). Longwu Township was also home to three minority schools and a minority teachers college. In fact, Tongren was recently honored as a National Historic-Cultural Renowned City (*Quanguo Lishi Wenhua Mingcheng*) for its Tibetan culture, the only town of its kind in the province.

These positive policies and measures towards Tibetan people and culture, coupled with the resurgence and popularization of Tibetan Buddhism among both Tibetans and Han,[17] fostered pride in Tibetan ethnic culture and a celebration of Tibetan ethnic identity among Tibetans. For example, among my informants, some Tibetan elites were particularly keen to adopt the word *bodajingshen* (extensive knowledge and profound scholarship) to describe their culture.

Education as the means to upward mobility

The largely top-down creation of opportunities for occupational mobility gave Tibetans, both rural and urban, a strong incentive for better social status and quality of life. This section considers the different ways in which these opportunities created incentives for parents from rural and urban backgrounds to value education for their children.

Rural Tibetans observed the life opportunities enjoyed by their compatriots in state work units, and became aware that their lives could improve if they too could become cadres. They saw education as the most direct route to upward mobility. This perception was not confined to the younger generation. Members of the older generation also prioritized education for their children, partly because they missed out on these opportunities for themselves. As some of my interviewees said, they would definitely secure the opportunity for their children to study in schools even if they had to ask for loans or postpone plans to build new houses.

Individuals from rural backgrounds who managed to escape farm and pastoral life through employment in a state work unit had a particularly strong sense of the importance of education. Some of these people were recruited into state work units because of their talents in aspects of Tibetan culture, for example *Zang xi* (Tibetan drama), while others received work unit employment as compensation after land was requisitioned from their village. These people personally experienced the contrast between the hard and bitter life of laboring in the countryside and the easy and relaxed life and regular wage that comes with being in a state work unit. Daily experiences in their new urban working lives further revealed to them the importance of Chinese language education. One informant told me: "this is what I can never forget – I cannot even write a *qingjia tiao* (a note asking for leave) (in Chinese). If I could have gone to school in those days, I would have probably been a county magistrate (*xianzhang*)" (Interview 030103).

Long-time urban Tibetans also valued education, though for different reasons to those who came recently from the countryside.[18] Whereas people from rural families had land for their children to fall back on if they failed in college entrance examinations (*gaokao*), the only outlet for established urbanites was to find temporary jobs such as being a waiter or shop assistant in the township area.[19] These jobs could not guarantee a financially stable life, particularly given the low levels of economic development in the area. The enthusiasm for and investment in education by these families therefore became a priority. This can be seen in their undiminished enthusiasm for education even after the government abolished the job allocation system for university and college graduates in 1996.[20] Under the new policy, when students graduate, they are not guaranteed a job by the state but need to find one by themselves. This meant they were at risk of unemployment after graduation (*biye ji shiye*). But this did not stop them from investing more energy and money in education, and many parents encouraged if not forced their children to study harder in order to enter high schools and ultimately a university.[21] Some parents went further by encouraging their children to try their best to enter a key or famous university (*zhongdian daxue, mingpai daxue*) whose graduates were better able to find a good job.

Among all Tibetans, but especially ones with better access to information, there was a growing tendency towards pursuing education abroad, a development that mirrors nationwide trends. This is not surprising given that many Tibetans felt a closer affinity with foreign countries than with China on account of the politicization and internationalization of the "Tibetan question". Some of my interviewees told me that they had relatives working abroad, and that they expected their overseas kin and relatives to sponsor their education, and perhaps even help them go abroad if they could demonstrate good school performance. These kinds of expectations were usually fostered by their awareness of others who had enjoyed such support.

To sum up, rural people identified education as the main way of freeing themselves from poverty and hardship, while urban dwellers saw it as a means for moving up the social ladder, and eventually joining the elite group wherever this was possible. Tibetan people's evaluations of education were therefore positively equated with material well-being and upward social mobility.

Two schools: an "ordinary" school and a "minority" school

As is common in many minority areas, Tibetan students in my fieldwork site could choose to be educated in either an ordinary or minority school. School choice is fundamental to the citizenship formation of individuals, because as is also discussed by Wang (this volume), the category of school influences the types of labels that are placed on students, the kinds of cultural knowledge that they obtain, and the set of resources and opportunities to which they ultimately receive entitlement. Among four high schools in Huangnan, Huangnan High School and Huangnan Minority Senior High School were under the administration of the Education Bureau of the Prefecture; the other two schools, Tongren County Minority High School and Yifu Minority Junior High School fell under the jurisdiction of the Education Bureau of Tongren County. In this section, I compare the two prefectural schools – Huangnan High School and Huangnan Minority Senior High School.

Huangnan High School is a prestigious local school. After it merged with Tongren County High School in 2002, it became the sole ordinary school in the Longwu area. Consequently it experienced a noticeable increase in the number of the minority students in general, and Muslim students in particular. According to figures provided by the school official, in the academic year 2002–2003, there were over 800 junior and senior school students in six grades, of whom nearly half were female. Among these, minority students made up 65.21 percent. The ethnic breakdown of the minority students was Muslim 31.63 percent[22] and Tibetan 24.09 percent.[23] With a slightly lower percentage than the Han (34.79 percent), the Muslim students comprised the second largest group in the school. In other words, the only ordinary school in Longwu Township was significantly "minoritized". All the Tibetan students were from urban areas and were residents of Longwu Township; many had parents working in state work units at county or prefectural level, while a few had a parent working as a self-employed business person. The students usually paid 400 or 500 *yuan* (Chinese currency unit *renminbi*) per semester, for tuition, facilities (computing), textbooks and exercise books, and some miscellaneous fees.

Of the 76 teachers at Huangnan High School, 9.21 percent were Muslims and 25 percent Tibetans while the remainder was Han.[24] There were no teachers of music and fine art, and there was a shortage of teachers of physical education and English. Qualifications-wise, 100 percent of the teachers for the junior grades met the requirement for an associate college degree (*dazhuan xueli*) or higher, while 46 percent of those who taught senior classes held a university graduate degree (*benke xueli*) or higher.

Like other high schools in China, Huangnan High School very much "danced to the baton of college entrance examinations" (*genzhe gaokao zhihuibang zhuan*). This was clear in both discipline and course arrangement. The students in year three at junior level (*chusan*) and above were required to spend in excess of nine hours per day in school during weekdays, and nearly eight hours devoted to classroom study. In addition, they had to attend school for five hours on Saturdays. When key examinations such as national college entrance examinations were pending, they even attended school on Sundays.

The school had rules and regulations that rewarded students for high achievement and punished them for truancy or other disruptive behavior. Once a student had been punished officially (*chufen*), he or she would be unable to get credentials issued by the school if the punishment had not been discharged by the time of graduation. On the whole, both the school and the teachers were satisfied with the attendance rate of the students, and few students dropped out.

Teachers at Huangnan High School were subject to strict punitive regulations for teaching performance. For instance, if a teacher did not meet the required number of teaching hours, he or she had to pay a fine. This was despite the fact that the insufficient time usually resulted from the school official not allocating the requisite number of teaching hours to the teacher. One of the regulations that the teachers complained about most bitterly was that they were fined when the percentage of students who had passed the end-of-year examinations fell short of the number designated by the school official. Almost every teacher had been punished for this "transgression", and the amount they had to pay varied depending on the percentage of failing students. Fines generally ranged from 40 *yuan* to some 6,000 *yuan*: for reference, the teachers' monthly salary was usually between 700 and 2,500 *yuan*. The key criticism towards this policy was not that the school had introduced such a regulation, but rather, that the criteria was not justifiable: the school had not set the percentage according to local conditions and abilities but according to standards in Xining, the capital of Qinghai province, where the quality of education was the highest in the province.

Like schools in other parts of China, the students were divided into two different classes when they entered *gao'er* (year two at senior level): *wenke ban* (class for liberal arts) and *like ban* (class for science). This eventually led to their study of specific subjects in universities. The school complied with the national curricula, and so used standard issue textbooks (*quanguo tongbian jiaocai*). Because of a shortage of teaching staff, music and fine art were not offered; once-offered courses in manual dexterity (*laodongjishu*) and demography (*renkou*) were also cancelled. Additionally, there were some textbooks on local history and geography that were distributed to the students mainly for self-study, such as *Qinghai Lishi* (Qinghai History), *Qinghai Dili* (Qinghai Geography) and *Minzu Zhengce Changshi* (General Knowledge of the Policy on Ethnic Minorities). The medium of instruction was exclusively Chinese Mandarin (*putonghua*, lit. common language).

Huangnan Minority Senior High School had a much shorter history than Hunagnan High School, but it enjoyed a high profile nevertheless. In 2002–2003 it attracted nearly 500 senior school students in its three grades. The student body comprised Tibetans (60 percent), Mongolians and Tu, and equal numbers of males and females. All the students were Tibetan speakers. They studied in the minority primary schools and junior high schools before attending Huangnan Minority Senior High School. Most of the students came from agricultural or pastoral areas, and boarded at the school. The frequency of home visits varied greatly according to the distance between home and school – once a week at one end of the spectrum, once a semester at the other, though most returned once every one to two months. The students paid 200–300 *yuan* per semester for their study and boarding, and received a grant-in-aid (*zhuxuejin*) of 40 *yuan* per semester from the government.

Students were expected to spend more than eight hours a day in school, with more than seven hours of classroom study. There were no classes on either Saturdays or Sundays. The students also had to go out for physical exercise (*chucao*) at 7am, five days a week.

The school had rules and regulations that rewarded and punished students, but compared with Huangnan High School, discipline was quite lax. Unlike Huangnan High School, there was no school uniform for the flag-raising ceremony or any other special occasions. But like the ordinary school, the attendance rate of the students satisfied both the school and the teachers, and there were hardly any dropouts.

There were 35 full-time teachers at the school and half of them were Tibetan, nearly half were Han, and a few were from other ethnic backgrounds. The teachers were well qualified with 85.70 percent of them having an undergraduate degree. Even so, there was a strong need for physics and chemistry teachers. Unlike Huangnan High School, there was no serious punishment system directed at the teachers' work.

Apart from the courses that were commonly offered in both the ordinary and minority schools, Huangnan Minority Senior High School offered a course that had been tailored in accordance with government policy, that is, *Zang yuwen* (Tibetan language and literature). This was the only course delivered in the Tibetan language at the minority school; all the others were taught in Chinese. *Han yuwen* (Chinese language and literature) and *Zang yuwen* were the only two courses that used *Wushengqu Tongbian Jiaocai* (uniformly compiled textbooks by five provinces and regions in west China where there are Tibetan residents, namely TAR, Qinghai, Sichuan, Yunnan and Gansu provinces). Fine art was also a Tibetan-related course in which the students could learn Tibetan Buddhist painting (*Tangka*), and for which Tongren was renowned both within and beyond the Tibetan area.

As in Huangnan High School, the students in the minority school were divided into the arts and sciences streams from year two (at senior level) onwards. They were entitled to sit college entrance exams in Tibetan.[25] The majority of the students would enter local minority colleges or universities and major in Tibetan literature or science. In the past few years, the number of the students who chose science subjects increased and was now slightly higher than those who chose Tibetan literature, the most popular subject in the past. This was possibly in part influenced by the abolition of the job allocation system. In the past, university graduates were guaranteed jobs regardless of whether or not there was a social or economic demand for their subject. Since students had to find their own jobs, subjects had to be chosen with more attention to the job market. So even though the scientific subjects were among the most difficult for the students in Huangnan Minority Senior High School,[26] they still tended to devote themselves to these subjects. There were nevertheless a high proportion of students who chose Tibetan – this choice usually enabled them to enroll in a minority university or college more easily.

The parental dilemma: where to send children?

There were the differences among Tibetan parents with regard to school choice. Generally speaking, rural parents, farmers or village government officers, and working class parents in state sectors sent their children to (Tibetan) minority (primary) schools in their villages of origin. The parents chose this type of school because of lower fees, convenient travel to and from school, Tibetan language instruction and Tibetan students and teachers. Students with this kind of early schooling usually continued their education in minority junior high and then senior high schools, which tended to be located in urban areas.

Parents preferred to keep their children within a Tibetan minority school environment because they feared that their children would not perform as well as their Han peers if they attended an ordinary school. Conversely, they thought that it would be easier for their children to study in their mother tongue and in a Tibetan cultural environment: language and thought are inseparable and Tibetan students often experience difficulty in grasping concepts and communicating within a Han language and cultural environment. For example, in the ordinary schools, Tibetan students could hardly understand commonsense aspects of the school routine that were taken for granted by the Han. So, even a brilliant Tibetan child who was able to perform excellently in a minority school remained, at best, an average student in an ordinary school.[27]

Parents who decided to send their children to minority schools were aware that many people in the larger society saw the Tibetan language as useless. But these parents felt that the language would nevertheless be useful if the student had a good command of it. This meant that when their children came back to Huangnan Tibetan Autonomous Prefecture as university graduates, they could still work in the government, for instance, in a law court or village governmental sectors, where cadres need to know the Tibetan language to deal with local people. The view that Tibetan is useful stemmed from a belief that children would normally return to Huangnan Tibetan Autonomous Prefecture after graduation. This was because Tibetan parents thought that their children lacked the knowledge, social contacts and cultural background to be able to compete with Han people in finding employment outside the Tibetan areas.

Parents also preferred the minority schools because they believed that their children – and themselves as well – should be able to speak Tibetan before studying other languages, cultures or subjects. To justify their choice, they also addressed the negative effect of studying in ordinary schools. They said that their children would be affected by the Han way after studying in Chinese language and cultural environment and would adopt a Han way of thinking. As a result, the children would become disobedient and lazy and demand too many material comforts like those children from better-off families.

Many parents told me that nowadays a Tibetan child could learn everything in a minority school that they could in an ordinary school. They pointed out that due to the adoption of the national curriculum in all state schools, their children could learn advanced knowledge like Chinese, English, and computing even in a minority school. At the same time they could also learn some Tibetan subjects like painting, literature and language, and some dance and song in regular or extra-curricula classes and so acquire their own ethnic culture in a Tibetan environment.

The parents who sent their children to an ordinary school usually worked in state work units at either county or prefectural level (but not as manual workers) and had been educated in Chinese in ordinary schools, or else they had been educated in minority schools followed by recruitment into a state work unit where the working language was Chinese. Their primary concern in school choice was the limited opportunity to use the Tibetan language because "even in this Tibetan Autonomous Prefecture" Chinese was the working language in the state work units, including Tibetan-related institutions such as the Prefectural Ethnic Song and Dance Ensemble, the Regong Art Gallery, and minority schools.[28] Some examples they gave were that all documents from the authorities had to be drafted in Chinese, although these were also usually coupled with a translation into Tibetan, and the formal language in meetings and conferences was Chinese, even when the majority of the participants were Tibetan.[29] The conclusion was thus that one must learn Chinese regardless of whether one stays in Huangnan or moves elsewhere. In their understanding, the dominance of the Chinese language was determined by its status as the national language, and by the fact that it is the first language of the Han majority. Competence in Chinese would enable a Tibetan student to study in Chinese at a regular rather than a minority college or university, and this would definitely be an advantage when looking for a job in competition with the Tibetan graduates from minority colleges or universities.

In short, a good command of Tibetan without Chinese caused inconvenience in daily life, and became a ceiling to personal occupational advancement. Importantly though, no one who held this view explicitly endorsed the idea of giving up Tibetan. They still expressed willingness or claimed to require that their children master oral Tibetan, and to a lesser extent, written Tibetan. Another consideration in discouraging children from learning or using Tibetan was that, as Huangnan Tibetan Autonomous Prefecture was a multiethnic area (*minzu zaju qu*), it would be inappropriate to adopt Tibetan as a major means of communication. Moreover, many parents also argued or implied that the quality of education in ordinary schools was higher than that in minority schools.

Some other reasons that informed the choice of parents who sent their children to ordinary schools were beyond an instrumental concern with language or quality of education, but were more ideological. One opinion was that Tibetan culture was closely connected with Buddhism, particularly when it went up to certain levels. As a religion, Buddhism was a good choice in cultivating one's moral character and nourishing one's nature (*xiushen yangxing*). But this was not very useful for the progress and development of society, and could even play a hindering role in this respect. This was a popular view among some middle-aged Tibetans who were educated during the Great Cultural Revolution when religion was uniformly criticized as feudal superstition (*fengjian mixin*), and as backward and opposed to advanced materialism (*weiwu zhuyi*). Another disadvantage in studying Tibetan culture was the view of some parents that such study could cultivate an antagonistic sentiment among Tibetans towards the Government and the CPC and, further, foster a consciousness of secession.

Where do the students want to study?

In Huangnan High School, ten out of the eleven Tibetan students in my investigation expressed a preference for studying in Huangnan Minority Senior High School. On the whole the students saw life in Huangnan High School as unattractive and boring. This was because major courses (*zhuke*) were usually too demanding on account of focusing on the college entrance examinations; the students would have preferred to study minor courses (*fuke*) and extra-curricula activities such as music, art and sports. In addition, they would have welcomed the opportunity to study courses such as Tibetan language and literature. But these options were either not offered or were reduced to a bare minimum. For example, even though there was ethnic minority content in the textbooks, many teachers did not bother to cover this material in class, and instead instructed the students to read it by themselves. The content of some teaching materials on ethnic minority issues was often perceived by Tibetan students to be antagonistic, and this sense of antagonism was exacerbated by the negative ways in which some teachers spoke about Tibetan customs.

They said that in contrast Huangnan Minority Senior High School students studied not only all subjects offered in Huangnan High School, including Chinese, English and computing, but also a range of minor courses in ethnic culture. In discussing why it was not possible for them to study the kinds of ethnic culture courses offered in Huangnan Minority Senior High School, the students at the ordinary school explained that their school could not offer such courses because they were not part of the core content of the college entrance examinations. Moreover, educational planners assumed that Tibetan students obtained culturally relevant knowledge from their families anyway (Interview 020101). When asked why they were keen to study their own language and culture, more than 90 percent of them described their embarrassment about their insufficient Tibetan, and explicitly expressed their need to improve their Tibetan. They thought that one should master one's own mother tongue – "the Tibetan language is a symbol of (our) ethnic group" (Interview 010204). They felt that it would be disgraceful if their descendants were not able to speak Tibetan and that poor Tibetan made it difficult for them to communicate with their Tibetan compatriots, with whom they spent most of their time. As for their interest in and enthusiasm for studying their own culture and religion, they explained that it was always good to acquire more knowledge; (their) religion advises people to be virtuous; they would have enough motivation to study excellently if the school offered courses in their culture and religion, and this would enhance their confidence in learning other subjects.

In addition to curriculum issues, the overly stern discipline and the cultural chauvinism of the teachers exacerbated their boredom with school life. Generally the school and teachers kept requiring students to study hard in order to be able to enter a (good) university. Meanwhile, as mentioned earlier, in order to keep up academic competitiveness, the school official also set strict punitive regulations for teacher evaluation. The teachers therefore faced punishment if exam targets were not met, so they transferred this pressure onto the students through harsh discipline, for instance, giving an official punishment, or beating or scolding students. In contrast, the students perceived that their counterparts in Huangnan Minority Senior High School were not disciplined so harshly. They believed that the teachers in the minority school respected and understood the students, treating them as their own children, because "they are also Tibetan" (Interview 010205).

When it came to the practice of ethno-religious customs in Huangnan High School, the students told me that the practitioners of religion were teased by the fellow students and even by fellow Tibetan students. They explained that some teachers did not even allow them to share or explain their customs: they told the Tibetan students not to bring "minority things" (*minzu de dongxi*) into the school, because they might be eccentric (*xiqiguguai*) and unhealthy (*buliang*). Some more informed students pointed out that this was because the school culture was based on the Han culture. The students of Huangnan High School also had the impression that the Minority High School did not discipline its pupils too strictly because they were able to wear their ethnic clothes and other ethnic- or religion-related accessories like Buddhist prayer beads.

A final reason that Tibetan students at Huangnan High School thought that they would have preferred to attend the Minority High School is because their classmates would be fellow Tibetans who they perceived to be more straightforward, authentic, broad-minded and cheerful. By contrast, they saw their fellow Han students in Huangnan High School to be tricky, hypocritical or narrow-minded. Moreover, some of their fellow Han students were not interested in making contact with the minority students. This tendency was presumably embedded in the Han self-perception of their higher intellectual quality; this led the Han students to believe that they could have a higher academic achievement in the school, and consequentially a higher socio-economic status in society. Tibetans therefore faced the prejudicial view that they were intellectually poor, and could not perform as well as the Han students. Although a couple of Tibetan students said that they did not make friends along the lines of ethnicity but personal character, they expressed a preference for the personality that was usually perceived to be possessed by Tibetan students as mentioned above.

In Huangnan Minority Senior High School, 25 out of 41 students in my investigation said that they would have preferred to study in Huangnan High School. Language was the first concern: they believed their Chinese would have improved if they had studied in the ordinary high school. They also held a positive view towards the teaching quality and educational standards of Huangnan High School. And they felt that they would have benefited from studying alongside the Han students who they saw as knowledgeable and academically talented. Relatedly, they thought that studying at Huangnan High School would have the added advantage of enabling them to make new Han friends.

Among Huangnan Minority High School students who expressed a preference for staying in their own school, language was the main consideration; with poor Mandarin they felt that they would not be able to keep up with their Han classmates if they studied in the ordinary high school. This is understandable if we consider that ever since primary school they had received instruction in their mother tongue of Tibetan. The perceived academic superiority of the Han students in Huangnan High School was another factor that prevented some of them from feeling confident enough to choose Huangnan High School over Huangnan Minority High School. While recognizing the social function of the Chinese language, they were not particularly interested in the Han culture; even among those who would like to study in Huangnan High School, only 1 out of 41 students expressed an interest in Han culture. By contrast, the minority school students showed high enthusiasm for their own culture, religion and language. This was another key attraction of the Huangnan Minority High School – that they could study their own culture, language, religion and history. Lastly, to study in an environment of Tibetan compatriots made them willing to stay in Huangnan Minority High School.

To be "ordinary" or minority: citizenship dilemmas

Tibetan students and parents both valued education as a way of producing useful people who could benefit their own ethnic group, their family and themselves. In other words, they were not content with the status quo. Conversely, they strived so much for socio-economic mobility that sometimes this resulted in a desperate pattern of study without break and serious frustration with the ineffectiveness of their study, particularly in Huangnan Minority High School.[30]

Apart from the instrumental function of upward mobility, education was symbolically important for Tibetans because it was seen as a way to transform the traditional image of themselves as a backward people (*luohou minzu*) into an advanced people (*xianjian minzu*). One of the most often used words in interviews was *xianjin* (advanced). They sensitively avoided employing "*luohou*" (backward) to describe their ethnic group by simply emphasizing that Tibetans needed to absorb or study the advanced culture in order to "get the traditional culture reformed and nurtured (*buyu*)". Without this reform and nurture, they feared being "phased out". In their mind, the advanced culture was *Zhongyuan wenhua* (Central Plains culture, i.e., Chinese Han culture), and *waiguo wenhua* (foreign culture) (Interview 030106, -07, -09). In this vein, some of them even argued that when sending children to study in school, it was also necessary to teach the children how to distinguish between *zongjiao* (religion) and *mixin* (superstition). Others emphatically explained to me that nowadays many Tibetan practices were not *religious practices*, but *customs* – custom was at the top while superstition was at the bottom in their ideological ranking system, with religion in between.

What is more, some Tibetans who migrated from other sinicized areas or with a sinicized education even acutely criticized Tibetan culture by claiming that the Tibetan modes of thought (*guannian*) in Huangnan Tibetan Autonomous Prefecture were outdated and backward, because Tibetan tradition was so deeply rooted in this area (Interview 030109 and an informal conversation with a Tibetan teacher in the minority school). What I found most striking was the comments of a Tibetan school administrator, who was also a teacher of Tibetan language and literature and a would-be reincarnation of Buddha. When discussing the achievement of the Tibetan students in his minority school, he kept repeating:

> Here it is a place the Tibetan people are concentrated, the modes of thinking (*sixiang guannian*) of the people are backward, and the economy is not developed, the desire for pursuing knowledge (*qiuzhiyu*) is low.
>
> (Interview 020201)

As a school official, he expectedly ethnicized economic and educational achievement by making a cause-effect link between cultural backwardness, economic underdevelopment and lack of motivation for education.[31]

This kind of view was echoed by Tibetan students from both Huangnan High School and Huangnan Minority Senior High School when they compared Han and Tibetans. They thought that the Han students had more aptitude for analysis and inference (*fenxi tuili nengli*), and were more knowledgeable, open-minded (*siwei kaifang*) and rational (*lizhi*). For instance, unlike Tibetans, a Han student commonly conceded to avoid trouble (*xishiningren*), while the former tended to fight to the finish. In their eyes, Han students had a higher study level (*xuexi shuiping*) and cultural level (*wenhua shuiping*), and so were of high quality (*suzhi gao*). The Han teachers in Huangnan High School also possessed more up-to-date knowledge. These factors allowed for a better study ethos (*xuexi fengqi*) in Huangnan High School. By contrast, they considered that Tibetan students had lower academic achievement, were more conventional (*chuantong*) or conservative (*baoshou*), and less sociable (*shejiaoshang buxing*). Essentially, Tibetans thought themselves to be of poor quality (*suzhi cha*) and morally degenerate (*daode baihuai*). As evidence of this they cited an inclination to drink or fight, which even scared some of their teachers. It was not surprising that the negative comments on Tibetan students were said in relation to those students at Huangnan Minority High School, and by the Tibetan students in the ordinary school.

The comments of Tibetan parents and students about the advancement of the Han and the poor quality and backwardness of the Tibetans suggested that they had internalized the critique of the dominant culture regarding their people, customs and cultural value. In this respect they resembled other marginal peoples such as the transnational Chinese youth described by Vanessa Fong (this volume), the migrant children described by Lu Wang (this volume), the farmers described by Rachel Murphy (this volume) and the immigrants described by Nicole Newendorp (this volume). Their resulting ambivalence about their own cultural identity could be seen at even a very young age. When jokingly asked by some adults "which ethnic group do you belong to", some young children who lived in a state work unit environment were very likely to identify themselves (and the people they had intimate relations with, for example, their mother) with Han, but regarded others (even their father or siblings, for instance) as Tibetans (Interview 030103, -09).

Although few parents or students explicitly stated during the interviews that they (or their children) had experienced discrimination, this did not seem convincing given the exaggerated tone of their denials. In fact, information about discrimination was evident in some of the stories they told. For instance, when a parent explained why he was not interested in attending parent-teacher meetings, he gave the example of a parent-teacher meeting that he had once attended when his daughter was in primary school:

> I asked the teacher "how is my kid performing?" "Your Tibetan kids are all like that" was the reply. There is more to it than meets the ear. At that moment I wondered to myself why he said that, "Tibetan students are all like that!" Like what? I did not fully understand but did not ask for his further elaboration. However he was the teacher of my kid . . . I have not attended a parent-teacher meeting since then.
>
> (Interview 030110)

Another parent told me that when his son was in the primary school, fellow students bullied him because he was a minority (*shaoshu*). The continued bullying slowly but surely reduced his enthusiasm for study and school life. This contributed to his mediocre academic achievement and disruptive behavior. His parent concluded by saying that if the teachers had intervened with these bullies, his son's situation would not have been so bad:

> The class head should have cared about and paid more attention to this kind of (minority) kid, rather than seeing them as the same (as the majority) (*yishitongren*) and then leave them there carelessly.
>
> (Interview 030104)

He finally sent his second child to a minority school.

Some of the Tibetan students mentioned a word that was usually used by the other ethnic students to describe them: *fan*. This word basically refers to the nature of a type of person who is slow to respond (*chidun*) and has mental problems (*naozi you wenti*). Sometimes even some of their teachers would make a connection between a student and rural Tibetan people when criticizing his or her stupidity by saying "you are just as stupid as those pastoral Tibetans (*muqu lai de Zangmin*)" (Interview 010202, 05). Here pastoral Tibetans were located in the lowest position in comparison to urban and farming Tibetans.[32]

This devaluation of Tibetan culture and people by the Han schools and society led to cultural ambivalence and alienation among Tibetans who had been sent to ordinary schools for their education. As some of my interviewees commented, in a cultural sense these Tibetans could barely harmonize with their own ethnic group, particularly with the older generation, nor could they integrate with the mainstream Han – though perhaps in the future their own children would (!). Knowledge-wise, they could not specialize in Tibetan language and culture, or Han. They then became "nothing" (*shenme ye bushi*) and only pain and tragedy remained.[33] They explained this to be the very reason why these Tibetans, after becoming parents, tended to send their own children to minority schools instead of following the example of their own parents and making sacrifices to send their children to "advanced" Han schools. Some other parents also expressed their regret about their choice to send their children to ordinary schools because it resulted in introducing and widening a cultural and linguistic gap between generations. They therefore wanted to stay in their village of origin after retirement so as to nurture their grandchildren with Tibetan culture. Some parents also tried to arrange some family tutorials for their ordinary school children in Tibetan culture and language. But most such "experiments" were ineffective due to the difficulty of finding time outside their children's school study, which focused on college entrance examinations. In addition, Tibetan culture and language lessons could also stir up conflict between parents and their children. A common response on the part of the children was: "now you are forcing me to study these, why did not you send me to a minority school at the very beginning?" (Interview 030110)

Compared to the ordinary schools, the average academic outcome for students in Huangnan Minority High School was limited, since it focused on preparing students for exams in many "useful" or "advanced" subjects like Chinese, English or science, to which students had little exposure in their previous rural and/or minority environments. At the same time, they were usually required or encouraged to study these subjects in Chinese, a language that was unfamiliar to them since the medium of instruction in their primary and junior high schools was Tibetan. In other words, their background and previous education did not equip them for dealing with Chinese language instruction in unfamiliar subjects. Following the *minkaomin* preferential policy of the state,[34] graduates from minority high schools usually entered local, mostly minority colleges or universities. The admission requirements for these institutions were usually lower than for regular universities. As a result, employers understandably preferred non-minority university or college graduates.

Ineffective study and a perception of the better quality of education in ordinary schools became the immediate dynamic which drove some of the minority students to dream of studying in ordinary schools, while simultaneously pushing others further away from ordinary school education. This desire to study in ordinary schools was informed not just by a concern with education alone, but also by an eagerness to become more "sociable" and "advanced". Because most of the students in Huangnan Minority High School were from rural areas, had few social relations with the outside world, boarded at school and were viewed negatively by both local urban dwellers and their counterparts in Huangnan High School, it was more difficult for them to socialize with off-campus society. All these reasons plus their language difficulty isolated them from both their far-away home community and the host community of their school.[35]

Attending minority schools reduced considerably both the competitiveness of Tibetan graduates in the job market and their opportunities to acquire a modern self-image. Under such circumstances, Tibetan students in the Minority School became increasingly devoted to the "useful" subjects associated with advancement and socio-economic mobility, which were taught in Chinese. At the same time, they needed to master Chinese and the unfamiliar subjects taught in Chinese meant that they must de-prioritize their own ethnic cultural studies. Furthermore, in minority schools the opportunity to study minority cultures was very limited – the only tailored course for ethnic minorities was minority language and literature, which according to the teachers of Tibetan language and literature was no more than a training in language and composition (*xiezuo*) skills. Another difficulty was that the impracticalities of distance limited students' opportunities for home visits. These factors contributed to a fall in the standard of Tibetan language among the students. Some Tibetan language teachers feared that this diminishing exposure of minority school students to Tibetan would lead to their alienation from their community, people and culture, which would eventually undermine the ethno-religious community as a whole.

This picture was quite different from that perceived by the parents who sent their children to minority schools. They claimed that their children had access to all the necessary knowledge of their own culture. But the study of necessary "useful" knowledge nevertheless resulted in ineffective study and the ethnic cultural content of the curriculum was reduced to the minimum. The only appeal of the Huangnan Minority High School, apart from practical reasons (lower fees, grant-in-aid, boarding, etc.), was that the majority of the school people are Tibetan. The reason forty percent of students in this school said they preferred the idea of staying in their own school and did not want to attend the ordinary school centered on the idea that they wanted to feel safe rather than be exposed to a competitive, uncertain and even humiliating environment. In my investigation, the only Tibetan student who had studied in a minority school and then opted to attend Huangnan High School, transferred back to Huangnan Minority High School after the first semester. She listed the reasons as follows: I could not get used to the teaching methods they used there, and also wanted to strengthen my Tibetan and learn more about our ethnic culture. I can better settle down to study (*geng anxin de xuexi*) in an environment of my own ethnic compatriots (Questionnaire 144).

At a superficial level, staying at Huangnan Minority High School seemed to be a voluntary decision on the part of parents and students. Most Tibetan students at that school, however, felt that they had no other choice. Likewise, few students from Huangnan High School had actually transferred to Huangnan Minority High School despite the large proportion of them who expressed a desire to do so. Both the students and the parents were very aware of how much they may lose for their future if they pursued education in a minority school. Like the migrant children described by Lu Wang and the immigrants in Newendorp's chapter (this volume), the Tibetans that I met in Huangnan recognized the need to be absorbed into the mainstream in order to progress. They prided themselves on being more advanced than their counterparts in minority schools. This idea was evident in the fact that I was told on some informal occasions that there was a much higher proportion of Tibetan children in the most prestigious primary ordinary school compared to one or two decades ago.[36] One parent explained that this was because Tibetans are "no longer biased against learning the Han Chinese language" (Interview 030109) while another suggested that this happened under the pressure of the state policy (Questionnaire 153).

Conclusion

In the process of making decisions about schooling, Tibetans in both ordinary and minority schools found themselves in a predicament. While they struggled against the perceived threat of being "phased out" economically or culturally by studying hard and emulating the Han model of "advanced culture" and "high quality", this seemed to devalue their own culture and put them at risk of losing contact with it. They were therefore placed in a situation where they voluntarily pursued education but then found themselves involuntarily alienated from their own culture and, further, degraded as the owner of their culture.

Tibetan parents, students and intellectuals responded by starting to think about what kind of education they needed. Some argued that transmitting Tibetan culture and language was not only a private responsibility, but also the obligation of public institutions like schools. For instance, some individuals started to appeal for Tibetan to be the medium of instruction at all levels in minority schools. Others advocated combining the advantage of monastery culture and rural culture with school curriculum in order to preserve and develop the local culture.

Yet it seemed unlikely that both the preservation of Tibetan culture and the education of Tibetan people for socio-economic mobility could ever be achieved. Factors from two sides contributed to this pessimism. First, on the side of schools and society, schools discouraged the desire for a Tibetan relevant curriculum in favor of the mainstream national culture. One of the typical remarks on this issue came from a top administrator who was also a history teacher in a mainstream school:

> [A student] is a secondary school student first, and then a minority student ... Minority students should be equal with Han and other

students and cannot surpass the other students. The school treats all students from different ethnic backgrounds the same (*dui ge minzu xuesheng dou yishitongren*) . . . [When the students are] in the school, they should hold back (*baoliu*) some of their ethnic or religious customs; otherwise it will bring about a negative effect (*buliang yingxiang*) in teaching and among their fellow students. As for curriculum, we offer courses of ideology and history in order to educate students with the correct view towards ethnicity and religion. For example, in history lessons [we] teach [students] the tradition of upholding unification of the country . . . We are an ordinary school rather than a minority school, even though we also have minority students. But if we practised distinguishing features (*gao tedian*), it would become purposeless for the state to run schools (*shiqu guojia banxue de zongzhi*).

(Interview 020105)

Even if a school, particularly a minority school, was willing to equally incorporate Tibetan language, religion and history into the curriculum, this would not be enough to counter the potency of a national mainstream ideology that devalues Tibetan culture. Indeed, as one interviewee noted, "the school is run by the state" (Interview 020201).[37]

The other source of pessimism was the self-depreciation of the Tibetans themselves. The national agenda centered firmly on "fitting" Tibetans into the mainstream and this had the effect of cultivating among Tibetans a "self-loathing" or "an internalized devaluation" of their culture and group (Young 1990:165). The deep internalization of this mindset was exemplified by the ways in which Tibetans criticized their own group and culture. For instance, when one girl's parents invited some Lamas to perform rituals to supplement the hospital treatment of an unwell family member, she asked uncomfortably: 'Isn't it enough that we just see a doctor?' (Interview 030110)

Through the dual process of being-made and self-making (Ong 1996), Tibetan culture and groups in Huangnan were clearly pushed to the periphery in opposition to the mainstream center. Yet from this marginal position, they still had to face the question of where, what and how to study. In other words, they had to choose, or had no choice about what they needed to sacrifice in an attempt to "catch up" – catch up academically, economically or culturally? This suggests the need for policies that could endow Tibetan and other minorities with full cultural membership in the larger society on their own terms.

Notes

1 Western China traditionally refers to three minority autonomous regions (*minzu zizhiqu*), Tibet (TAR), Xinjiang (XUAR) and Ningxia (NHAR), six provinces, Shaanxi, Qinghai, Gansu, Sichuan, Yunnan and Guizhou, and one municipality,

Chongqing. This is a region where over 50% minority population is concentrated. In the government's "Go West" program (Xibu Da Kaifa), Inner Mongolian Autonomous Region, Guangxi Zhuang Autonomous Region and some areas in Hunan province with a concentration of ethnic minorities are also incorporated in this category; the minority population in "West" thus amounts to nearly 80% of the total in China. (GRPB and GTRSKT 2002). I will adopt the older categorization of Western China.

2 While the CPC (Communist Party of China) believes that religion is a historical phenomenon that follows an emergence-development-disappearance law, the Party also holds the same viewpoint towards nationality (*minzu*), i.e., *minzu* will eventually disappear. See for example Jiang 1992, D. Li 2000 and R. Li 2002.

3 In terms of education, this freedom appears in some religion-related practices like diet, dress, funding of religious schools or even inviting a few religious clergy to act as language teachers (Gladney 1999:84; Mackerras 1999:38, 43–44; Postiglione 1999:6).

4 This alleged collaboration or unity is conclusively reflected in the influential concept of *Duoyuan Yiti* (plurality and unity) that was first put forward by the eminent Chinese anthropologist and sociologist Fei Xiaotong in 1988 in a lecture in the Chinese University of Hong Kong (Fei 1989).

5 According to the Fifth National Census, the rural population in Western China amounts to 72.10% while the percentage of the coastal provinces and municipalities is 42.18% (Beijing, Tianjin, Shanghai, Shandong, Jiangsu, Zhejiang, Fujian and Guangdong) (Zhongguo Guojia Tongjiju 2000 (data online)).

6 There are ten officially recognized ethnic minority groups committed to Islam in China, who can be basically divided into two blocs, those mainly residing in XUAR (Kazak, Kirgiz, Tajik, Tatar, Uygur and Uzbek) and those across all China but especially in the Ningxia-Gansu-Qinghai borderland areas (Bonan, Dongxiang, Hui and Salar). Unlike the former, who are indigenous to the XUAR, the latter are mainly the descendants of local people and of Muslims who migrated to China for business reasons or in the wake of war between the seventh and 14th centuries from the Middle East or Central Asia. Academically, Muslims in the XUAR are labeled *Turkic and Indo-European Muslim* while the majority population of the other bloc, Hui, is *Chinese Muslim*.

7 Due to the time limit, I did not interview the students in the minority school. Instead, I designed a different questionnaire for them which contained additional questions. These additional questions covered the same content as those that I asked the Tibetan students in the mainstream school in the personal interviews.

8 The Mongolians are concentrated in Henan Mongolian Autonomous County (99.34 percent) while the vast majority of Muslim (Hui, Salar and Baoan) reside in Jianzha (70.53 percent) and Tongren (25.08 percent).

9 The figures are from the Fifth National Census (see HZT 2002:93–112).

10 Xunhua is the only Salar Autonomous County in Qinghai as well as in China.

11 The detail of this demographic transition, which was mainly caused by the move of Muslim population from the county part to the prefecture part, can be found in Yi 2005 of my PhD thesis on Muslims and Schooling.

12 This does not necessarily mean that they are also appointed as the top leaders of the Party committees, i.e., to the real top positions in the government system.

13 The people working in state work units are traditionally called *ganbu* (cadre), who are in opposition with *laobaixing* (ordinary people) or *qunzhong* (the masses), the rural people (e.g., numerous Tibetans, Mongolians, Tu) and self-employed urban dwellers (mainly Muslims). This is to say that *ganbu* have *tiefanwan* (iron rice bowl, i.e., a secure job), which entitles them to full state

welfare services ranging from an urban residence permit (*chengzhen hukou*) to health care, education. In this sense, *ganbu* can also be used to refer to working class people in state work units, despite the fact that their socio-economic status is far lower than those non-working class *ganbu*. Recently there is a tendency that in many ways the line between *ganbu* and *qunzhong* is coming to be blurred under privatization and marketization, but the titles are still popular for the reasons of tradition and the fact that nowadays in China, especially in remote areas like Huangnan, the disparity between *cadres* and the masses is still conspicuous, though in some different ways. Therefore "cadre" in this chapter will be referred to people working in the state system.

14 Zhonghua Renmin Gongheguo Minzu Quyu Zizhi Fa (Self-Autonomous Law of Ethnic Minority Regions in People's Republic of China) (see Wang and Chen 2001:285–314); Huangnan Zangzu Zizhizhou Zizhi Tiaoli (Self-Autonomous Rules in Huangnan Tibetan Autonomous Prefecture) (see HZZBW 1999:1605–1615).

15 Extracted from the local government documents.

16 Regong is the Tibetan name for Tongren, renowned for its Tibetan painting, sculpture and the similar art works. Regong Art Gallery is a collection place of these art works.

17 About this resurgence among the Tibetan in general, see Goldstein 1998 and Mackerras 1999.

18 Actually most urban Tibetans usually have an extended family based in rural areas, where they are originally from.

19 Because the local cadre team is approaching saturation point, it is getting more and more difficult to become a cadre, particularly a non-working class one, without a degree, although there has been the policy that privileges Tibetans in recruitment into state work units.

20 This is a system in which the government institutionally rather than individually contracts with university/college/school students to assign them to a job in a state work unit when they graduate.

21 Traditionally for financial and some other practical reasons, they tended to let their children have a job earlier, for instance when children finished their junior high school study, their parents preferred to send them to *zhongzhuan* (high specialized school), where they could learn some practical skills (*shiyong jishu*). There were basically two benefits they could get by doing so: the period of time they needed to sponsor their children became shorter, and their children could start to earn money earlier, i.e., supplement family income earlier.

22 The Muslim students are made up of the Hui, Salar, Bonan or their mixture.

23 The number of Tibetan students offered by the school official is quite different from my investigation. My estimation, which is based on over 90 questionnaires and 50 interviews as well as observation, informal conversations with the people in this school, is that the number of the Tibetan students in terms of naming, language, heredity and psychology is around 10 percent. This will also be the figure used in the following analysis. The higher proportion provided by the school official is mainly a result of the change of nationality (*minzu chengfen*) among some Han and Tu. For these Han, they will benefit from the preferential policies for ethnic minorities after changing for minorities; the Tu who changed their nationality are either not satisfied with the categorization of them by the state or because compared to the Tibetan, they are less visible or heard culturally or politically.

24 These are again different from my investigation: the proportion of the Han, Muslim and Tibetan teachers is respectively 75 percent, 9.21 percent and 2.63 percent.

25 This is the policy called *minkaomin*, an idea that allows minority students to sit college entrance examinations in minority languages. Also see Sautman 1999.

26 According to some teachers in this school, most students in the past got less than 20 percent of the exam questions correct in college entrance examinations.

27 Correspondingly, they also pointed out that a Han student would not be able to perform as well as Tibetan students if she or he were studying in a minority school.

28 To adopt Chinese as the medium of instruction in minority schools does not seem to be compulsory though this is encouraged by the local government policy, particularly in senior high schools. For instance, my investigation shows that Huangnan Minority Senior High School is the only one of its kind in the township where Chinese is thoroughly used as the medium of instruction, while the other two minority schools only partially do so. This is interesting concerning the cultural background of the head-teachers in three schools: the head-teachers in Huangnan Minority Senior High School are Han and those in other two minority schools are Tibetan.

29 I was told that the only opportunity when Tibetan is employed as the main means of communication is during the period of Two Conferences (*Lianghui Qijian*), i.e., of Prefectural People's Congress Conference (PPCC) and Prefectural Committee of the People's Political Consultative Conference (PCPPCC).

30 There are two examples that are worth mentioning. A teacher in a minority school told me that some of his students had to spend 40 minutes just trying to memorize a physics theorem in Chinese (so they are regarded as intellectual inferiority). Secondly, many students I investigated in the minority school eagerly requested in their questionnaires that I taught them how to study effectively.

31 On how hegemonies of race, civilization and economy are entangled with one another, Ong provided some interesting and insightful cases (Ong 1996).

32 According to Harrell, Crossley also observed a similar view of difference between pastoral and farming populations (Harrell 1995:19).

33 An interesting point of comparison is the language ability of Tibetan students in inland boarding schools where they study all subjects in Chinese, with the obvious exception of Tibetan language. This has made their language ability in Tibetan inferior to that of their counterparts who remain in Tibet while their Chinese ability is not necessarily strong though surely better than those remaining in Tibet. For more information see Postiglione, Zhu and Ben 2004.

34 See footnote 25.

35 This segregation becomes more serious with Tibetan students studying in inland boarding schools. Details can be found in Postiglione, Zhu and Ben 2004.

36 I used to be a pupil in this primary school more than 20 years ago. I still remember that among my some 100 fellow pupils, there was only one who was Tibetan.

37 However, as can be seen from the discussions elsewhere in this chapter, the Party's principles (for instance, its constitution), policies and practice on ethnic minority peoples and cultures are, to a large extent, contradictory. This reflects the Party's ambivalence towards the relationship between cultural and political loyalty and cultural tolerance when trying to integrate the ideas of political control, cultural diversity, citizenship cultivation, etc., into a coherent whole. This is particularly salient in the religious issue as can be seen from Potter's comprehensive arguments over the Party's contested attempt to maintain a balance between political loyalty and popular autonomy (2003). In other words, there is still a bottom line of loyalty that guides and also complicates policies and practice regarding ethnic minorities.

5 Legal Report
Citizenship education through a television documentary

Yingchi Chu

Introduction

This chapter examines how a television documentary, *Legal Report* (*Jinri shuofa*), served as a top-down form of citizenship education that sought to strengthen the legitimacy and power of the state by presenting people at the margins of Chinese society as examples of how the rights and responsibilities of citizenship should and should not work. Unlike other chapters in this volume which consider citizenship education activities aimed at social groups at the margins of Chinese society, such as the farmer education campaigns described by Rachel Murphy and the pedagogy for the urban poor described by Tianshu Pan, this chapter examines citizenship education that targets a mainstream Chinese audience of over 900 million. Aware of their huge reach, the producers of *Legal Report* felt a tremendous responsibility to use the programme content to make Chinese society more advanced and sophisticated by inculcating in the audience an understanding of modern legal knowledge and a legalistic outlook. Most particularly, the documentary producers sought to affect a shift from a public mindset that saw justice in terms of traditional morality to one which recognized the importance of law in everyday life. But in trying to change public consciousness, the documentary makers were forced to confront the tension that existed between traditional and modern ideas about the rights and responsibilities of Chinese citizenship. The chapter addresses the role of the documentary *Legal Report* by looking at its background, case studies, narrative structure, and conceptualizations of Chinese citizenship.

If we accept the idea that 'education for citizenship is not an optional extra, but an integral part of the concept of citizenship', (Heater 1990:319) then citizenship pedagogy via the electronic media is central to our understanding of citizenship in China today. *Legal Report* was specially designed by the Chinese media ministries for the purposes of citizenship pedagogy, with its content focusing on the tension between *fazhi* (governing by law) and *dezhi* (governing by morality) in real life social situations.

The *Legal Report* is the inadvertent progeny of a film which Zhang Yimou presented to the public in 1994. The film, a social realist comedy called *The Story of Qiuju* (*Qiuju da guansi*) follows the trials and tribulations of a pregnant woman who takes her *cunzhang* (village chief) to court. In a minor dispute, Qiuju's husband insults the *cunzhang* by telling him that his family line will soon be terminated. Outraged, the village chief kicks the husband in the genitals, injuring him seriously. Qiuju asks for a *shuofa* (an apology or an official statement explaining the reason), which is refused. Much of the film shows the pregnant Qiuju travelling from her village to courts in the district, town and city, seeking justice. Justice seems finally to be done when the *cunzhang* is taken away by the police. But Qiuju is confused by the result and the film ends with a medium shot of her puzzled face: she did not want her *cunzhang* to be arrested – all she wanted was a *shuofa*. Two years later, the first of more than a thousand episodes of *Legal Report* was made, with the documentary series becoming a cornerstone of government-sponsored citizenship education.

The background of *Legal Report*

Television programmes are potent tools in citizenship education because they easily reach the population at large. Television producers in China are intuitively inclined to emphasis the pedagogic content of their products in part because of the inheritance of a traditional aesthetic in literature and art represented by the maxim *wenyi zaidao* – 'The function of literature is to convey the morality.' The view that the arts should have a didactic function was revived by Mao Zedong's Yan'an 'Speech on the Arts' in 1942, where he declared that art must serve politics. In both the planned and market economy, television, along with print, radio and film has been powerful in serving politics by disseminating political propaganda, providing information about government policies and promoting norms about the qualities of productive and civilized citizens.

In the current market economy, television must be both commercially viable and politically responsible, a dual mandate that is realized by creating and manipulating public opinion (*yulun daoxiang*). To this end, the policy-making department in the CCTV and the editorial departments in local television stations coordinate (*tongyi koujin*) their public messages (Zheng, 2002:201). As Zheng declares,

> Those positive views control and direct the public's consciousness in order to guide its behaviour. As to negative views, instead of ignoring them, we should immediately reveal the truth to stop them from spreading. Thus we will be able to lead the social psychology and emotions of the masses to support positive ideas.
>
> (Zheng 2002:200)

This reveals that even in the new market economy television cannot be viewed as primarily market and profit oriented. Rather it is a market institution which is simultaneously an effective tool for political control (Yu 2002:9). Being unable to exploit the market means reduced political influence. The basic condition for a television station to operate in the market economy is to adhere to government directives. This is why 'what' is to be produced continues to be more important than 'how' the programme will appear to the market. The challenge facing television makers in the market economy is therefore one of guiding public opinion via profitable products. As a result, TV citizenship education in the 1990s has evolved into various forms of didactic entertainment, with an emphasis on documentary modes.

Television documentary was one of the most popular genres in the 1990s, ranking third after news and dramas. Documentary thrived on the appearance of reality, location shooting and the recording of places, events, people, materials and issues that can be identified in actuality. In China, documentary has been advertised as a genre in which *laobaixing jiang ziji de gushi* (ordinary citizens tell their own stories). The popularity of this genre is not all that surprising given that the genre was underdeveloped in the pre-communist era, used by the government only for presenting news, education (science, history, geography, ethnography) and information (travel, sports and autobiography).

Only since the late 1980s when a number of documentary programmes, such as CCTV's *Difangtai 50* (Local Station 50 Minutes), *Jiaodian* (Focus), *Caifang* (Interview), Shanghai television's *Bianji shi de gushi* (Stories from the editorial Room) began to present the lives and lifestyles of ordinary citizens in realist style, have documentaries been able to draw the market's attention. These documentary programmes contain episodes varying between 15 to 30 minutes and ranging in style from news to investigative reporting. The emergence and popularity of these programmes can be explained by the following three observations. First, the market needs 'real' stories, realistic representations of society, and 'realistic' views after decades of promoting heroic deeds under Communist ideology and a planned economy (Gao 2003:2–3). Second, the government is keen to be seen as close to ordinary citizens. Their commitment to documentaries shows the government's intention to regain the trust and confidence of the people by presenting the government's media as the people's media with stories about ordinary citizens from the perspective of ordinary citizens. Third, documentary programmes are supported by screen scholars and cultural critics who now measure the quality of a television station by its ability to produce documentaries (Gao 2003:11). It is against this background that the enormous popularity as well as pedagogic efficacy of the *Legal Report* should be viewed.

Ironically, media events often turn out to be more real in terms of their effects than ordinary events, such as crimes or road accidents, and the *Legal Report* is no exception. The *Legal Report* screens each day on China Central TV2 between 12:30–1:00pm following the lunchtime news. The programme aims to introduce concepts of law and the mechanisms of the legal process to the public through documented case narratives. This is why the programme is commonly referred to as *Zhongguo ren de falü wucan* (Chinese People's Legal Lunch). The programme consists of two sections. The first section is a documentary report on a case with a duration of between 15 to 20 minutes. The second section involves a discussion about the case between the host(s) of the programme and the special guest expert, usually an academic from a university jurisprudence faculty or some other legal specialists. Since 2 January 1999, the *Legal Report* has produced more than a thousand episodes. There are about 50 documentary makers – producers, journalists, cameramen, sound recorders and editors, in front and behind the camera. The programme is broadcast nation-wide to China's 900 million television audience, maintaining top ten rating from the first day, capturing 1.78% to 5.24% of the population and a growth rate for a while of 2 million viewers per day. The station receives more than 1,000 letters every day. There is a professional team ready to respond to audience queries via a 24 hours telephone answering service. A sizeable number of Chinese citizens involved in actual law suits approach the *Legal Report* team for professional advice. A website and e-mail service enhances the interactive character of the *Legal Report*, guaranteeing the highest possible degree of public involvement, including the wider audience of the Chinese diaspora.

The English titles 'Legal Report' or 'Law Today' do not quite capture the significance of the cultural and political connotations of the original Chinese *Jinri shuofa*. '*Jinri*' means 'today', while *shuofa* can be understood as 'statement' or 'the way you reason a matter'. '*Shuofa*' is borrowed from *The Story of Qiuju* in which the protagonist, Qiuju, makes a superhuman effort in requesting the law courts to provide an official *shuofa* (statement, reason) why *cunzhang* (the village chief) should be permitted to kick her husband's reproductive organs without having to offer an apology. *Jinri shuofa* targets millions of Chinese TV viewers who, like Qiuju, experience injustice on account of particular forms of social and political marginalization and at the same time lack the legal knowledge and representation needed to address their grievances. The chief editor, Yin Li explains the purpose of the programme as follows:

> Over the 20 years since the economic reform, the creation of laws has accelerated to such an extent that 300 new laws have been established. 'Governing the country by laws' has been written into our constitution, Qiuju's '*taoge shuofa*' (begging for an 'official' statement or reason) has entered the homes of thousands of families over night. However, how many people in 1.2 billion have received education on the legal process? How much do they know about laws? How much do they use laws as principles (ways) to protect themselves and, at the same time, as principles to regulate their own behaviour?
>
> (Yin 2001b:Vol. 3)

Put in such a context, the title *Jinri shuofa* could be understood also as 'today's reason(ing) from the authority'. Implicitly the title indicates that we are dealing with an official explanation of individual cases involving a legal dispute. The title could also be understood to refer to a programme with a certain temporal limitation: legal reasoning for today rather than reasoning applicable to the past and the future.

There are a number of reasons why millions of Chinese, like Qiuju, lack knowledge about the law. First, in Chinese traditional society, law was mainly associated with punishment. The law existed 'to protect rulers' and regarded 'citizens as subjects to be controlled'. In this sense the 'law does not protect citizen's property rights, nor does it recognise the individual right of freedom' (Li 2001:167). Civil law was only gradually developed out of the government's emphasis on criminal law (Li 2001:167). Second, in the Mao period from the 1950s to the early 1980s, the concept of law was undermined to the point of an absence of the law, since *zhengce*, or policies, more or less replaced the legal process. The main citizenship responsibility in the Mao era was to be a member of the proletariat (workers, peasants, or soldiers) who actively participated in political movements by following the Party's instructions. As citizenship is a relationship between an individual and the state, and as the Chinese constitution stated that the CCP is the only governing Party of the nation, good citizenship during the Cultural Revolution was measured by a citizen's closeness to Party rule. Only from the 1980s when the Party introduced the principle of *yifa zhiguo* (governing the country by law), was legal consciousness promoted on the Party's agenda for nationwide education. For most of the 20th century China has been governed by a mixture of traditional morality (Confucian values, *liangxin* 'conscience') and CCP's policies. The *Legal Report* still reflects this mixture.

The *Legal Report* is one of the first television programmes to respond to the Government's call for mass education in legal matters. It is also a highly successful media product sponsored by an authoritarian government in tune with China's market economy. The main purpose of the programme is to complement the government's current political and social campaigns, with an emphasis on civil rights and responsibilities. For instance, on 4 December 2002, China's Law Promotion Day, the programme presented a documentary of a citizenship ceremony under the national flag accompanied by the tune of the national anthem – a ritual with thousands of children, all 16 years old, swearing to become good citizens. About half the cases portrayed were from government sources, police stations or courts, with about a quarter adapted from local newspapers and the remainder developed from audience requests demanding that the CCTV conduct further investigations. To illustrate how topical the *Legal Report* can be, since the spreading of the SARS epidemic, the programme has offered a series of documentaries and discussions on the legal aspects of SARS, explaining and backing official policies and regulations. Predictably, all episodes receive government permission before broadcasting.

The central aim of the *Legal Report* is to develop China's legal culture by assisting the masses in developing a legal consciousness – to use laws to regulate social behaviour, and to establish mass confidence in China's legal system. The motto for the programme is *zongzai pufa* (making laws accessible), *jiandu zhifa* (inspecting how laws are being carried out); and *chujin lifa* (encouraging laws to be established) (Yin 2001:3). This directive covers matters dealing with civil laws: marriage, extra-marital affairs, family, inheritance, adoption, children rights, property rights, civic matters; criminal laws; traffic laws; security; administration; law scrutiny; business laws: contracts, product quality, business fraud, insurance, advertising, enterprises, consumer rights; labour laws; intellectual property rights, natural resources, land management, elections, and organisational laws. At the same time, the traditional idea of morality is never far from the central intent of the programme. For example, on 30 May 2002, the *Legal Report* organized a quiz show dedicated to the theme of 'Knowledge of Citizenship Morality' screened nationwide.

As the sample analyses show, the programme supports the ideological apparatus of the government, while at the same time catering for the needs of a vast and growing market. The popularity of the programme is due partly to society's demand for knowledge of the law, partly to a structured format combining story telling with expert discussion, and partly, of course, to viewers' voyeuristic interest in the transgressive actions of individuals at the margins of Chinese society. Given its aim of nurturing a new legal consciousness in society in the style of fast-food consumption, the *Legal Report*'s formulaic programme structure is well suited to providing introductory lessons in law within a half hour time slot at lunch time to a mass audience.

The majority of cases televised over the last four years (1999–2003) fall into three broad categories: (1) introducing the audience to laws and the legal process; (2) examining the efficiency of the way laws are being applied; and (3) situations in which the law has been deficient or absent. But no matter how we may wish to categorize individual episodes, they are all variations on the deep theme of the intricate relationship between legal process and moral behaviour. With this proviso, the chapter now turns to an interpretive description of five selected *Legal Report* episodes covering three cases.

Case studies

1) *Hainan (Ocean Accident)* is about an investigation into the compensation awarded the families of fourteen victims of an accident at sea. The fourteen victims, all fishermen, drowned as a result of a collision between their trawler and a large commercial fishing vessel. The accident occurred on 6 April 1997. Although the courts granted the families of the victims' full compensation, the money was never received. *Ocean Accident* consists

of two episodes, *Hainan* (I) and *Hainan* (II), exploring the details of the fraud.

The first episode opens with three images setting the scene and theme of the investigation:

- Image 1: a rural, middle aged woman, the wife of one of the victims, tearfully describes the moment when her family receives the news of her husband's death. 'My child is in tears, wailing "How can I live without my father? I want my father."' Below the image the caption reads: 'Perished in the ocean, the fishermen will never return';
- Image 2: an old man, the father of one of the victims, speaking in anger: 'My name is false, all of these names are false.' The caption reads: 'Inventing false names; who is responsible for the theft of 1.26 million *Yuan* in compensation?';
- Image 3: a middle aged woman in her court uniform admits: 'The court too has been cheated.' The caption repeats the title of the episode.

The *Legal Report* usually opens its episodes with attention-grabbing images announcing the investigation of a crime and the search for social justice. *Ocean Accident* is a story of fraud which could not have occurred without the involvement of officials in government and the legal institutions. Soon after the accident, the Ningjing Fishing Company, which had employed the fishermen, paid RMB15,000 to each family for their loss. At the same time, the company asked the bereaved families to sign an agreement that they would make no further claims should the ship responsible for the accident not be found. However, within less than a year the ship was identified by the Company. Without informing the victims' families, the Ningjing Fishing Company initiated legal action. The Company first sought documentation from the Rongcheng Court, Rongcheng City testifying that the victims had families and therefore a compensation claim should be pursued on their behalf. The Ningjing Fishing Company then employed a lawyer to represent the victims' families in the Qingdao Ocean Affairs Court to seek two separate compensation claims, one for the Company's loss of its boat, the other for the victims' families. The Qingdao Ocean Affairs Court resolved that a total of RMB2.2 million must be paid by the convicted party, 1.4 million to the fourteen victims' families, and 800,000 to the Ningjing Fishing Company.

However, the Ningjing Fishing Company, the lawyer and the guilty party decided to settle out of court to the effect that the compensation claim was to be reduced from 2.2 million to 1.26 million. As the Ningjing Fishing Company was a state-owned company of the Town of Ningjing, the Deputy Mayor instructed the lawyer to transfer 1.06 million to the Ningjing Government minus legal fees and other deductions. The Government then drew 200,000 *Yuan* from the account, paying for road construction, and transferred the rest to the Lingye Fishing

Company, which happened to be a branch office of the Ningjing Fishing Company.

The fraud proceeded smoothly mainly because the victims' families had been excluded from the legal proceedings. As Professor Zhao Ling, guest law expert in the episode, pointed out, the fraud could have been stopped if the Rongcheng Court had followed the rule that the court could issue death certificates only after checking the identities of the victims' family members, the family registrations, and the marriage certificates. The fraud could also have been terminated had the lawyer met with the families whom he was supposed to represent in court. The Rongcheng Court inspector, while admitting their error, insisted that they themselves had become victims of fraud. Likewise, the lawyer conceded that he should have met with the victims' families to discuss their case. The question that is implicitly posed then is whether this massive fraud was the result of no more than a few deplorable acts of unprofessional behaviour.

In the episodes of *Ocean Accident* broadcast over two lunch times we are given three perspectives. One is provided by the reporter of the *Legal Report*, Sun Hui, who is also the narrator and the investigator of the crime. The second perspective is that of the host of the *Legal Report*, while the third is the analysis offered by the guest of the show, a legal expert. Sun Hui represents the victims' families. She interviews the families, the deputy court judge and inspector, the lawyers, the Party Secretary of the Ningjing Town Government, and unsuccessfully pursues the Director of the Ningjing Fishing Company for an interview. She appears non-aggressive, modest and yet determined. Her investigation is presented from the victims' families' position and their claim for compensation. Her investigation proceeds from the families to the Qingdao Ocean Affairs Court, the Rongcheng Court, the lawyer, the Ningjing Government, and finally the Ningjing Fishing Company.

As part of the documentation of the case, Sun Hui uses the strategy of the hidden camera to record encounters between the victims' families and the lawyer, the Party Secretary and herself. Her sympathetic attitude towards the defrauded families is shown in her relationship with the family members, the corrupt and unresponsive governmental officers and lawyers, and the critical images taken of government buildings. We see her sitting closely with the families in the rural family yard. We also see her casting herself in opposition to government officials, the Rongcheng Court inspector, the Qingdao Deputy Judge, and the lawyer. She employs her hidden camera to capture the Party Secretary's unsophisticated manner and lies. In between, the sequence cuts to a shot of Mao's words 'Serve the People' which is painted in large characters on the government building. The montage leads the viewers to judge critically the function of government against Mao's motto for the CCP. Almost all the images of the government buildings, the courts and the offices are composed from low angles to highlight their authoritative, if not oppressive, status. The two *Hainan* episodes end with symbolic images of the reporter, Sun Hui, in relation to the plaintiffs and the government: the peasants in tears seeing Sun off at the village gate, grateful for her efforts to present their case; and Sun climbing up the steps leading to the Qingdao Ocean Affair Court with her concluding remarks, 'hopefully the relevant institution will be able to make an early and speedy decision'.

While Sun investigates the crime on behalf of the victims, the program host anchors the themes and conclusions by commenting and asking questions from the perspectives of ordinary citizens. The host does not ask questions such as 'Should the Rongchen Court be sued for failing to check the identities of the families?', 'Should the court be punished for breaches of the laws?' or 'Should the Ningjing Government be sued since without their support, the Party Secretary and the Deputy Mayor, the Ningjing Fishing Company and the lawyer could not have been successful in committing the crime?' Instead, she points out that the old man, the woman, and the children are all too trusting, though she admires their faith in the legal system and justice. Rather than challenging the authorities and asking what kind of punishment they should face, the host directs the viewers to sympathize with the victims. Two messages appear to be suggested by the host and the guest speaker: first, that one can sue lawyers for failing their duties; and second, that the misfortunes of the families portrayed are the result of the authorities' inability to guarantee justice.

The questions posed by the host address the reasons why such frauds can occur in the legal process, why it is possible for a lawyer to represent his clients without informing his clients about his presence, and alter a decision made by the courts on behalf of the victims, and what the defrauded families can do in pursuing their claims for compensation. These questions are understood by the audience not only as revealing the legitimate legal concerns of the public but also as rightly provoking general moral outrage. 'What kind of persons could be so cruel', she asks, 'to cheat the old, the women, and the children?' As frequently in the *Legal Report*, the reference to morality serves as a method to guide the audience's attention to the question of what has gone wrong in the application of the law.

The guest of the program, a legal expert, offers a third perspective, though his answers are constrained by the host's questions and comments. In *Ocean Accident*, Professor Zhao Lin identifies the Rongcheng Court and the lawyer as responsible for the crime since they have failed in their professional duties. He also points out that the Ningjing Government has failed in its responsibility to distribute the legally allocated money to the families, and that the lawyer should be sued for failing to perform his professional duty of transferring the money to the victims. Zhao further informs the viewers that a lawyer has no right to alter a court decision without being reappointed by his clients. Accordingly, the 1.26 million *Yuan* should, in his legal opinion, belong to the victims' families *in toto*. As to a solution to the problem, Zhao offers two choices: one is to reopen the case, the other is to redistribute the compensation funds to the families. In addition to this legal advice, Professor Zhao's concluding remarks emphasize the moral issues involved in the case:

> Whatever the option, I think, as a public institution, the Ningjing Government should show their sincerity in their support of the suffering families and so conclude this matter in peace.

(2) *Jiayao de laili* (*The Origin of Fake Medicine*) is likewise presented over two episodes. While the first episode informs the viewers about the law on consumer rights, the second develops from an investigation of the source of fake medicine to an exploration of government corruption. Both episodes aim to solve a puzzle: Where is the fake medicine from? As usual the reporter is the investigator as well as the narrator. While the episodes praise the government's achievement in market control, they expose at the same time corruption and unprofessional conduct, as well as inefficient supervision of the market by certain government officials.

The first episode introduces viewers to consumer rights, while also addressing the question of morality in the medical profession. The opening contains:

- Image 1: The victim, 47 year old factory worker, Jing Gang, asking, 'the medicine comes from my *danwei* (the state government workplace where I work), how can that be fake?' with the caption reading: 'after having taken false medicine, Jing *shifu* (master) *paian erqi* (slams his fist on the table and rises angrily to his feet)';
- Image 2: The distributor of the medicine, claiming innocence, conceding: 'Yes, we distributed the fake medicine. This is a fact, and we have admitted the mistake from the beginning.' The caption reads: 'Insisting that he has been implicated unjustly, the distributor tells his story in detail';
- Image 3: The accused, the state clinic manager, saying 'He (Jing Gang) did not give any evidence.' The caption repeats the title of the episode; 'The Origin of Fake Medicine'.

The episode introduces legal knowledge that most people in China are unfamiliar with. It presents the viewers with two types of law that consumers are able to invoke in the case of justifiable claims for compensation. After a serious cancer operation, Jing Gang is advised to take medicine provided by the state factory clinic. A year later Jing becomes seriously ill. Assuming that his cancer had returned, he terminates his employment, awaiting his inevitable fate. His wife, somewhat more sceptical however, urges him to look at the possibility of a connection between his sickness and the prescribed medicine, as Jing often vomits heavily after having taken the medicine. Jing takes her advice and writes a letter to the pharmaceutical factory to inquire into the reason for his sickness. To his surprise the factory informs him that the medicine he has been taking is not the product of the factory. Worse, the medicine he has inquired about turns out not to exist officially at all. In disbelief, Jing takes the medicine to the Bureau of Medicine Inspection, where the result is confirmed. In anger, Jing takes the state clinic and medicine distributor to court for damages suffered. The court decides that the clinic should return Jing's medical fees, and furthermore, that Jing is entitled to receive a RMB10,000 compensation for mental stress from the clinic and the distributor.

In the dispute between Jing and the accused, a moral question is raised by Jing's lawyer. Both the clinic and distributor have argued that there is no evidence to show Jing's sickness was caused by the medicine he took. The distributor claims that 'like animals, humans get sick without taking medicines'. In defending themselves against the payment of compensation for mental stress, they argue that their relationship with Jing was no more than a contract between a seller and a buyer. Hence, they say, compensation for mental stress does not apply. In reply, Jing's lawyer has this to say:

> You prescribed the medicine, and my client took it in good faith. Your medicine is fake, and now my client is getting sick from taking it. How can you say that you have done nothing wrong? Strictly speaking, this is not a question of law; it is a question of *liangxin* (conscience or morality).

Professor Ni, legal expert and guest in this episode, addresses the concept of contracts between seller and buyer; the notion of violation of customer rights; laws governing compensation for mental stress; and the regulations for the control of the pharmaceutical market. He explains that the court's decision was rightly based on the consequences caused by the clinic and the distributor. In spite of the fact that they themselves have been defrauded – trusting products issued by government agencies – they are guilty of failing in their professional duty to check the products they sell. By selling fake medicine they have violated Jing's rights as a consumer, leading to the termination of his employment and considerable anxiety.

The second episode exposes unprofessional conduct and corruption in local government, as well as the tension between the central government's determination to control a poorly regulated pharmaceutical market, and the resistance by local officials to the uncovering of the scandal. The investigator of the episodes, the reporter, leaves Baoji for the capital city of Shaanxi province, seeking the answer to the question of 'how fraudulent medicine is able to infiltrate government controlled channels of distribution.' However fruitless the search for an answer to the question proves to be, it reveals more than the viewers were led to expect.

After the manager of the head distribution in Xi'an has admitted that they did not, as a matter of course, check pharmaceutical products supplied by providers before they released them onto the market, the reporter travels

to Puning, Guangdong province in South China, with Xi'an's receipt signed
by the provider Xu Chuangshen, *Canrong* Company. It turns out that Puning
has already been listed as one of the centres in China known for producing
fake medicines. From September to March, the local government has dealt
with 90 such cases, with 16 people given 6 to 10 years' jail sentences. The
local official praises this achievement by saying that RMB30,000 rewards
for informers have not been claimed since March that year, and the
reporter concludes the introduction by remarking that 'the methods to
eradicate the crime employed by the government of Puning leaders are
forceful; and their strict ruling put us at ease'.

The next scene introduces us to the corruption of local officials. The
manager of the Canrong Company is summoned for interview by two officials from the local Bureau of Medicine Inspection, of which the uncut
footage presents the following dialogue.

> *The reporter in the background*: Can I trouble you to speak Mandarin?
> *The officer to the manager of Canrong*: You speak Chaozhou dialect
> with ease. Let him (the bookkeeper, the other official) write whatever
> he wants to write. Let's meddle things around, and the trouble will
> pass. Just say there is no such a person called Xu Chuangshen. The
> person is a fiction. Say you have never produced such medicine.
> *The Bookkeeper*: But how are we going to explain the receipt?
> *Officer*: Have you used this invoice before? Which date? November
> 2000? Just say that the stamp has nothing to do with your company.
> You haven't used this stamp since 1996.

As a northern Chinese, the reporter does not understand the local dialect.
The scene makes sense to him only after he returns to Beijing, when someone familiar with the dialect exposes the fraud. The documentary ends with
a promise made by the Director of the Bureau of Medicine Inspection in
Puning that the Puning government has established a special committee to
investigate the case. The reporter comments that 'his promise makes us
believe that the case will be cleared up and that the people involved in the
production and distribution of fake medicine will not escape punishment'.

In discussing how it is possible for fake medicine to enter the market, the
guest for the episode, Professor Qu, points out that cover ups by local
government have made the system dysfunctional. He explains further that
the central government has various kinds of punitive control for such crimes,
ranging from heavy fines to the death sentence. By way of conclusion, the
host lists government achievements for the previous year, including the
handling of about 50,000 cases, worth 40 million Yuan; the arrest of around
1,000 people; the suing of 197 companies for producing fake medicine; and
the termination of 14,219 distribution contracts. The episode demonstrates
that the media has played its role in guiding public opinion (*daoxiang
yulun*) and by doing so has stabilized society.

(3) The episode *Wang Honger de bugui zhi lu* (Wang Honger's Road of No Return) conveys three messages: rape needs to be reported; bigamy is a crime; and a woman should ask for custody of her children and a fair share of finances and property in the case of divorce. These three messages are delivered through the portrayal of a marginal rural woman who has killed her ex-husband. As usual, the episode starts with three images presenting the major parties involved in the case.

- A policeman describes the cruelty of the murder 'it is very cruel' against the caption 'With a single wave of his hand, her ex-husband passed away';
- Wang, in hand-cuffs, weeping, says 'I have suffered too much', with the caption reading 'Whispering her secret with a sigh of regret';
- Wang's daughter's memory of happier days with her parents. The opening lures the viewer into Wang's secret motivation for the murder, the caption reading 'She has suffered; she has also been loved; why choose murder?'.

Wang's story is presented in a realist manner by a non-sympathetic male voice, the reporter. Images are the collections of Wang and her husband's residences in their rural home town in Anhui and Shanghai, with cuts in between the interviews of Wang, her children, her husband's second wife and policemen. This short documentary begins with Wang's confession in the police station on 13 June 2002. Eighteen years ago, Wang recalls, she was a raped by her ex-husband. After she discovered her pregnancy, Wang married the rapist. Though they lived in rural hardship, Wang conceded that the first 15 years of marriage were reasonably happy because of her husband's devotion to their three children. In 1996 the husband left the village for Shanghai.

Two years later Wang is told that her husband is living in a de facto relationship with a younger woman. In disbelief, Wang travels to Shanghai, only to return to her village realizing that her husband has started divorce proceedings, claiming custody of her three children and all of their finances. Wang accepts his demands for the sake of her children. She starts a new life in China's northwest. Two years later, the husband calls her asking her to abandon her job and new family in order to return to him. He offers her the chance of remarriage. However, Wang soon discovers that the husband has no intention to divorce his younger wife. With memories of having been raped, forced into marriage and divorce, and betrayed once more, Wang is unable to suppress any longer her tortured feelings and assaults her ex-husband with a hammer until he is dead.

The discussion of Wang's case focuses on female crimes in China, and their relation to gender difference. No doubt, Wang's tolerance reflects the traditional moral rules for women, the 'three forms of submission and four virtues'. From the point of view of traditional morality she has done everything to serve her husband's needs! Wang's case is an example of the negative consequences that adherence to traditional moral codes can have on women. Interestingly, neither the host nor the guest speaker mentions the role that traditional patriarchal culture plays in such cases. Instead, their explanations remain within the confines of the debate of the 'natural' characteristics of the female sex. This also shows that existing elements from public morality about male and female traits are reworked into current citizenship education.

According to Professor Li, the guest speaker of the episode, the weakness of women, in tolerating violence and repressing their needs inevitably leads to social catastrophe. Leaving aside the question whether this is a characteristic unique to the female sex, the result of biological factors, or shaped by the cultural environment, Li argues that Wang's murder is caused by years of tolerance and repression of her husband's crimes of rape and bigamy, and the loss of her children. In her transformation from 'an obedient, dutiful and kind woman' to a murderer, Wang is not uncommon among female criminals. A list of statistics is provided on the screen to demonstrate the relationship between women, crime and personal relationships:

> The two most common crimes by women are murder and financial fraud.
> 60% of women who commit crimes are married;
> 60% of violence and murders are caused by unhappy marriages and love relationships;
> Victims are usually close associates, including husband, lover, and children.

In Li's analysis, the suggestion that women should use the law to protect themselves is based on the assumption that women are especially in need of legal protection because they are oppressed and marginal. Wang is shown to be a victim of traditional morality. To avoid the tragedy, Li suggested, Wang should have sought legal protection at least three times in her life: after she has been raped; after she has discovered her husband's bigamy; and during her divorce. What is new is that 'legal consciousness' is now encouraged to enter the private domain, such as the domestic relationship between husband and wife. Yet 'thinking about laws' is still articulated from the perspective of traditional moral assumptions about gender. As the host concludes the episode, he says:

> We all have misfortunes in life. Women have more misfortunes than men. In addition, women's ability for bearing misfortunes is inferior to that of men. When facing misfortunes, we should remember that every choice we make leads to options that will change our fate. So the best way to protect oneself is to use laws.

Narrative structure

Two narrative patterns are dominant in these documentaries. The major pattern portrays how and why a perpetrator has committed a crime. The minor narrative pattern is the investigation of a dispute. Even in this structure, some incidence of injustice usually opens the story. Both structures involve real events, real people, specific temporal frames and actual spatial co-ordinates. The story of *Wang Honger's Road of no Return* is a typical example of the first narrative type. The reporter gives the date and the place where Wang Honger, in the company of her daughter, tells the police that she has just killed her ex-husband. The story then explores the reasons why Wang has committed murder against the background of her being portrayed as a 'kind', 'submissive wife and dutiful mother' and her ex-husband as 'hardworking' and 'always willing to help others'. A similar story (5 December 2001) deals with a woman who has killed her second husband in order to protect her first disabled spouse. Again, the reporter investigates the motivation that has led a 'kind and dutiful wife' to commit murder. In each case, the reporter's narrative is based on data available in police and court documents and recorded during interviews.

The other, less frequent structure, the one concerned mainly with some kind of dispute, typically shows how an investigator presents a disputed case and interviews the various parties involved, including third parties and witnesses who present their views. The law is usually portrayed as providing a solution to the dispute. *Ocean Accident* and *The Origin of Fake Medicine* are two examples in this narrative pattern. Another representative episode in this mode is the case of a resident who sues her district security for failing to protect her home against robbery (10 April 1999). After the court decides that her evidence is insufficient a jurisprudence expert explains the court verdict. In another case, a child is the victim of alleged medical malpractice in the Yidou Central Hospital in Qingzhou (24, 25 April 1999). During a small operation the boy is given an anaesthetic overdose resulting in brain damage. The parents complain to the local police who after an investigation write a comprehensive report which they send to the court. When the Bureau of Health is informed about the case they object to the intervention of the police, arguing that they should have been approached in the first instance. A dispute arises about which is applicable for governing medical accidents, criminal law or regulations. Yet another case in this mode deals with an eight year old girl who is seriously injured by a motorbike in a National Park, Shenzhen (10 May 1999). When the parents sue the National Park authorities for damages a dispute arises as to where the complaint should be lodged. The park authorities argue that such a case is not covered by park regulations but falls under general civil or road accident law and therefore is a matter for the police who should apprehend the motorcycle rider. In the end the court decides that all three parties are responsible to some degree: the parents because they have neglected their duty of care, the park authorities because the accident occurred within the park precinct and the motorcycle driver because he failed to take appropriate care.

In all episodes, the investigator's narration is the dominant voice within the 15 to 20 minute time frame. The interviews are selected for the reporters to demonstrate different sides of the argument; the interviews are highly focused, direct, with no additional, alternative or multiple explanation. The reporters have very clear aims. The messages they present are straightforward and the style of the investigation is kept simple. There is no room in these narratives for psychological development or other forms of narrative evolution. A glance at the basic features of documentary narrative structure supports these summary observations.

Documentary Style

- Tight image sequence of 15–20 minutes;
- News report style of documentary: narration by the reporter dominates; images and interviews are selected and cut to fit the narration;
- No location sound except during interviews;
- Although the narration tends to be fast (a complicated case explained within 15 minutes), it appears 'objective' and 'calm' in the style of news presentation; most of the reporters are invisible; they tend to be situated as sympathetic to the victims and seem to know who the perpetrator is from the beginning, quite apart from the process of investigation;
- Real events (location and time are actual); the parties involved do exist;
- Opening questions – what happened? Followed by an investigation of motivation and who is responsible for the crime;
- Cause and effect relations: every cause is shown to lead inevitably to an effect(s); the impression of documented event and an investigation contradicts the fact that all the events, as well as their investigations, have been completed before shooting the film;
- Cases are sometimes unfinished either because the courts have not yet given a verdict or because the perpetrators have disappeared;
- The majority of cases happen in the rural areas; or in small or medium cities; 99.9% cases involve lower middle class families; few celebrities appear in the stories;
- Corruption cases mainly refer to the lower cadres, such as village chiefs, township Party secretaries, low-ranking clerks in legal institution, and lower rank of policemen;
- Cases of civil law are the rule: family issues (children and parents; marriage, extra-marital affairs, divorce, adoption, children or senior parents rights); business (fake products; contracts); disputes (between relatives, neighbourhood etc); accidents (traffic accidents, work related accidents);

- Violence and sex are barred; most cases are unusual, some have comic effects, most are attention-grabbing: vistas of private backyards, portraits of uneducated peasants, rural leaders, exploration of corruption, family gossip, the display of emotions, such as anger or despair.

Representative events, acts, and agents

1. Haozhuang xiangshui yu Village in Taiyuan has rat problems apparently caused by the pillows used by the villagers (3 December 2001). The reporter interviews the workers in the pillow factory, who it turns out never use the pillows themselves because they stuff them with biodegradable rubbish, as witnessed by the camera. Using a hidden camera, the reporter interviews distributors and retailers at the market and more than ten shops, to find out if they are aware of the fraud. The reporter then hands the case over to Consumer Affairs, which bans the pillow production and fines the factory owner.

2. On world AIDS day, 1 Dec 2001 the programme portrayed Wenlou village in Henan (Population 800) where two thirds of the population are HIV-positive. The cause of the disease is traced to the villagers' habit of selling blood to untrained blood bank personnel. The documentary first shows the details of the blood trade, then switches to a national report on the 600,000 AIDS patients in China. Two blood merchants admit that they are not aware that they are breaching any law; all they wanted was 'to earn some money'. The two are charged, awaiting a court verdict.

3. A two and half year old child dies after falling from a balcony when nanny goes to take the rubbish away (16 December 2001). A number of interviews flesh out the background to the accident: the child's parent say that they had not asked the nanny to do any work except looking after the baby; the nanny, a 50 year old woman from the country is crying helplessly, unable to speak; the court rules that she has to pay RMB 60,000 compensation; her husband says to the interviewer, 'her fault is that she has been trying to do too much'. The discussion informs the audience that Shenzhen has just passed China's first nanny regulations, including rights and duties of nannies.

4. In Gongyi, Henan province an old man drives without a licence and kills a person on the road (7 December 2001). His son goes to the police to confess to the accident. He is then sent to jail, while the daughter-in-law, deprived of a husband, fights with the father. Later, the daughter-in-law tells the truth to the police. The father asks whether he can go to jail so that his son could be released. However, his son is charged with concealing a crime. When the villagers are interviewed they refer to the proverb *Fu zai zi huan* (A father's debts are paid by the son). In their view, the son behaved responsibly, and he should not be punished for his filial piety. The discussion addresses

why the proverb does no longer apply to the legal processes of a market economy.

5. An 87 year old sick lady, a widow of 58 years, takes her 63 year old son to court for failing to look after her (6 February 2001). The son explains that he has an agreement with his elder brother who is to care for their mother in exchange for inheriting their mother's property after her death. The court rules in favour of the old woman, arguing that the agreement between the two brothers is illegal. The discussion emphasizes that nobody has a right to ignore the duty to look after parents.

6. A man leaves a will according to which his superannuation and half of the property are to be given to his de facto spouse (with whom he has a four year old daughter, whom he has treated well, though he has never acknowledged her publicly) (26 November 2001). His legal wife discovers the will after his death and challenges the will. The de factor spouse takes the wife to court, but only attends the court at the beginning of the case when she faces pressure from a hostile public. The popular opinion is that the court should protect the wife even if the marriage had not been satisfactory and in spite of the fact that the husband had requested a divorce, which however was rejected. Some community members are outraged that a mistress should be able to sue a legal wife. They are concerned that if the de facto spouse were to be successful in her claim this would amount to society supporting the legitimacy of having a mistress. After the hearing the vast majority of people attending the case applaud the court's decision that the man's will is illegal. In the discussion existing marriage laws are explained and the notion of a de facto relationship rejected as inappropriate for Chinese society.

7. A dispute has arisen with an 87 year old woman who loves an old tree she planted many years ago and from which she earns a living by selling its fruit. However, her brother's son claims that the tree belongs to him as it is in his garden (7 February 2001). According to forest law, the tree belongs to the woman, but according to the land law, the tree belongs to her nephew. The court decides that the tree belongs to the old women, but the profit from selling its fruit must be shared between the two families. The host of the episode reports that the old lady had died two months after the court decision, perhaps because she could not bear the thought of strife between the two families and concludes by saying: 'I believe laws can solve certain problems, but shouldn't we be more tolerant, more giving and loving when we face disputes between friends and relatives?'

Other episodes address such matters as China's entry into the WTO and the effect of this event on Chinese laws; copyright laws and pirate control; extra-marital affairs; a girl suing her parents for not providing tuition fees;

a tourist taking a travel bureau to court for false advertising; a woman filing a complaint against the wine industry for failing to point out that alcohol consumption may lead to death; and hundreds of episodes in a similar vein, addressing a broad spectrum of social events.

By focusing on criminals and victims at the margins of Chinese society, *Legal Report* titillates viewers with a look at transgressors who test the limits of citizenship. Yet the lesson of the show reinforces rather than transgresses cultural and legal norms promoted by the Chinese state. At the end of many of the episodes of the *Legal Report*, the discussion addresses the fact that public awareness of the law has certainly increased and that it is useful to know how to use laws to solve certain problems. At the same time, the discussion acknowledges that traditional thinking which tries to avoid such problems in the first place still has a role to play in Chinese society. And this is why, the host argues, we should continue to support people who defend some moral values, no matter whether they win or lose in court.

Thematics and audience response

All episodes of the *Legal Report* are constructed as variations on the theme of the tension between traditional morality and the new legal process. Depending on the topic of each individual case, the different structural components of the episode are weighted towards the one or the other. As a result, the *Legal Report* as a whole presents a picture of morality being tempered by laws and the law as modified by moral expectations.

Television audience feedback is not merely an incidental, additional attraction of the *Legal Report* to keep the ratings up, but integral to the didactic effectiveness of each episode, as well as the legal consciousness-raising of the series as a whole. By involving the viewers on a massive scale via e-mail, telephone and letters, the editors are able to plough public response back into the evolving series, resuming topics, referring back to earlier discussions, and keeping the debate topical and alive as if in a vastly extended college lecture theatre.

Narrative formula

It is possible to distil from the core pattern of the empirical story a succinct narrative type. The myriad variants of the *Legal Report* share a common narrative structure which incorporates ten main ingredients. These ingredients include an initial situation of injustice or suffering (a crime, a dispute, an accident, a moral infringement); a confrontation between one or more perpetrators of a crime and its victim(s) or between opponents in a dispute; an investigating reporter; interviews; a court verdict (given or pending); an expert providing specialized legal knowledge; a discussion of the case and its legal and moral implications; a tension between traditional moral expectations and the legal process; audience response; and an overarching ideological, didactic component: citizenship education in legal matters.

In the fleshed out individual episodes these core ingredients all play their part in forging a new kind of citizenship through media pedagogy. What is new in these exemplars and their emphasis on morality is the legal argument introduced by professional experts and a certain degree of democratization via investigative journalism and audience feedback. In this way, the producers of *Legal Report* tried to use the stories of people at the margins of Chinese society as cautionary tales to legitimate and popularize the Chinese state's conceptualization of the rights and responsibilities of Chinese citizenship.

Legal Report and Chinese conceptualizations of citizenship

Specific themes and motifs help to explain why Zhang Yimou's film *The Story of Qiu Ju* became the pilot for a TV documentary series at the centre of current citizenship education. These include the traditional motif of an initial injustice requiring the righting of a wrong; the theme that a request for justice remains unsuccessful until someone in a position of authority takes an interest in the plaintiff's case (Lyotard 1988); the idiom of *taoge shuofa* (begging for an official explanation); and the pervasive tension between expectations of traditional morality and the law. In the *Legal Report* these themes have been integrated into a highly successful narrative formula which has kept millions glued to the television screen since 2 January 1999.

The interaction of a new legal awareness and traditional moral thinking was at the heart of a number of TV documentaries other than the *Legal Report*, which have likewise been designed to teach ordinary Chinese, many of them without recourse to legal processes, to learn how to reconcile their traditional values with an increasingly complex legal perspective. Appreciating this relationship requires an interpretive framework within which both TV documentaries aimed at citizenship education and their focus on the relationship between law and morality make sense. Such a framework entails abandoning clichéd views such as 'Western citizen standards are individualistic and adversarial whereas those of Asia are communitarian and consensus-seeking' (Davidson 1999:222).

In formulating an appropriate analytical framework I consider first the concepts of citizenship that inform recent discussions of citizenship in the Anglo-sphere and Europe, showing that these are inapplicable to the Chinese situation. Next I turn to Chinese sources to propose an alternative conception of citizenship which better illuminates the ways in which Chinese viewers are urged to think about justice, rights and responsibilities.

According to Rolf Dahrendorf, 'there is no more dynamic social figure in modern history than The Citizen' (1994:292). The most radical use of this dynamic social figure is perhaps the concept of the 'global citizen' or 'world citizen', which understands people as being primarily 'citizens of the world' (Dower and Williams 2002:1). This kind of citizen not only accepts a global ethical framework, but also belongs to and participates 'in a wider community which finds expression in a variety of institutions within global civil society' (Dower and Williams 2002:40). From this perspective, citizenship 'ceases to be synonymous with nationality' (Delanty 2000:127). While this 'decoupling of citizenship and nationality' (131) and the accompanying picture of a 'fluid world' in which 'the ironic citizen needs to learn how to move on, how to adjust and to adopt to a world of cultural contingencies' (Turner 2000:30) could be applied to the kinds of transnational Chinese described in Fong's study (this volume), it cannot be applied to the vast majority of the Chinese population who are unable to attain flexible, transnational citizenship. The Chinese state's conceptualization of citizenship do not mention anything like the 'polyethnic rights' of 'multicultural citizenship' (Shafir 1998:171;167) 'regional citizenship' (Falk 2002:23f.), 'supra-societal rights' (Turner 1994:473) let alone 'differentiated citizenship' and 'special rights' of underprivileged groups (Young 1998:288).

A special handicap in Western perspectives on citizenship and citizenship education if applied to Chinese social phenomena is the assumption that ethics, especially in their utopian global form, should be premised on the way in which morality has emerged out of religious traditions. While it may be true that 'there will be no new world order without a global ethic' (Küng 2002:134), such an ethic is not necessarily tied to any form of religion. The tenacious emphasis on morality in China today is the result of several thousand years of non-theistic and secular moral practice as well as its continuous theorization.

A more appropriate interpretive path suggests that China is gradually warming to the concept of modern citizenship, so long as its leadership is confident that it can restrain the dual forces of democracy and capitalism. With capitalism on a leash, early ideas of European citizenship appear relevant, especially those that emphasize responsibilities rather than rights, from the Treaty of Westphalia (1648), through the writings of Pufendorf, Mendelsohn and Kant, to the '*devoirs*' of the French Revolution in 1789. If, as Kenneth Minogue notes, the trajectory of citizenship curves from 'compliance' towards 'participation' (Minogue 1995:16;13), China could be said to be gradually approaching the latter, having achieved in its recent history at least some of the requirements stipulated by Thomas Marshall in 1950, such as old-age pensions, unemployment benefits, public health insurance, legal aid, a minimum wage, and a modicum of some other entitlements.

From a Chinese perspective, one could approve of Dahrendorf's view of citizenship as 'the institutional counterpart of rationality, not merely an idea but a reality, the crystallization of rationality into a social role' as long as such a reality does not 'cross a line beyond which it defeats its own purpose', a threat that he terms the 'suicidal strain' of citizenship

(Dahrendorf 1994:307). Perhaps the transformation of the workers of European modernity into postmodern consumers signals to the Chinese authorities the crossing of that suicidal line.

What is more realistic for contemporary China is the transformation of a society grounded in public morality under state control into a community under more specific legal constraints, what Dahrendorf calls a 'Rechtsgemeinschaft' (Dahrendorf 1994:292). Certainly, as public announcements, as well as a massive wave of media pedagogy, suggest, Chinese authorities have taken seriously the task of educating their citizens towards a better grasp of the role that the law increasingly plays in their everyday lives, for in the past, as Li and Wu observe, 'the dignity of the law has been a foreign notion for most Chinese' (Li and Wu 1999:165). What has been familiar to all Chinese instead has been the long-standing tradition of common morality. In the absence of a history of familiarity with a complex and detailed body of laws, the new citizenship education programme appears as timely as it is necessary if China is to optimize its position in a rapidly globalizing world.

Today China has its own practices and interpretations of citizenship, a social phenomenon in which morality plays a fundamental role. The term 'morality' here refers loosely to what remains active of traditional Confucianism: the particular way of understanding the nation-state, government, and the relationship between rulers and subjects. The signifier 'nation-state', in Chinese, is constructed as two characters guo (country, kingdom) and jia (family): guojia, a family of nation-state, or a nation-state as an extended family. This notion of seeing the state as an extended family is illustrated by Li and Wu's observation of the relationship between state and the citizens on the issue of right and duties. 'For most Chinese, the rights of citizens are given by the government, and a citizen is part of the state: citizens perform their duties and, in return, government gives them their rights' (Li and Wu 1999:165). The relationship between state and citizens in China mirrors the family relationship in that children are an integral part of the family; the parents give children certain restricted rights, while in return the children do as they are told. This perspective is reflected also in the popular Chinese saying, Guojia younan, pifu youze (when a country is in difficulty, every ordinary citizen has responsibilities).

The emphasis on the state as an extended family foregrounding duties rather than rights is invoked by a leading intellectual of the late Qing, Liang Qichao, when he admonishes the guomin, the people, to increase their efforts to strengthen China in the face of Western imperialism. He felt that it was a 'lack of a sense of obligation – to pay taxes and serve in the military, for example – rather than the lack of rights, [that] constituted the root cause of China's problems' (Goldman and Perry 2002:6). So it makes sense that even in the twenty-first century, Chinese patriotism and nationalism are still built on the idea of an extended family. For instance, in the discourse of Chinese nationalism, Taiwan, Hong Kong and Macau

Chinese are referred to as *Taiwan tongbao, Gang'Ao tongbao,* that is, as full brothers and sisters of the mainland Chinese, while minorities in Chinese are seen as cousins and nephews of the Han.

The Chinese view of nation-state as an extended family transfers the singular relationship between the state and the citizen into a complicated dual relationship between citizen and the state, and citizens and rulers, where the rulers are perceived as parents responsible for running the family. In Western terminology, citizenship focuses on the relationship between state and the citizen, on rights and duties through ideas of 'justice' and 'equality'. But in China, citizenship is complicated by the relationship between state, rulers and individual. As the state is an extended family, the rulers of the state and the rulers of the family become interchangeable: it is not the state that looks after the citizen, but rather the rulers of the state who perform the duty of looking after their 'children'.

In Chen Yuanbin's novel *Wanjia shusong* (1991), on which Zhang Yimou's The *Story of Qiuju* is based, Qiuju complains,

> *Cunzhang* (the village chief) is in charge of the whole village, just like being in charge of a big family. The person who is charge is, of course, allowed to hit and scold his subjects. But he should not kick my husband's *yaoming de difang* (his place of life). I asked him [the chief]; he didn't even have a *shuofa* (reason).

When the Chief is taken away by the police, Qiuju does not understand that *cunzhang*'s behaviour of hitting a villager is a breach of law. What she understands is that the Chief has a right to punish the villagers (his children), but not by assaulting that particular part of the body. Since Qiuju does not yet know the gender of her unborn baby, her husband's reproductive organs are crucial to the continuation of the family line.

Seeing the ruler as the senior (parents) of the family connotes a sense of gratitude for the contribution he has made to his subjects, a well established theme of Confucianism. This makes it difficult to see citizens' rights as a product of a contract between individual and state on an equal basis. And it is likewise difficult to see how an ordinary citizen (son/daughter) should participate in decision making in the affairs of the state (family) on an equal basis with the ruler (parents).

As a consequence of this metaphoric and yet powerful extension of the family relationship to that between rulers and citizens, people in China tend to 'accept' situations where the relation between state and citizen is overruled by decisions made by the rulers of the day. For instance, in the CCP's categories, people (*renmin*), nationals (*guomin*), citizens (*gongmin*), the *renmin* enjoyed the rights to elect or to be elected, have freedom of thought, speech, and the press, while *guomin*, which includes *diren* (the CCP's political enemies within China), were required to perform their duties but could not necessarily enjoy all the political rights and liberties of the *renmin* (Li and Wu 1999:158). Between 1954 to the late 1970s, Mao's 'two kinds of contradiction' between people and enemy certainly overruled the legal notion of the citizen. Furthermore, as the meaning of *renmin* has changed to meet the Party's needs, so has their rights and duties.

This authoritarian and pastoral practice of citizenship only works so long as Confucianism plays a role more significant than the rule of law. Throughout 20th century China, rulers and intellectual elites developed a series of moral criteria to guide citizen behaviour. In the 1910s, the national government and the intellectuals called for citizens to perform their duties to make China strong. In the 1930s, Chiang Kai-Shek's nationalist government called for the return of Confucian morality in the *xin shenghuo* (New Life) movement proclaiming that every *guomin* (national) had a duty to participate in nation-building. In the 1950s, the Communist Government developed the *wuai* (five loves: love the nation, the people, work, science, and socialism), the standard measurement for a *hao gongmin* (good citizen). In the 1960s and 1970s, following the Party's fast changing instructions was the sole measurement for a good citizen. Lei Feng, a Communist solider killed in a road accident was the government's example for a good citizen for his unselfish and collective spirit.

As China entered the period of economic reform, the idea of 'governing the country according to law' became the new and not so revolutionary idea. The government gradually realized that a market economy could function without a highly complex legal system. In 1979, one year after his return to power, Deng Xiaoping stated that China 'needs to develop a high degree of democratic and comprehensive system of laws'. He urged the government that the People's democracy must be systematic and legal: *'youfa keyi, youfa biyi, zhifa biyan, waifa bijiu'* (We must have laws that we can rely on, we must carry out the laws we established, we are strictly abiding by our laws, and we will investigate to the end if our laws are breached.). In September 1979, the CCP developed the new concept of *shehuizhuyi fazhi* (socialist legal system). In April 1980 at the National Congress, the government launched the idea *yifa zhiguo* (governing the country by law). In November 1985 the Central Party and the State Council declared the *yifa zhiguo* a principle, and passed five five-year plans for mass education in law. In 1996 at the fifteenth Party Congress *'yifa zhiguo'* and 'establishing a law governed country' became the nation's fundamental credos for running the country. In 1999, basic strategies of governing the country by law were written into the constitution (*xiuzhen an*).

However, while the nation gradually changed into a society governed by law, government and conservative intellectuals expressed concerns about the demise of the nation's morality. Questions were raised, such as: What is the role of morality in citizenship education? Is it sufficient to govern the country by law? What if citizens are more aware of their rights than the morality that guides their duties? (You 2001:27). There was a fear that, while awareness of laws was rapidly increasing, moral education was lagging behind.

Even for those who saw no contradiction between law and morality, the former was seen as inferior. Wei, for one, argued that the law was the lowest form of morality (Wei 2001:199–121). The law was regarded as punishment enforced by the state; a set of rights and duties, and restrictions imposed on both self and others. Most importantly, in Wei's perspective, the law could act as a basis for all social relations. In contrast, he argued that morality was the highest status of human beings; it rested on beliefs and cultural values; concerned sacrifice and the performance of duties; and could modify all existing social relations as well as predict possible social relations in the future. For Wei, morality should be recognized as the supreme law.

A somewhat different view was offered by You (You 2001:21–24). He argued that law was a nation's legal spirit, a state's value system and a basis for judgement, whereas morality involved differences between class, institutions, race and ethnic groups. Law, he explained, required a formal process to be carried out within the institution, whilst morality relied on self-evaluation within social constraints. All social relationships covered by laws were also covered by morality, but not all social relations covered by morality could be covered by laws. Morality was a treasure of Chinese traditional ideology. Morality was the basis, law was the method. Law belonged to political construction and had a political spirit; morality involved ideological construction, reflecting the spirit of civilization (*People's Daily, Editorial*, 1 Feb 2001). Like many other Chinese, You insisted on the need for a return to moral education, for 'if there is only the law, then there is no spiritual civilisation' (You 2001:27).

The government embraced the idea that moral education was not only necessary in the long run, but was also an immediate and urgent task in citizenship education. State planners recognized that the nation was facing a moral crisis caused by 'the contradiction between a fast developed economy and a moral system that is lagging badly behind' (Jiang 2001:241). As Hao wrote:

> We had a socialist morality but that was the morality of the planned economy which was relative simple and direct (in organisational for-mat, employment methods, distribution of wealth). Now we are in the market economy, and our system is empty.
>
> (Hao 2001:15)

The document, *Gongmin daode jianshe shisi gangyao* (*Outline for Carry-ing Out the Citizenship Moral Construction*), issued by the Central Com-mittee CCP on 20 September 2001, argued that the current moral degradation would seriously 'disturb the economy and social order' if the following social phenomena could not be stopped.

In some social areas and aspects, moral degradation is on the rise. Boundaries between right and wrong, kind and evil, beauty and ugliness, are being violated. Materialism, hedonism, and individualism are increasing. At times we forget what is right at the sight of profit, and seek private gain at public expense. Loss of credibility and cheating are harming our society. Corruption and the use of power to gain private benefits are serious issues.

The calls to establish *minde* (morality for the masses, the ordinary citizens, or people) and *guande* (morality for the officials) grew louder (Jiang 2001:247–9). In January 2001, the then general Party Secretary Jiang Zemin declared that 'in the process of developing a socialist market economy, we must persist in strengthening the socialist legal system, in order to govern the country by law. At the same time, we must also persist in constructing and strengthening socialist morality, in order to govern the country by morality' (Meeting of Media Ministers).

What precisely was this morality the CCP was calling for? How did the morality that they had in mind differ from the Confucian ideal, especially in its perception of the relationship between state and individual? Did the morality that the CCP wanted assist in changing the perspective of rulers and society as an extended family to a legal contract relationship between state and individual? The CCP acknowledged that the notion of 'governing the country by morality' was inherited from a cultural tradition that informed the management of ideology and the state apparatus (Gao and Liu 2002:3). The Party also acknowledged that the differences between distinct kinds of morality stemmed largely from the differing ideological positions that produced them. Hence the CCP produced a 'system of socialist morality' that best suited their idea of a 'socialist market economy' (*People's Editorial*, 1 Feb 2001 and *Xinhua Daily*, Feb 13, 2001). This moral blue print contained as its core message: serving the people; the principle of collectivism; the five loves (of the nation, the people, work, science and socialism) and three domains which morality was to be primarily employed, the social, the profession and the family. These guidelines were echoed in the *Zhongguo gongmin daode shouce* (*Chinese Citizenship Morality Handbook*) which highlighted knowledge of morality; learning about the law; social behaviour; the idea that law was subordinate to morality; and *wuai* or the 'five loves' as the legal duty and moral responsibility of every Chinese citizen.

Citizenship education has always been at the centre of the government's agenda under the guidance of the CCP since 1949. The main difference between the Mao period and post-Mao period lies in the content rather than the methods, namely, mass education through campaigns and movements. In the post-Mao period, political ideology has been reduced. In its place, awareness of the law now occupies centre stage in citizenship education to ensure China's smooth transition from its planned economy to that of the market. In the planned economy, social rights and responsibilities were the most important aspects of citizenship, as social and familial problems were usually solved through government mediation with the help of party committees in the workplaces and neighbourhood, with an emphasis on the spirit of collectivism, harmony, and various moral codes. In the emerging market economy, however, the government encourages citizens to use laws as solutions to their problems. This new focus on the civil and legal aspects of citizenship involves a new way of thinking, including evaluating the individual's position in relation to family, society and state.

Although Jiang Zemin's slogan 'govern the country by law' significantly accelerated the public's thinking in terms of a contractual relationship with authority, Jiang did not want to let go of the notion of morality, though what he wished to retain was a 'socialist morality' suitable to the new 'market economy'. While in Mao's period morality was subsumed under 'political ideology', the CCP under Jiang's leadership revived a modified notion of morality compatible with the demands of the market. In 1990, the Jiang Zemin Government insisted that moral education was to remain part of citizenship education. In 1996 the government specified that a modern citizen should have these qualities (*suzhi*): ideologically correct morality (*shixiang daode*); knowledge of science and culture (*kexue wenhua*); and awareness of the law (*minzhu fazhi guan*). In 2001, Jiang proclaimed that while 'governing the country by law is important', it is equally important to 'govern the country by morality'.

Throughout Chinese history, then, governments defined and redefined 'morality' to accommodate what they felt was required for the specific circumstances of their rule. In their studies for the methodology of governing the country by morality, Gao and Liu (2002:4–5) argued:

> The [Jiang's] 'morality' in 'governing the country by morality' refers to a socialist and communist' morality. The ancient morality is the morality of slave society and feudalism. Morality under socialism and communism emphasizes unity between individualism and collectivism, between the interests of the nation and those of whole human beings, between collectivism and self interest.

The tension between collectivist obligation and the interests of individual citizens has remained a pervasive theme in Chinese society. It is therefore not surprising that TV programmes which contribute to citizenship education reflect this tension. In the *Legal Report* the relationship between collectivist obligation and the rights of the individual are negotiated within a complex structural dialogue between morality and the law.

Conclusion

In this chapter I have analysed how the documentary TV programme, the *Legal Report,* functions as an important source of citizenship education in

China. In its more than a thousand episodes to date the *Legal Report* reflects an anxiety deeply embedded in the social pathology of Chinese society today. On the one hand, there is the realization by government, the intelligentsia, and the leadership in technology and commerce that the development of a complex network of laws and legal processes is a *sine qua non* if China wishes to compete successfully in the global economy. On the other hand, China fears that the shift towards a legally managed rather than authority controlled social system could seriously damage its time-honoured, pragmatically proven, and all-pervasive, ideational system of traditional morality.

As my analysis of the case study episodes shows, the dialogic tension between law and morality is not only present as a motif throughout episodes of *Legal Report*, it informs its every structural feature from the reporter's data collection to audience feed-back. The staggering popularity of the *Legal Report* has been traced to a highly formulaic narrative structure able to meet a number of viewer expectations at the same time: informative topicality, practical applicability, legal and moral pedagogy, and narrative entertainment that takes advantage of viewers' fascination with those at the margins of Chinese society. In this, the programme revives, in a televisual mode, the traditional Chinese demand on art to convey morality – *wen yi zai dao*.

What, I want to ask at the end of this chapter, are the effects of this kind of citizenship education? Or, to speculate about government expectations in sponsoring such programmes, what is the political purpose behind the *Legal Report?* Perhaps the following summary propositions will provide at least a tentative answer to both questions. The consistent thematics and didactic direction of the *Legal Report* appear to achieve a new social awareness that combines increasing knowledge of legal processes with traditional moral values, perhaps resulting in a renewed social cohesion. It is also no accident that the *Legal Report* should emphasize something that is essential to the functioning of late capitalist democracies: an intricate web of laws. Instead of aiming for Western global citizenship aspirations, however, China appears to have embraced the more realistic goal of striving for compatibility between its rapidly changing cultural, political, technological and economic systems. In this, the kind of citizenship education offered by the *Legal Report* plays a crucial and effective role. While it is true to say that the notion of the 'dignity of the law' is foreign to China, it is equally true that the dignity of morality remains a mainstay of Chinese thought.

Note

The author would like to thank Professors Xu Congde, Lü Shilun, Tim Wright, and Horst Ruthrof for their helpful input, and the *Legal Report* producer Liu Zhongde for his generous assistance.

6 "Civilizing" Shanghai

Government efforts to cultivate citizenship among impoverished residents

Tianshu Pan

Introduction

This paper is an ethnographic examination of community-building practices in Bay Bridge, a poor, marginalized neighborhood in Shanghai City, China. Based on field research conducted intermittently between 1998 and 2002, I explore how cadres in neighborhood organizations defined and promoted social and cultural citizenship while dealing with contradictions between the modernizing visions of policymakers and the harsh realities of the city's marginalized "lower quarters."

I cast street officers and committee cadres as movers and shakers in the process of civilizing a notoriously marginalized "lower quarters" slum locality. I show that Chinese policymakers' efforts to define and promote certain kinds of cultural citizenship were constantly subject to the manipulation of individual and institutional actors within the neighborhood. Instead of lumping street officers and resident committee cadres in the rather broad category of "local officials" or "neighborhood organizations cadres," I distinguish between these two groups of agents of change in the local social milieu. I argue that the street officers and committee cadres differed from each other not only in terms of their ranking in the job grade system but also in their levels of education and the degree to which they identified with the local community.

This paper is organized into three sections. I begin with a discussion of local ideas about the "lower quarters" and "upper quarters," which corresponded to different and unequal kinds of social and cultural citizenship. From the colonial past to the late socialist present, these notions were among the most meaningful categories for articulating one's status and position in society. The persistence of such a dichotomy in everyday discourse indicated the limits of socialist attempts at eliminating inequality and disparity within and between various residential quarters.

In the second section, I examine professionalization programs designed by the reform-minded technocrats of the Shanghai Municipal government who attempted to turn the neighborhood organization from an arm of state authority into a service-oriented network of social workers. By comparing the experiences of two generations of neighborhood organization workers, I highlight the dilemmas faced by a younger, supposedly more professional generation of street officers (i.e. "the textile sisters") who lacked the social skills and political incentives of their predecessors (i.e. "the granny cadres").

The last section on showcasing citizenship examines the impact of the global flow of knowledge and ideas in the late 1990s on community building practices at the local level. The younger generation of street officers hoped that selecting a "lower quarters" neighborhood for transformation into a showcase "civilized community" would help the "lower quarters" attain the kind of social and cultural citizenship previously reserved for the "upper quarters." The "granny cadres," however, were concerned that such gentrification efforts only exacerbated the gap between rich and poor in the lower quarters.

Location-based cultural citizenship: lower and upper quarters of Shanghai

The Shanghainese cultural citizenship described in this chapter bears a strong resemblance to the "First World citizenship" discussed in Vanessa Fong's chapter (this volume) in that both forms of citizenship are defined in terms of access to material and symbolic resources. Shanghainese cultural citizenship can thus be seen as a particular combination of Fong's "First World citizenship" and a historically defined locality-based citizenship. People of Shanghai's "upper quarters" have long been cosmopolitans who wore their civic pride like a badge of honor. They have been called the Londoners, Parisians and New Yorkers of China. Their sense of civic pride derived from their colonial past, as the "upper quarters" were once concessions run and occupied by wealthier, more powerful countries.

The large-scale changes that affected every part of Shanghai since the early 1990s made it easy to assume that territoriality has become less an issue that it was in the recent past. Over the course of my research, however, I came to realize that the age-old dichotomy between the lower quarters and upper quarters has not been blurred by broader transformations. I found, rather, that the lower/upper quarters dichotomy has remained a linguistic device strategically appropriated by both local residents and neighborhood organization cadres. They use this device to map out residential communities in their mental universe. The kinds of social and cultural citizenship available to them corresponded to the particular socioeconomic echelons and spatial terrains they inhabited.

In the Shanghainese dialect, the location of one's residence or workplace in the "upper quarters," the so-called *shangzhi jiao*, could be viewed as the equivalent of the English terms "uptown" or "the right side of the tracks." The term "lower quarters," or *xiazhi jiao*, on the other hand, was the equivalent for "downtown" or the "wrong side of the tracks." Social historians have often noted snobbery based on distinctions between the lower and upper quarters (Honig 1992; Lu 1999: 15, 376). As reflections of both historical imagination and social reality, the two "quarters" remained the key terms used self-consciously by the local residents, municipal officials, and real estate agents as a strategic device to position themselves in everyday social life. Over the past 150 years, the twin processes of urbanization and industrialization transformed Shanghai from a rural county seat into a cosmopolitan metropolis, and in the process, produced these two echelons which represented different lifestyles, local histories, native place identities, and living environments. Historically, the "upper quarters" were the neighborhoods with enclaves of foreign populations – the French, the British, the Americans, and the Jews who fled Russia and Eastern Europe. Within the "upper quarters," a beautiful house with a garden and backyard well protected by an iron-gate and thick walls was often the residence of a top government official. Yet in the same neighborhood, an apartment building of colonial style could be occupied by more than a dozen families who moved in after the original owner fled Shanghai on the eve of the communist takeover in 1949. It is important to note that for most of the ordinary residents living in the former International Settlement and the French Concession, their sense of superiority derived from the very location (*jiao*) of their home and not necessarily their actual housing conditions.

In local terms, the "lower quarters" used to be a synonym for shantytown housing or simply shacks (*penghu*) and had always been associated with stereotypical images of narrow lanes inhabited by the Subei people, the descendents of migrants and refugees from northern Jiangsu who spoke a dialect distinctively different from Shanghainese. The derogatory term "Subei" might be just a term that was conceived by those residents elsewhere in the city and not necessarily an objective description of their place of origin, as Honig rightly argues (Honig 1992: 28–35). Yet the "lower quarters," the very source of prejudice against the Subei people in Shanghai, had remained a material reality and a mental category for decades. Shanghai's lower quarters were seen as the armpit of the city, and were stereotyped as places where one would expect to see a vicious circle of urban poverty, illegal housing, family breakdown, and social disorganization.

The dichotomy between "lower" and "upper" quarters was a key point of reference for the city administrators trying to identify the social and economic characteristics of a particular neighborhood and mark out the boundaries of residential enclaves. After 1949, the Districts within the entire Shanghai Municipality were reorganized so that a District became an administrative region of several sub-divisions. Each sub-district formed a constituency governed by the Street Office appointed by the District Government. Because of Communist city-planners' desire to eliminate if not minimize the inequalities in income and housing conditions between districts, the goal of redistricting was to combine administrative spheres that fell into the pre-1949 categories of the "lower quarters" *and* "upper quarters." The boundaries that separated poor districts from rich ones disappeared on the city map of New Shanghai. Yet, within each newly configured district, the boundaries that used to separate the "lower quarters" from "upper quarters" continued to exist.

While demarcation lines between the "quarters," such as walls, fences, and paths, became less visible, the establishment of subdistrict street officers served to reify the difference between the socioeconomic statuses of those inhabiting neighborhoods that represented two totally different social worlds. In everyday bureaucratic practices, as social historian Lu Hanchao notes, the leaders of the Street Office actually acknowledged existing differences by establishing residents' committees based on the types of neighborhood, the living conditions, and even the native-place origins of the inhabitants (Lu 1999: 316). The alleyways and lanes within the jurisdiction of the street office as well as the allocation of space to particular uses and sizes of buildings therefore became an overt expression of the total gamut of behavior characteristic of a certain residential quarters. As if to rid the city of its colonial past and to reflect the changes brought by the founding of New China, the English and French names of the streets within the "upper quarters" were changed into Chinese ones. Ford Lane became Fu Jian road and Route Lafayette, Fuxing road (which literally meant "the street of revitalization"). The street names within the "lower quarters" for the most part, were purposefully kept.[1] If the post-1949 "upper quarters" continued to stand for modernity and civilization, the "lower quarters" beyond the neon lights, would remain a symbol of backwardness and underdevelopment.

One should not be much surprised if "revolutionary leaderships, consciously or unconsciously, come to play the lord of manor," as Benedict Anderson cautions us (Anderson 1991: 160). Anderson makes it clear that it was the leadership not the ordinary people who came to "inherit the old switchboards and palaces" (*ibid.* 161). As Chairman Mao Zedong and his marshals took residence in the imperial mansions in the vicinity of the "Forbidden City" of China's last Dynasty, his comrades in Shanghai quietly moved into the colonial style manor houses located in the former French Concession which had always been off-limits to ordinary people. The privileges the communist victors enjoyed made a mockery of the socialist ideal of egalitarianism and illustrated what Bahro refers to as "social stratification under actually existing socialism" (Bahro 1978: 163–182; see also J. Watson 1984: 1–15; R. Watson 1994).

When I began my fieldwork in 1998, I was struck by the continuing presence of both "upper quarters" and "lower quarters" in Luwan District. As I walked from the northern Luwan to Bay Bridge, I could detect a gradual change in housing patterns, from the fancy little European style villas sandwiched between the postmodern high rises, to the more traditional terraced houses which blended into rows of match-box shaped apartment buildings. Within Bay Bridge, the match-box shaped buildings (five or six story walk-ups) and the century old and poorly maintained wooden houses were the most representative form of housing for the local residents. Occasionally, one could even find traces of squatter settlement in Bay Bridge's oldest housing community nicknamed "the commoners village."

What set Bay Bridge apart from other comparable underclass neighborhoods in the City's periphery was, however, its proximity to the northern section of Luwan District, which claimed "upper quarters" status because it had been part of the French Concession. To the best knowledge of the urban planners I interviewed, Bay Bridge was among the very few "lower quarters" in the City that was in the vicinity of historical landmarks, the architectural representations of "monumental time" (Herzfeld 1991) of modern Shanghai. To its north was the restored holy site of the "Birthplace of the Chinese Communist Party (CCP)" where the First Congress of CCP was held in July 1921. To its south was Jiangnan Shipyard (which began as an Arsenal during the later Imperial era), which was called the "Cradle of China's Proletarian Class" in the official historiography. To its east, the "City of Temple Gods," a walled City for the Chinese residents in the colonial days, was a showcase exhibiting the Shanghai local cultures and customs. Located to its far west was a Catholic Cathedral known for its pivotal role in promoting the Chinese understanding of the West three centuries ago.

The marginalized "lower quarters" status of Bay Bridge was reified, as I gradually learned over the course of fieldwork, because of the additional sources of stigma attached to the entire locality. First, a well-developed funeral service connected with less prominent guilds prior to the 1949 communist takeover was believed to have disrupted the system of geomancy that regulated the forces of "wind" and "water" (*fengshui*). The locality was further "polluted" due to the notorious Japanese bombing of Shanghai in 1937 that had effectively turned Bay Bridge into one of the city's biggest graveyards where thousands of dead bodies were discarded without proper burial. During the Civil War (1947–49), the "ghost land" of Bay Bridge became a haven for both the bandits of the defeated Nationalist Army and the landlords who had fled their home villages in the aftermath of the Communist Land Reform (1945–1950). Even during the present construction boom, the inauspicious indications of an unspoken *and* unspeakable past often disturbed those living in the present as human bones and skeletons were unearthed in virtually all the sites upon which high-rise office and apartment buildings would be built.

Apparently the pre-1949 Bay Bridge had more than enough attributes to qualify as the most marginalized of the city's "lower quarters" – graves and garbage, dirty ponds and creeks, squatter settlements, beggars and tramps, mosquitoes and flies. The historical connection with death and funerals as well as the starving beggars became a major source of stigma that reinforced the marginalization of the neighborhood even after 1949. The lack of a decent school confirmed its social and economic status.

As "the people without history" (to paraphrase Eric Wolf 1982), the people of Bay Bridge could never expect to be treated equally by those with full Shanghainese social and cultural citizenship in the "upper quarters," even though they had been legally registered as the permanent residents of Shanghai under the *hukou* system for generations (see for example, Honig's pioneering work on the Subei people in Shanghai [1992]). They were deprived of full social and cultural citizenship as long as they retained their marginalized "lower quarters" status. Small wonder that the local cadres dispatched from the District Government (which was, ironically, located in the "upper quarters," the former French Concession) referred to Bay Bridge as "Luwan's Siberia."

In the summer of 2000, I presented a young Bay Bridge street officer with a report on the undocumented history of the pre-1949 past of Bay Bridge with the hope that he could use some of my findings for an upcoming exhibition on the past and present of the neighborhood. To my surprise and dismay, the street officer and his colleagues showed very little interest in what I wrote, and wondered at the time and effort I took in "writing so much about so small a community." They implicitly criticized me for being too obsessed with the past of Bay Bridge, since the past had practically nothing to do with their present, let alone the future they envisioned for themselves.

Until it became an officially designated "Model Community" in 1995, Bay Bridge had been considered "matter out of place" (Douglas 1966) even though it was within walking distance of all the historical landmarks often associated with images of colonial gentility and postsocialist prosperity. As the biggest territorial subdivision of Luwan, occupying an area of 3.07 square kilometers inhabiting 81,634 registered residents, Bay Bridge was hardly mentioned in the 244 pages of the District Gazette, which contained a mere two pages of introduction of its population and neighborhood organization structure.

The cadres of Bay Bridge seized every possible opportunity to improve the status of their neighborhood and develop various strategies of competing for community resources, media coverage and attention from the municipal officials. The community construction movement, beginning in the early 1950s, became their best chance to change the image of the "lower quarters" by erasing its unspeakable past and monumentalizing its present for the sole purpose of creating a community as the model for a civilized and scientific way of living in a modernist city. Each generation of street officers shared the idea that, as a typically marginalized "lower quarters," Bay Bridge was no more than a blank sheet of paper on which they could paint beautiful pictures. Some of the pictures, as I show in the following sections, became faded as time went by while others turned into hollow showcases, or even figments of their imagination.

Managing the debris of socialism in Bay Bridge

As Rachel Murphy and Yingchi Chu noted (this volume), modernization ideals have had a profound impact on local bureaucratic practices. Along with the introduction of western concepts of efficient business management, Shanghai officials have replaced outmoded socialist jargon with such terms as "social work," "sustainable development," and "community service." These terms were used to authorize gentrification and revitalization processes aimed at giving residents of the marginalized "lower quarters" access to the social and cultural citizenship they had long been denied.

As casualties of the structural reform of state enterprises, millions of unemployed industrial workers in China found themselves in a painful process of adjusting to a new way of life centering on their community rather than their workplace. Growing unemployment drastically enlarged the marginalized sector of Chinese society officially labeled as the "hardship population" which had traditionally included the elderly, disabled, and sick in the neighborhood. Lacking a well-developed social safety net, officials in the Chinese Civil Affairs Ministry have been implementing community-based programs aimed at improving existing welfare functions. Meanwhile the steady increase in the proportion of the population who were elderly (an unintended consequence of family planning practices) and the rise of compulsory early retirement caused a pressing need for new social security schemes.

Despite the fact that Shanghai had arguably the most sophisticated social welfare scheme in post-Deng China, the fight against urban poverty was an uphill battle. This was largely because of Shanghai's historical position as the nation's industrial base, the locus of hundreds of state-owned textile factories, steel plants, shipyards, and mechanical works. As government officials engaged in a relentless bid to regain its pre-1945 status as the financial center of Asia by renovating the colonial style bank buildings and constructing high rises for foreign companies, state owned factories located in the city's peripheral area (including most "lower quarters") were approaching the end of their productive life.

The modernist visions of the young technocrats who began to dominate the leadership of the Street Office were in great tension with the harsh conditions of a marginalized lower quarters neighborhood like Bay Bridge. By the 1990s, the state factories in the neighborhood were either shut down or on the brink of bankruptcy. Most of these factories were built in the 1950s to replace the temples, shrines, and guild halls as new landmarks. Back then industrialization was the Chinese approach to urbanization. Chimneys puffing out smoke were auspicious signs for the future of socialism. Four decades later, the chimneys had stopped puffing black smoke. This was not because the managers were concerned with the environment but there were simply no jobs available for the workers. In Bay Bridge, many recently unemployed workers were psychologically unprepared for the sudden loss of the "iron rice bowl" of secure lifelong employment. They were afraid of re-entering the labor market because they thought that they had long lost the ability to compete. Whenever they became nostalgic for the "good old days" when the chimneys of their factories were still puffing out smoke, they felt they were being short-changed. They were overwhelmed with a sense of disorientation, betrayal, despair, and misplacement because they could no longer wear a badge of honor as members of the vanguard class.

Municipal officials perceived unemployment as a source of instability. They devoted considerable amount of time and energy to accommodating the needs of the unemployed and underemployed because they were well aware of the tradition of rebellion in the birthplace of the proletarian class and the Chinese Communist Party (e.g., Perry 2002). As a section chief of the district police confided to me, confronting the desperate unemployed workers ("who had nothing to lose") in the local community was much more of a challenge than handling the student protesters back in 1989 or the crackdown on the Falungong sect a decade later. Small wonder that Shanghai's Party Secretariat repeatedly told the street officers that "any social conflicts must be resolved at the grassroots level."

While the current urban crisis had re-emphasized the role of the neighborhood organization as the buffer between the state and the people, Shanghai officials were still facing the dilemmas of social and economic transitions: without a well-developed social safety net, who would be willing to care for those who are "not making it" in the new, globalizing economy? Within the local community, who would possibly be able to manage the debris of the system created under the Maoist regime?

"Granny cadres": enforcers of responsibilities and defenders of rights

In Bay Bridge, the "granny cadres" or the "bound-foot police" had been remarkably successful at building social and cultural citizenship among the poor. The power of these seemingly weak elderly women derived from the legitimacy built up slowly over the several decades they had worked for the community. Most of them started working as volunteers or activists for the neighborhood organization in the 1950s or the early 1960s. Even in the 1990s, these "granny cadres" still remained an indispensable and formidable force in maintaining the order and stability of the local community.[2] In the absence of a well-structured judiciary court system, the residents' committees often played an important role in settling disputes among feuding neighbors and even between relatives. During the student demonstration of 1989, many granny cadres in Shanghai were much more skilled in maintaining community order than the professional police.

It was difficult for me to know for sure how the granny cadres managed to dissuade potential "dissidents" in the community from participating in street demonstrations (or even acting as bystanders) a decade ago. From what my informants in Bay Bridge told me (with a sense of pride), they effectively kept the "usual suspects" (high school and college students as well as the unemployed and the ex-cons) at home by allowing them to gamble through playing poker and mahjong. Later the women cadres justified their decision to legitimize the mahjong game in the neighborhood without formal approval from the superiors of the Street Office and District Police Station[3] as a useful tactic of diverting the attention of the local residents from the potentially explosive events on the streets. Apparently the committee cadres (many of whom were themselves expert mahjong players) succeeded in their lobbying efforts so that the district leaders eventually gave informal consent. This immediately made mahjong the most enjoyable pastime in many Shanghai neighborhoods.

The stereotypical view of the snoopy and nosy "granny cadres" as community enforcers of social responsibilities was promoted not only by foreigners but also by those working in the Chinese entertainment industry. In almost any film about urban life in contemporary China, the audience could expect to see scenes of elderly women with watchful eyes poking their noses into the private lives of others. Young couples who recently moved into the neighborhood would be easy targets for the "granny cadres," especially if the newcomers failed to produce evidence of a legal marriage.

I managed to trace the granny cadres' derogatory nickname "bound foot police" to a comedy skit performed in a variety show shown by China's Central TV Station on Lunar New Year's Eve. The comedy featured the plight of a migrant couple who fled to Beijing because they violated the birth control policy. While in the city, they were afraid of being caught by the residents' committee cadres they called "bound foot police and detectives." The term "bound foot police" was most likely a misnomer. In the neighborhoods of Beijing and Shanghai where I conducted fieldwork, the women cadres who had worked for the residents' committees ranged in age from 60 to 80. Footbinding was on the wane by the time they were born, and most of them could not have had their feet bound because they had worked as child laborers in textile factories and tobacco plants before 1949.

Terms such as the "bound foot police" downplayed the dual role played by granny cadres working for the neighborhood organizations, both as civilizing agents who promoted social responsibilities and as public servants who defended social rights and promoted cultural citizenship. In the early 1950s, when they started out as volunteers or activists of the "fire and crime prevention team" in Bay Bridge and elsewhere in the city, they were newlyweds or young mothers. They were persuaded by chief officer of the District work team to "come out" (*chulai*) to work for benefit of the entire community of Bay Bridge. Many of them did courageously "come out" to join the parade for the District wide celebration of March 3 (International Women's Day) and May 1 (the International Labor Day). To "come out" (*chulai*) represented a kind of liberation from traditional family life to explore the possibilities of realizing their value in public rather than private spheres. Young and restless, these newly recruited residents' committee cadres presented themselves as examples of how local women were capable of "becoming socialist women" and gaining access to the more prestigious kinds of social and cultural citizenship. The literacy classes taught in various housing communities in the early and mid-1950s in Shanghai had enabled many working class women to master writing skills – something they had never dreamed of before 1949 (Zhang 1993: 75; see also Honig 1986).

Throughout the 1950s, the neighborhood organizations in Bay Bridge enjoyed a considerable degree of local popularity for their role in increasing disempowered residents' access to social and cultural citizenship. Some retired street officers I interviewed called this period the "golden age of our offices and committees." By organizing neighborhood activities and connecting residents with the broader political culture, residents' committee cadres encouraged residents to have a sense of belonging in the broader culture of Maoist socialism. The social citizenship these cadres promoted consisted not only of responsibilities to obey state policies, but also of rights to food, medicine, security, and emergency assistance. Because a large percentage of the local population were the descendants of refugees and laborers, social welfare assistance had always been an integral part of the routine work of the residents' committees ever since the formative years of the sub-district "winter crime and fire prevention station." To wealthy, self-sufficient residents who lived in the "upper quarters" of Luwan, a residents' committee cadre might have been seen as an unwanted intruder, tiresomely reminding them of the responsibilities of social citizenship. In the District's marginalized "lower quarters," however, residents' committee cadres served as champions of social rights, and were thus welcomed by the majority of the residents.

Championing social and cultural citizenship for the poor: two street officers' stories

One such cadre, Feng Ting, had been a street officer in the "upper quarters" of Luwan District for over five years before she was assigned to work as the representative of the Women's Federation in Bay Bridge in 1960. On the fifth working day of every month, usually in the early hours of the afternoon, Feng Ting would come to collect her pension, and would have a boxed lunch with the other retired cadres and staff members. I found this to be the most convenient time to engage a personal conversation with her over a cup of hot green tea.

Feng Ting was well into her seventies but still had excellent memories of her life and the events she had experienced as a cadre in the local community before she retired in the early 1980s. Recalling what happened in the prime of her life kept her awake and energetic as we talked during the post-lunch rest break, when most of the people in the Street Office would take a nap (*wushui*). Despite her complete fluency in Shanghai dialect, she surprised me by telling me that she was already in her late twenties when she first came to work in Luwan with her husband on job transfer after 1949.

During the Land Reform in the 1940s, the women's liberation projects in Feng Ting's home village in Shandong Province had resulted in the dramatic increase of divorce cases. Many of these cases involved the former "little daughter-in-laws" who had married their adopted brothers after betrothals arranged by their parents when they were only children (M. Wolf 1972). The cadres from the communist work terms were hardly prepared for the divorces caused by the new policy, which was intended to promote gender equality and women's freedom in marriage choice. As the leader of the newly established women's township federation, Feng Ting was given the task of dissuading (rather than encouraging!) the unfortunate "little daughter-in-laws" from divorcing their husbands for the sake of maintaining stability in the revolutionary base area. Too young to see the discrepancy between the communist ideals and the actual local conditions, Feng Ting complied with the order from the work team and tried her best to fulfill this impossible mission. She reflected on her experience as an unwilling mediator back then and admitted that "I was naïve but they (the township authority) were just as stubborn as the feudalists (the husbands of the little daughter-in-laws)."

Feng Ting jumped at the chance when she and her husband were recruited to work in Shanghai's new District Government. What attracted Feng Ting, however, was not the affluence of China's biggest city but the opportunity to work in the birthplace of the Chinese Communist Party. This birthplace was only two blocks away from the District Government, which, ironically, was located in a peaceful neighborhood in the city's former "French Concession." Only a couple of months after she settled down in her new home and workplace, Feng Ting began to feel uncomfortable dealing with those well-dressed housewives in the "upper quarters" who always maintained a distance from the local cadres. Like the rural migrant children described by Lu Wang (this volume), Feng Ting experienced discrimination from lifelong urban residents who were arrogant in their sense of superior social and cultural citizenship. At the bottom of her heart, Feng Ting believed the class difference between those living in this rich neighborhood and people like her with a rural background would never be eliminated.

In order to change to a different work environment, Feng Ting surprised her colleagues in the District Government by volunteering to be "sent down" to the Street Office of Bay Bridge nicknamed as Luwan's "Siberia." Unlike her predecessors most of whom were originally from the city's "upper quarters" who kept complaining about the bad conditions of Bay Bridge, Feng Ting immediately fell in love with the place and its people. A strong contrast to the rich and pompous in the District's "upper quarters," the residents here greeted her with smiling faces. She was particularly impressed with the local women who were, as Feng Ting put it, "not only brainy but also marvelous with their hands" (an idiom which could be literally translated as "clever and deft"). They taught her how to make the best use of leftovers to cook a delicious meal and how to weave traditional cloth with beautiful patterns.

As in other "lower quarters," the socioeconomic status of working class women in "Luwan's Siberia" remained virtually unchanged during the 1950s. The local residents who benefited from the post-1949 industrialization process were primarily men who worked as the officially categorized "physical laborers," such as longshoremen and steel plant workers. The majority of women in Bay Bridge were uneducated and had no choice but to stay at home to look after the children and cook for the entire family. Feng Ting felt so frustrated at hearing about so many cases of young housewives being mistreated by their husbands and mothers-in-law that she decided to change the situation. She firmly believed that "the political liberation of women was meaningless if they were still deprived of economic rights." For one thing, women who lacked decent jobs not only earned no salary but also had only two thirds of the monthly ration coupons as their male counterparts.

Taking full advantage of the political atmosphere and the personal connections she cultivated while working in the District Government, Feng Ting formed several "women's groups for studying Mao Zedong Thought" (a euphemism for women's production teams). For Feng Ting, this was the very first step toward realizing her goal of enhancing Bay Bridge women's access to social and cultural citizenship. Most of the women below the age of forty-five joined the production team, and only a few chose to remain at home. Through hard negotiations with factory managers in the Shipyard (previously known as the Jiangnan Arsenal) area, Feng Ting secured part time jobs for these women who became contract laborers and were later entitled to have a small salary and some benefits. Eventually they were all officially offered an "iron rice bowl" which included a full wage and a complete welfare package.

Feng Ting gradually discovered that food and medicine were vital for improving the health of local women who could not afford to go to hospitals. She recalled the time when she and her comrades went out early in the morning in search of wild plants of medicinal value and returned home at dusk with bunches of herbaceous peony. They made for themselves herbal medicine that proved to be a good cure for bronchitis and anemia prevalent among the local women. Feng Ting and her team members earned for themselves the nickname "barefoot doctors" (after the rural medics who brought basic healthcare to China's countryside).

But Feng Ting's superiors "up" in the District Government (in Luwan's "upper quarters") were not at all happy with what she was doing "down there." In the 1960s, the institutionalization of local government gave rise to a new generation of communist bureaucrats who avoided making further progress for fear of making mistakes. Satisfied with the status quo, they felt it was not in the social and political interest of the district leaders to engage women in the industrialization process.[4] They saw Feng Ting's project as essentially "troublemaking" and wanted to discipline her, fearing women in other sub-districts would emulate her.

From Feng Ting's point of view, these District Officers shared the mentality of her superiors in the work team back in her home village. She labeled such a mentality the root cause of "bureaucratism" (*guanliao zhuyi*), which she had fought during her entire career. Feng Ting decided that she would not give in to such pressures from the top this time and fought back without any hesitation. To justify their cause, she reminded the people around her that: "Didn't Chairman Mao say that every one has the right to eat a bowl of rice?" She strategically used Mao's words of wisdom as a shield against the accusations from the district leaders. Eventually, Feng Ting became a role model for her colleagues in other sub-district committees and gained official recognition as a model cadre for her achievement.

More than two decades later, those of us who critically examined the effects of the Maoist women's liberation project might be disappointed to find that Chinese women for the most part, were still confined to their own sphere with allocated menial jobs. However, according to Feng Ting, without such menial jobs, things could have been much worse for women in Bay Bridge. Feng Ting told me that those who chose to remain at home instead of joining her team continued to suffer at the hands of their mothers-in-law and forty years later, their daughters-in-law! "For women, economic rights are everything," Feng Ting said, "then and now." She was clearly alluding to rising unemployment in the late 1990s. She particularly felt sad that among the unemployed were many women in their late thirties and mid-forties.

While the Maoist project of women's liberation failed in many ways, it did provide an opportunity for many working class women to "come out" and claim the entitlements of full social and cultural citizenship – to find their niche in an androcentric society and display their organizational skills and revolutionary spirit. Their energies were unleashed and their life had never been so meaningful, retired street officers recalled with nostalgia. Most of the community production teams, day care centers, even public canteens, were transformed into the affordable service providers for the neighborhood. They withstood the test of time because they performed a function in serving social needs. More importantly such undertakings laid important groundwork for the development of a community-based service industry during the 1980s.

Originally a member of Feng Ting's women's production brigade in the early 1960s, Mei Ling was among the very granny cadres who eventually made it to the Street Office. Hardly as eloquent as Feng Ting, Mei Ling began her career as a low-level woman cadre (until very recently, street officers were employees of local government agencies while most of the residents' committee cadres were either volunteers or contracted part-timers). When

Shanghai was affected by the post-Leap food shortage in 1960, Mei Ling volunteered to go back to her home village to participate in agricultural activities.[5] Two years later she was transferred back to Bay Bridge to work for the resident committee with very little compensation. For almost twenty years, Mei Ling had managed to take personal care of more than a dozen of the elderly and widowed on a routine basis in her residential community – a unit in which she was both its resident and caretaker. She was later promoted to the street office and became the representative of the women's federation after Feng Ting retired in the late 1980s.

It is tempting for us to view committee cadres in hundreds of thousands of urban neighborhoods as basically the "ears and eyes" of the party-state, or a tool of government control in urban China. The danger of doing so is to ignore the fact that on the ground level, both in the socialist past and the late socialist present, these cadres assumed an important role as caretakers for the community, or the "servants of the people" as they would like to call themselves. My field research suggests that long before the state initiated its campaign to professionalize its various social service agencies in the 1990s, committee cadres such as Mei Ling had been key promoters of the rights as well as the responsibilities associated with social and cultural citizenship among Shanghai's poor.

Reflecting on her own work experiences, Mei Ling did not regret being used as a "government tool of control" in these old, innocent days under Maoist socialism. In fact it was during the short-lived Communist Project of City People's Commune that she met her future husband, a sub-district cadre then in charge of the workshop constructions in Bay Bridge. In retrospect Mei Ling was rather proud of having functioned as a "peg in a machine." Her words were reminiscent of the model soldier Lei Feng's comments about contributing to a new socialist tradition of community assistance. Even in the formative stage of neighborhood organizations, residents in dire needs of food and medicine saw local cadres as their only hope for improving their lives. The elderly, the sick, the disabled, the widowed, and the relatives of "revolutionary martyrs" (parents and widows of deceased military personnel) had long been the beneficiaries of state welfare policies that recognized their social citizenship. Committee cadres not only implemented but also "humanized" these policies.

Mei Ling insisted that a committee cadre should not be considered as qualified or "doing a nice job" if she simply delivered the relief funds and/or food stamps (or other forms of coupons) to the recipient's family. She should at least be prepared to spend some time chatting with the old and sick especially the childless elderly. Mei Ling expressed a great deal of concern over the possible loss of such a tradition of caring that she and many of the veteran cadres prided themselves upon as the government attempted to professionalize the social services and its local agencies. Mei Ling's concern was not entirely unjustified. In the absence of truly autonomous charitable organizations or high rates of voluntarism,[6] the role of residents' committee cadres as the last stronghold of welfare assistance to the urban poor would become increasingly important.

Although seldom treating these "granny cadres" as their equals, the current generation of forward-looking street officers and District leaders confided to me that these old ladies had been crucial in helping implement state policies such as birth control and crime prevention at the "base level" (*jiceng*) in the past decades. Unfortunately, the street officers also believed that the historical mission of the "granny cadres" had been fulfilled and that these old women could no longer function effectively to deal with new challenges. Since the mid 1990s, the "granny cadres" in Bay Bridge were gradually replaced by the "textile sisters" (*fangsao*), previously the laid-off workers from bankrupt state owned factories. After these "textile-sisters" went through a program of re-employment sponsored by the District Government, they were recruited by the Street Office as part of the ongoing scheme to professionalize the neighborhood organizations.

District officials' quest for global cultural citizenship

In order to make sense of the official commitment to professionalizing civil and social services at all administrative levels, we must first situate our analysis in the context of Shanghai's quest for First World cultural citizenship. Throughout the 1990s, catch phrases such as "linking to the international track" and "heading toward sustainable development for the 21st century" were frequently used by bureaucrats at all levels. From Wang Daohan (former mayor, mentor of Jiang Zemin) to Zhu Rongji (who was premier of China at the time), Shanghai had been ruled by two generations of technocrats who were college-educated and open-minded/cosmopolitan/or anything. But conservative and narrow-minded. Wang, who initiated the professionalization of administrators at the municipal and district levels in Shanghai, was said to be a close friend of local economists and political scientists who proposed the idea of "developing the new area of Pudong" in the mid-1980s. Former Mayor Zhu himself never hesitated to refer to the "positive" effects of Shanghai's colonial experience, which he claimed made "Shanghai bureaucrats" particularly good at accepting new ideas and honoring business contracts. Xu Kuangdi, who was mayor of Shanghai at the time was an academician himself and was known for his expertise in chemical engineering as well as his obsession with the "western spirit of science and rationality."

In 1995 Jian Wang became the first Head Street Officer of Bay Bridge with an MA degree in public administration from the extension school of a top university in Shanghai. It was also remarkable that Jian Wang was a non-native who used to reside in Luwan's "upper quarters." Before Jian Wang was transferred to the District government, he taught English in a magnet school with a history traced back to the days of the French Concession (1843–1945). Shortly after he took office, Jian Wang and his colleagues started to concentrate their efforts on designing a series of pilot projects to explore innovative ways of building social and cultural citizenship among Shanghai's poor. Jian Wang had much more discretionary power than his predecessors in his quest to streamline administration and explore alternative ways of building up a localized network of social ties, thanks to the post-Deng official urban management principle that promoted a "small government and big society."

What set Jian Wang apart from his counterparts was the connection he had established with scholars from the universities and the academy of social sciences who were interested in "community studies." Assuming the unlikely role of a "scholar-bureaucrat," Jian Wang formed an affiliation with the academic community, which in turn helped to make Bay Bridge a "research base" for college students and fieldworkers. He believed that Bay Bridge could compensate for its lack of institutional connections with the rich and powerful by establishing new ties to local scholars interested in community development issues.

Beginning in the mid-1990s, local scholars in the fields of sociology and political science had been involved in the professionalization process as they directed their attention to empirical studies in particular neighborhoods within the city. One of the unintended outcomes of such interactions between the ivory tower and bureaucratic institutions was that more and more college graduates were recruited as staff members in street offices. After his stint as a part-time intern, Wei Dong, who had an MA in public policy and administration from Fudan University, decided to accept an offer from Jian Wang to direct the "Research & Development" section in the Street Office of Bay Bridge. Young and ambitious, Wei Dong became the most educated local cadre in neighborhood Shanghai and the designer of a series of pilot projects, which, in his own words, "would make history in China's local political development."

Although working in Bay Bridge occasionally made Wei Dong feel like he was immersed in a "sea of paperwork and a mountain of meetings" (*wenshan huihai*), Wei Dong was never content with his relatively insignificant role as the speech writer and press secretary for Jian Wang. An avid reader of western philosophy and a political activist back in his college days, Wei Dong was deeply involved in planning and implementing a pilot project aimed at professionalizing the residents' committees in Bay Bridge. Turning the poorly educated committee cadres into professional "social workers" would therefore not only strengthen the status of Bay Bridge as an "up and coming" model community but also secure the future promotion of the street officers.

One of the pilot projects was intended as the first step toward a structural transformation of the residents' committees from a bureaucratic institution of social *control* into a community affairs *management* center. The committee cadres would soon assume a new role as "social worker" (*shegong*). They would be hired as contracted full-time employees. As professional social workers, they would receive a monthly wage of 500 to

1,000 *yuan* but would be advised not to engage in entrepreneurial activities within the residential community where they worked.

Recall that in the recent past, the residents' committee cadres helped alleviate the unemployment problems in the community while making the best use of the resources at hand to serve their own social and political purposes. The proponents of professionalization, however, from the Street Office insisted that all the business activities of the residents' committees should be terminated after professionalization because the social workers of neighborhood organizations should focus on serving the community rather than on making money. Cadres would thus have fewer resources they could use to satisfy the growing need for welfare support.

In order to make the neighborhood committee a more autonomous organization and "increase grassroots democracy" (which had become a political slogan in urban Shanghai), Wei Dong and his colleagues sought to experiment with a rather innovative form of local governance. According to their scheme, the structure of the neighborhood committee would be altered in such a way that it would perform the functions more like those of a community center. The committee cadres would be re-labeled as social workers whose chief responsibility was to serve the people in the neighborhood.

The Street Officers expected that in the near future, an elected neighborhood council[7] made up of local residents would make the final hiring decisions about all social workers within the community. The election of the neighborhood council was indispensable to the professionalization process. The council members were expected to work as volunteers and received no compensation. They would routinely report to the council and hold monthly meetings to discuss community affairs. The council members would also evaluate the social workers' performance annually. The social workers and neighborhood council members thus represented two levels of administration in the re-structured community. The former would act as the "doers" and the latter as the "talkers." More importantly, the social workers would be subject to supervision not only by the street officers but also by the neighborhood councils. Giving neighborhood councils power over cadres also meant that cadres would need to focus primarily on helping residents secure their social rights, and less on compelling them to fulfill their social responsibilities.

The second step the Street Officers took was to create a situation whereby all the current neighborhood committee cadres and staff members would have to learn to be professional social workers "for the new millennium." Like the municipal officials at the top, Jian Wang and his colleagues considered education level and age to be the two key elements that would make a social worker truly professional. Despite the fact that all the committee directors had high school diplomas, most of the staff members had only elementary or junior high level of schooling. Examinations were administered in the community evening school in order to get a better idea of the overall education level of the local cadres. To be "professional" also meant to be healthy and young. The average age of neighborhood committee members in Bay Bridge was already less than fifty and most of them were from the generation that had spent part of their youth exiled to the countryside. In future all the social workers should ideally be less than forty-five years old, and they should have at least a high school diploma.

To gain more experience, Wei Dong and his colleagues conducted a mock interview of four candidates chosen from the residents' committee to determine if they would qualify as professional social workers. The candidates were asked to prepare short self-introductions and reports on their routine work as if they were applying for jobs as social workers. As expected, the four candidates appeared nervous in front of the elected neighborhood council members and the street officers even though the interview was not supposed to jeopardize their careers in the immediate future. All four candidates were over-prepared for the task. Some of them read an already written script that was full of political jargon.

Their nervousness and uneasiness were well justified especially as we considered their previous experiences as model workers of bankrupt textile factories. They used social connections to gain entry to a program of re-employment sponsored by the light industry bureau. Eventually these "textile sisters" (*fang sao*) were recruited by the Street Office as part of the professionalization scheme to gradually replace the old generation of so-called "granny cadres" and "nosy aunts." Would a younger generation of professional social workers necessarily be as capable of dealing with all kinds of social crises in the neighborhood as their predecessors? It is premature for me to give any definite answer at this stage of professionalization in Bay Bridge. However, as of my fieldwork period, these newcomers had yet to develop a new work style that would enable them to feel completely at ease in a residential community. As the legal documentary examined by Yingchi Chu (this volume) suggests, Chinese officials often struggle with contradictions between their desire to promote the kind of impersonal, objective law enforcement deemed necessary for modernization and their desire to adhere to the personalistic morality that has long governed Chinese social relations. In their effort to embody impersonal professionalism, the new social workers found themselves unable to deal with problems that the granny cadres had been able to resolve through personalistic morality.

The difficulties of promoting social citizenship in an era of declining social rights

As the economic reforms decreased social welfare and increased the gap between rich and poor, both the rights and responsibilities associated with social citizenship declined, and the most prestigious kinds of cultural citizenship became increasingly inaccessible for residents of Shanghai's "lower quarters." Like the mainland immigrants described by Nicole Newendorp (this volume), poor residents of Bay Bridge had little sense of social responsibility toward a society that increasingly deprived them of both social rights and a sense of cultural belonging. By weakening the neighborhood businesses and personal ties that had helped neighborhood committee cadres champion social rights and enforce social responsibilities, district officials' idealistic professionalization plans actually exacerbated the difficulties faced by the newly trained social workers. These difficulties are exemplified by the case of Ah Ge, who was released from labor camp in 1990 and had been living with his widowed mother Ah Po in a small two-bedroom apartment in a six story walk-up ever since then. In his early 40s, Ah Ge was never fortunate enough to have any iron-rice-bowl kind of job like some of his peers. He tried to apply for welfare assistance but without success. Apparently the committee cadres of the Liyuan residential community (located in the northeast corner of Bay Bridge) thought he was young and healthy enough to find decent work. Because of his criminal record and humble background, Ah Ge had problems finding local women to date, and had remained single until he had found Ah Mei, who was originally from rural Yangzhou. Ah Ge and Ah Mei then fell in love and had been living together without getting married.

Ever since Ah Mei had moved in, she had become a huge problem for Ah Po's family. First, Ah Po had to retreat to a tiny room with dim lights because the couple had to occupy the bigger bedroom. Ah Jie, Ah Po's daughter, who volunteered to go to Jiangxi Province during the rustification campaign (1968–70), had eventually returned to Shanghai and found a factory job. A year ago she was laid off when her work unit could not afford to pay its employees. Ah Jie had no choice but returned to Shanghai to seek job opportunities. Since she could not even share a room with Ah Po because of Ah Mei's presence, she had to rent a small room in suburban Pudong (on the east bank of Pujiang) which was an hour and half away from the restaurant where she worked as a temporary kitchen staff. She was upset by the fact that Ah Ge and Ah Mei would not even allow her to pay routine visits to Ah Po to fulfill her responsibility as a filial daughter. The Liyuan cadres were very sympathetic about their situation but there was very little they could do.

The real trouble began when Ah Mei got pregnant. This time the cadres of Liyuan had to get involved to make sure Ah Mei abided by her social responsibility to obey the one-child policy. To Li Dan, a recently hired staff member in the residents' committee in charge of migrant workers and women's reproductive health (family planning), this was no small matter. Technically Li Dan could let both Ah Mei and Ah Ge off the hook since Ah Mei was not a permanent resident of Shanghai and therefore lacked a *hukou* status (household registration record). All Li Dan had to do was to alert the family-planning authorities in Ah Mei's hometown. But what if Ah Ge and Ah Mei would choose to get married before giving birth to their (illegitimate) child in Shanghai? According to gossip that Li Dan had heard in the neighborhood, Ah Mei might even have a husband somewhere and could even have a child. Moreover, Li Dan would have to learn about Ah Mei's reproductive history (i.e. how many children she had had before) in order to release a birth certificate. If Li Dan failed to resolve this thorny issue appropriately, her neighborhood could be found in violation of the one-policy, and lose its chance at being named one of Shanghai's Model Communities.

Like the "granny cadres" she was reluctant to imitate, Li Dan had to pay unexpected calls to Ah Ge's home in order to get hold of Ah Mei, who seemed to be elusive. The most unwelcome visitor to the couple, Li Dan was greeted by a curse each time she knocked at the door. In the end Ah Ge got so impatient that he would simply tell Li Dan that the only time she would be welcome was when she agree to give his family one more "green card" (i.e. the food stamps) in addition to what Ah Po already had. Totally unprepared, Li Dan would ask: "Why are you guys so shameless? And how much is your worth? Just twenty-five yuan?"[8] Li Dan apparently was not as patient as the "granny cadres."

Li Dan's experience was shared by many social workers, who found that their inability to improve residents' access to social rights meant that they also lacked the authority to get residents to fulfill social responsibilities. The plight of Ah Po's family reflected a whole range of problems in a rapidly changing local society in the late socialist setting: housing, the drifting population (rural-urban migration), welfare assistance for the elderly and the poor, domestic violence, women's reproductive health, unemployment, and the legacy of the rustification campaign. It was difficult for social workers to get residents to believe that they had full social and cultural citizenship as they lived in the debris of a collapsing socialist system.

During my field research I discovered that resident committee cadres often assumed the role of "jack of all trades" in their community and a power-broker between the state and the local population. A successful committee cadre not only pleased her superiors by showcasing a "beautiful community" to an inspection team from the District or the Municipal Government, but also gained legitimacy by doing good service to appease the neighborhood. Unlike the generation of "granny cadres," these "textile sisters" were not embedded in the local communities. Most granny cadres believed that as an ideal the workers of the neighborhood organizations should not only implement but also "humanize" (rather than professionalize) these policies. For the young generation of social workers, getting too personal with the welfare recipients was not their favorite work style.

The crucial question confronting the older cadres therefore was whether the skill at cultivating social and cultural citizenship that they developed over the socialist period would remain useful to address problems such as urban poverty in late socialist Shanghai. The young and relatively well-educated professional social workers lacked (and did not care to gain) the intimate local knowledge, interpersonal skills, and ability to strategize in an increasingly diverse urban environment that had enabled the snoopy and seemingly "unprofessional" cadres to serve as champions of social and cultural citizenship for the poor. Theoretically, the professionalization of neighborhood organizations represented a future that would improve residents' access to the prestigious kinds of citizenship defined by global standards of modernity and gentrification. In routine practice, however, the professional social workers were struggling just to manage the debris of socialism.

Showcasing citizenship and gentrifying the "lower quarters"

In the futuristic visions of Shanghai's ambitious leaders, community building served the long-term goal of turning a late socialist city into the financial center of East Asia. They needed to beautify both the "upper quarters" and the "lower quarters" so that Shanghai residents could claim the prestigious kinds of citizenship associated with global standards of urban wealth. The need to compete with other global cities became even more urgent after the Party Secretariat's visit to Rio de Janeiro and other Latin American cities in June 1995. The leaders of the Shanghai Delegation were said to be dismayed at the degree to which most of the Brazilian cities they saw were divided (Kang 2001: 232). The coexistence of scenic spots with rundown houses visible in the inner-city neighborhoods or *favelas* bore a strong resemblance to the remaining ramshackle huts in Shanghai's marginalized "lower quarters" and the emerging squatter settlements in the city's outskirts where illegal housing constructions went on everyday.

What had happened in Latin America today could be Shanghai's tomorrow. This was the lesson that the Party Secretariat insisted that his colleagues must learn while looking for the urbanization approach most suitable for China (Kang 2001: 233). The focus of the city-wide beautification campaign would be on both the lower and upper quarters. As base-level organizations, the street office and its residents' committees were once again on the front lines of campaigns for promoting social and cultural citizenship.

In everyday practice, such revitalization schemes were translated into a series of civilizing projects that captured the attention of the party-state, the mass media, and academics across the nation. Participation in model community contests were a top priority of Shanghai neighborhood organizations. Street officers in the marginalized "lower quarters" seized every possible opportunity to improve the social and economic status of their neighborhood and develop various strategies competing for media coverage and attention from the municipal government. The street officers invested a considerable amount of their time, energy, and resources in preparation for the monthly inspections and unexpected visits of the officials from the various departments of municipal and central governments. These official visits would often determine the final outcome of the neighborhood's annual bid for the model community award.

As of 1998, eleven street offices in Shanghai had been officially recognized for their achievement in community building as a reward for their effort in putting on a show that pleased the eyes and ears of the inspecting authorities. Among those who had successfully garnered the official awards was the Street Office of Bay Bridge, which had emerged as a "dark horse" in the competition for fame and honor. Many local cadres insisted that the current elevated status of Bay Bridge was indeed hard-earned considering its competitive disadvantages in location (as a marginalized "lower quarters" area) and the low educational levels of its residents.

Bay Bridge's achieved status, in the form of brass plaques on permanent display as a badge of honor at the entrance of the residential compounds, was proudly displayed as a symbol of prestigious cultural citizenship. Varying in size depending on what level of "model" the residential community was accredited (district or municipal), the plaques were all engraved with the same red characters, *wenming shequ* which literally meant "civilized community." But did it really make sense for cadres in Bay Bridge, an underdeveloped urban community often categorized as Shanghai's marginalized "lower quarters," to become so preoccupied with such a seemingly impractical fame game? How could they balance the overwhelming problems of the debris of socialism with the need to showcase citizenship in a less than community where the economic reforms were eroding residents' social and cultural citizenship?

In order to deal with these questions, we should first look at the connections between ongoing community-building processes and neighborhood gentrification during the 1990s urban reforms on the one hand, and institutional restructuring and individual strategizing at the local level on the other hand. With the almost overnight disappearance of old housing communities due to infrastructure reconstruction and the emergence of residential areas where the new and gated communities were built, the city landscape has undergone a series of transformations. As an observable housing pattern in the postindustrial world, the term "gentrification" has often been interpreted as middle-class settlement or resettlement in older inner-city neighborhoods formerly occupied mostly by working class and underclass residents. In this paper, however, "gentrification" refers to a social and political process that must be understood in the historical context of socialist engineering and community development during the reform era. As far as spatial reconfiguration in neighborhood Shanghai is concerned, we should be able to discern at least two forms of gentrification in the "upper quarters" and "lower quarters." "Upper quarters" inner-city neighborhoods had maintained their prestige despite signs of urban decay in certain areas. Gentrification efforts in the "upper quarters" manifested themselves in the restoration and renovation of old style villas and mansions along with the construction of skyscrapers and modern apartment buildings.

The disappearance of factories and plants in the City's depressed industrial areas in the 1990s coincided with the gentrification of Bay Bridge.

Gated communities managed by local or transnational real estate developers started to appear on the land acquired from the owners of bankrupt or poorly managed state owned factories. In a sense the built forms of high-rise apartments in a "lower quarters", such as Bay Bridge, were literally the sprouts of capitalism grown out of the debris of socialism. But the advent of gated communities did not immediately result in the relocation of poorer residents. A gated community in Bay Bridge was often in the same neighborhood as several "workers' villages" made up of dozens of six story walk-ups in the typical form of government housing projects built during the 1970s.

Between 1997 and 1998, two brand new housing complexes (named "the Volkswagen Town" and "Redbud Pavilion") were completed in north and southwest Bay Bridge. Accordingly, two residents' committees were established in order to manage the life of the newly arrived 3,552 (as of September 1998) residents who were total strangers to the neighborhood. "The Volkswagen City" for example was the fourth residential housing project in Shanghai funded by the famous German Automobile Company in order to improve the living conditions of its employees (mostly scientists and engineers recruited from throughout China). "Redbud Pavilion" was a residential community of 426 residents who were mostly mid-level government officials. With financial support from their own work units, they managed to buy homes in these modern apartment buildings.

The most active gentrifying agents in Bay Bridge were the young, well-educated street officers who formed an alliance with property and real estate developers, local entrepreneurs, and urban planners with the same visions of high modernity and scientizing principles divorced from the social and economic realities of a locality that used to be characterized as the marginalized "lower quarters." The new technocrats who took control of the entire neighborhood were pleased with the presence of "Volkswagen Town" and "Redbud Pavilion" because these gated residential communities were essential to a rapid process of gentrification that would "improve" the neighborhood by attracting residents with more prestigious kinds of cultural citizenship. The granny cadres of the residents' committees, however, became increasingly suspicious if these new residents in the gated communities would necessarily identify themselves with the rest of the locality that was once part of the marginalized "lower quarters." Such concerns on the part of the granny cadres proved to be legitimate because the community building schemes implemented in the late 1990s, served to justify the existence of various communities representing different interests in a "gentrified" Bay Bridge where social and cultural citizenship rights were not evenly distributed.

To promote a "small government and big society," the Shanghai Municipal Government launched a series of structural reforms to give more autonomy to the local community. Here "autonomy" refers to the increased discretionary power of the sub-district level street office in handling local affairs, *not* necessarily the freedoms associated with civil and political citizenship in Western societies. In the framework of "two levels of governance, three levels of management, and four levels of network," the street office and the residents' committee were positioned at the third and fourth levels respectively in the administrative hierarchy. Without the intervention from the municipal and district governments, the street level administrators were authorized to make their own decisions in community building process and on their own initiatives. By doing so the city officials hoped to cut red tape and allow the local cadres to explore innovative ways of managing the local social and political life. Even as the need for a social security system to substitute for the workplace-based "iron rice bowl" became increasingly pressing, the state was withdrawing from the realm of welfare assistance and trying to delegate to street offices and community-based voluntary associations the hard work of guaranteeing social rights that had previously been shouldered by higher levels of government agencies.

The discretionary power that street offices thus gained as a result of the upgrading in civil management varied with districts. Within the jurisdiction of the Street Office in Bay Bridge, the leaders were allowed a much larger role in urban planning and housing development. The street officers were allowed to give licenses to small business people such as restaurant and storeowners, exercise control over any building structures that occupied public space, issue permits to outdoor commercial advertising, and negotiate with potential trading partners for developing joint-ventures, etc. In the vocabulary that city officials often borrowed from the business world, the Head Street Officer would resemble a CEO running a local corporate state.

Among the bidders for model community status, Jian Wang stood out as an especially innovative street officer who succeeded in turning "Luwan's Siberia" (Bay Bridge) into a brand new model of community building and urban renewal in neighborhood Shanghai. In 1995 Jian Wang was assigned to work as the Director of the Street Office of Bay Bridge. Unlike most of his predecessors, Jian Wang was not only a doer but also a talker or in local dialect, *daojianghu* meaning "an expert in affective bull-shitting." He persuaded his superior in the District Government to allow Bay Bridge to be the first street office in Luwan to try out some of his community building initiatives. His logic was simple: Bay Bridge, as the marginalized "lower quarters" of the District, was just like a blank sheet of paper on which they could paint beautiful pictures. Such an allusion to Mao's original remarks about the backward conditions of pre-1949 China made perfect sense to the District Leaders, who eventually gave Jian Wang the go-ahead with his well-conceived plan.

The best educated local leader that Bay Bridge had ever had since the 1950s, Jian Wang summed up his secret for achieving overnight success in the following way: whenever you have an idea you have got to put it into practice right away. His tactic was "to get it done quick and dirty." Jian

Wang would make sure he was always the first in Shanghai to experiment with these novel ideas of community development. Although he looked young and even a bit nerdy, Jian Wang was hardly a green hand in dealing with local affairs and cultivating personal and official ties, especially with the media. If any of his projects failed to get the attention of the press, radio, and television, it would mean a waste of time, money, and energy. Jian Wang's projects were always in the spotlight unless he purposefully chose to keep a low profile.[9] During his tenure as Chief Officer (1995–99) Jian Wang fully utilized community building as an opportunity to perfect political skills for advancing a career as a successful technocrat in a global city. Moreover, Jian Wang's carefully cultivated social ties also led to a wide range of research interest from the academic community. Bay Bridge had quickly become a field site for scholars and students from the top research institutions and universities in Shanghai.

Gentrification, the quest for model community status, and the professionalization of the neighborhood committees advocated by idealistic modernizers like Jian Wang may indeed have been appropriate for wealthy new residents who needed no help in securing full social and cultural citizenship. The poorer residents, however, were increasingly alienated by the rising inequalities in their neighborhood and by the newly professionalized social workers who did not seem interested in promoting their social rights or cultural belonging. Like the minority teenagers described by Lin Yi and the impoverished farmers described by Rachel Murphy in this volume, many poor residents and granny cadres felt that their interests, identities, and demands for social rights were ignored and stigmatized by state officials' efforts to make them yearn for a kind of cultural citizenship they could never truly attain.

Conclusion

As gentrification started to turn Bay Bridge from a re-imagined socialist Community to walled and gated communities representing different social and economic interests, the street officers of Bay Bridge adopted selective showcasing as a viable strategy to attract media attention and official recognition. For the current generation of technocrats, the gated community, whose residents were total strangers in the neighborhood, represented the ideal form of a "model community" – a perfect showcase for cultural citizenship. For the young and forward-looking street officers, showcasing a garden-like "model community," supervised by an elected neighborhood council or owner's association should or would help the local people forget their forgettable past, restore their confidence in the present, and envision the future of Bay Bridge as a transformed locality. As a result, the newly established gated community called "Volkswagen Town," home to the staff members of the German automobile company in Shanghai was chosen to represent all of Bay Bridge in the model community contest.

Despite the publicity such showcasing events received in the mass media and the efforts of the local cadres, the model community contest as a whole failed to secure strong and sustained support from the ordinary residents who could not care less about the number of brass plaques their neighborhood received. Moreover, by adopting a selective strategy to represent a significantly improved "lower quarters," the street officers reminded the majority of those living in Bay Bridge of pre-revolutionary inequalities, rather than of a bright future in which social and cultural citizenship would be equally accessible to all. The remaining "urban villages" in the neighborhood were effectively airbrushed from the social and political map. Underneath the false façade of a harmonious, hygienic, and crime-free environment, Bay Bridge was nothing more than "dirt" – a matter out of place (Douglas 1966) in a city that aimed to become a showcase of affluent modernity.

Notes

1 According to my observation, it had been a common practice for the local officials to keep the names of the lanes within the "lower quarters" (e.g., those indicative of the residents' native place such as "Su-bei Lane" and "Nan-tong Lane") until the 1970s.

2 One would hardly be surprised to see that these granny cadres assumed their role of community watch-dogs in the recent SARS outbreak to make sure any "suspicious" visitors from Beijing and Canton in the neighborhood would be effectively quarantined.

3 Prior to 1989, the local police regarded playing mahjong in public as illegal gambling activity.

4 In retrospect, the dissatisfaction of the District Leaders was probably justified with the difficulty experienced by most state and collectively owned factories in absorbing laborers. In the aftermath of the Great Leap Forward (1958–60), approximately 400,000 workers became redundant in steel and textile industries. Some returned home and became housewives again. Some joined the troops of rustified youth heading for the countries' frontiers. And some tried to survive by working as part-timers in down-sized street factories (Shen and Li 1998: 6). It was estimated that between 1961–64, among the job-seekers (467,400) 173,000 fell into the official category of "housewives" (Shen and Li 1998: 71).

5 As a response to the nationwide famine and food shortage in the aftermath of the "Great Leap Forward" and People's Commune movement (1958-1960), the Shanghai City Government issued orders to its various institutions in the district and sub-district levels to encourage employees to go back to their "places of origin." This way the local state could manage to keep the population (or the "number of eating mouths") under control and thus help reducing the pressure of the food rationing bureaucracies.

6 To the best of my knowledge, charitable organizations such as the Chinese Society of Philanthropists, the Charity Funds, and the Shanghai and Beijing branches of YMCA are among the most important "voluntary institutions" but still not independent of the leadership of the party-state. Moreover, even though these NGOs contributed to the cause of poverty relief, they cannot function as a routine caretaker of the community like the official street offices and resident committees.

7 The Chinese term is *Juweihui*. But to avoid confusion, I translate "juweihui" as neighborhood council in the professionalization context.
8 Each food stamp allows its recipient to buy staple foods and cooking oils worth twenty-five yuan at designated grocery stores.
9 For example, the "free election" of neighborhood councils in the entire Bay Bridge area, a rather bold experiment with grassroots democracy, was not covered by any official media in Shanghai. This was because Jian Wang did not want his rivals in other parts of Shanghai to follow suit. He would wait until this brainchild of his to grow for 2–3 years into a real model of local democratic participation.

7 Teaching "responsibility"

Social workers' efforts to turn Chinese immigrants into ideal Hong Kong citizens

Nicole Newendorp

Introduction

Emily[1] was the youngest of the social workers at a Hong Kong government-funded social service center serving New Arrival[2] needs where I conducted research for fifteen months in 2001 and 2002.[3] She had just been working there for a few months when I began my involvement with the center's staff and clients. By the time that I interviewed Emily almost one year after first meeting her, she had begun to form clear opinions about the center's clients and her work with them. In particular, her interaction with numerous clients and the influence of the more experienced social workers had left her with the opinion that many of the New Arrivals who came to the center were not responsible, either in terms of their expectations of their lives after arrival in Hong Kong, or in terms of their planning before arrival. She told me about the interaction that she had with one client, who was pregnant, which had been especially memorable for her.

> She [the client] wanted to know if after she had the baby the government would give her any money to help support the child. I thought it was really strange to ask in this way! You should have a plan before having a baby. You should have financial support before having a baby. If not, you will be a very "irresponsible" mother! But she just answered me: "Why wouldn't the government help her raise her child?" And then I asked her: "After you have the baby, will you look for a job to help support the child?" And she said that she couldn't, because she didn't have anyone to help her look after the child. So, I suggested that by working, she would make enough money to hire someone to help her look after the child, or to place the child in a daycare or crèche. And then her answer was even stranger. She said, "No, that is not possible, because my baby must drink breast milk. The baby cannot drink milk powder, because it will not be nutritious enough and is not really good for the baby." I thought this answer was really strange, really "irresponsible." She had completely no sense of "self-help." That's why, after meeting more and more cases like this, it seems like you

really have to look and see if a client is worth helping. I just thought that this example was really odd.[4]

While the PRC state has sponsored educational campaigns that have promoted breastfeeding in urban Chinese hospitals, there have been no such campaigns in Hong Kong, where mothers rarely breastfeed.[5] As a result, Emily's refusal to acknowledge the health benefits of that practice to both mother and infant is understandable. Nevertheless, I was still struck by her apparent inability to empathize with a mother who obviously wanted the opportunity to be with her child rather than working at a job that would probably not even provide enough money for living expenses after her child's daycare expenses had been paid. Emily's explanation at the end of this quote, in which she noted that this client was not interested in "self-help," provides context for her reaction within a framework of local social work values – values which prioritize a client's effort to learn and act "independently" over inaction or "laziness." Clients who demonstrated a strong sense of social and cultural citizenship through their active involvement in resolving personal difficulties were "worth helping." On the other hand, clients who continued to demonstrate dependency on social workers or social welfare support, without any attempt to make any sort of personal "contribution" to society through their paid or unpaid work, were judged to be less aware of their citizenship responsibilities, and thus less "worthy" of help. This theme of "responsibility" pervaded much of the interaction that I witnessed between social workers and their clients during my period of participant observation at the center. Social workers often used the English term "sense of responsibility" as well as the Cantonese term, "*jaahtyahmsum*" (責任心), even though these terms were never a topic of conversation among clients themselves. Pervasive in discussions of self-reliance, learning, planning, consideration for others, volunteering, or making a contribution to society, the idea of "acting responsibly" (the Hong Kong way) was clearly an important lesson that New Arrivals in Hong Kong were expected to learn if they wanted to attain full social and cultural citizenship in Hong Kong.

The conflict between Emily and her client illustrates difficulties social workers and New Arrivals faced in their efforts to produce a specifically Hong Kong brand of Chinese cultural citizenship. Drawing on ethnographic fieldwork conducted among Hong Kong social workers and their clients, I examine interactions between these groups in order to elucidate the "everyday processes" (Ong 1996:737) involved in efforts to define and promote Hong Kong cultural citizenship. Focusing on the theme of "responsibility," I follow Aihwa Ong's theoretical example to examine the ways in which "civil institutions and social groups" serve as "disciplinary forces in the making of cultural citizens" (1996:738). I employ a narrative approach (see, e.g., Constable 1999) to explore the importance of the twin concepts of individual and social responsibility as they were promoted by social workers. This analysis of these concepts demonstrates that perceptions of client responsibility were highly influential in social workers' motivation in their work with individual clients. Furthermore, the various ways – such as budgeting for parties and reporting on homework assignments – in which these concepts were introduced to New Arrivals by social workers provides substantial information about the kinds of behavior that social workers felt immigrants needed to learn to become full social and cultural citizens of Hong Kong.

Since the mid-1990s, the majority of Chinese immigrants to Hong Kong have been the spouses (primarily wives) and children of Hong Kong men.[6] In 2001, during the period of my research, 85% of all immigrants to Hong Kong could be included in these two categories of wives and non-adult children of Hong Kong permanent residents (www.socialnet.org.hk). Strictly enforced immigration quotas meant that most of these recent immigrants had waited at least five to ten years to join their family members in Hong Kong. Although these women and children could have visited their Hong Kong family members using visitor permits that were issued as frequently as one or two times each year, many of them had only visited Hong Kong once or twice before their arrival in Hong Kong as "Hong Kong residents." Since 1995, 55,000 Chinese residents have been allowed to immigrate to Hong Kong each year. This quota has caused significant controversy among Hong Kong residents, the local Hong Kong government, and the mainland Chinese government. Twice as great as any previous quota, this quota caused Hong Kong locals to worry that the influx of largely untrained mainlanders will further undermine their once prosperous economy, which has been in decline since the Asian financial crisis of 1997. Furthermore, significant government funding has been spent on establishing services to aid in these immigrants' adjustment and integration to Hong Kong life, and many locals think that these funds should be spent on long-term Hong Kong residents rather than on newcomers. Nonetheless, this aid provides recent immigrants with access to numerous support services, including social work services and information about government resources, all of which are instrumental in educating immigrants about the roles and behavior expected of them as Hong Kong permanent residents.

This paper is based on the participant observation that I conducted between June 2001 and July 2002 at a government-funded social service center for New Arrivals in the Sham Shui Po district of Hong Kong. During this time, I participated as a volunteer member of all aspects of center life, spent substantial informal time with immigrant clients and their family members, and also completed thirty in-depth interviews with the center's staff and clients.[7] In this paper, I explore Hong Kong social workers' efforts to cultivate social and cultural citizenship among their New Arrival clients through skits, family counseling, and volunteer activity groups. Through all these activities, I found tensions between social workers' focus on the importance of social responsibilities and New Arrivals' focus on their desire for social rights and cultural belonging.

The responsibilities of citizenship

Citizenship is generally defined as a relationship between individuals and their society, in which individuals gain certain rights and responsibilities in return for the protection and other advantages they gain through recognized membership in a given society. Many current academic discussions of citizenship include some reference to the three components of citizenship – civil, political, and social – first identified in the 1950s by T.H. Marshall, referring, of course, to citizenship as it had developed in Western liberal democratic regimes (concomitantly with the governmental institutions which served both to protect the rights of individual citizens while also giving "social expression" to these rights) (Turner 2001:190). In the 1990s, however, anthropological writing about citizenship focused attention away from these formal definitions of citizenship to explore instead the relationships between culture and citizenship. The term "cultural citizenship" was first coined by Rosaldo to describe the "demand of disadvantaged subjects for citizenship in spite of their cultural difference from mainstream society" (Ong 1996:738). Aihwa Ong subsequently adopted the term "cultural citizenship" (changed to "everyday citizenship" in her most recent writings) "to refer to cultural practices and beliefs produced through negotiations of often ambivalent and contested relations with the state and its hegemonic forms that establish the criteria of belonging within a national population and territory" (*ibid.*, 2003). Like the essays in Holston and Appadurai's edited volume (1999), *Cities and Citizenship*, these theories of "cultural citizenship" highlight the divide between the formal status and actual practices which constitute citizenship and also inform our understanding of the cultural and historical variability of this legal concept (see also Borneman 1997).

Writing about the interactions between citizens and their governments in twentieth century China, scholars in recent years have demonstrated the applicability of various conceptions of citizenship to the Chinese case (e.g., Solinger 1999; Ong 1999; Goldman and Perry 2002; Smart 2003). Unlike the Marshallian theory of citizenship, which "was primarily a theory of entitlement" and therefore paid little attention to the "responsibilities" of citizenship, such as paying taxes or performing jury or military duty, (Turner 2001:190–191), the development of citizenship in the Chinese context resulted primarily from a foundational belief in "responsibility" over rights. As Goldman and Perry point out, the development of citizenship in China has emphasized social citizenship – in the form of a moral commitment to protect and contribute to the public good – over political citizenship (2002:5–6). Today in the People's Republic of China, "substantive rights" – that is, the rights associated with social welfare provision – remain much more important than the rights associated with personal freedoms that remain the hallmark of citizen and state relations in the West (Smart and Smart 2001). This focus is consistent with what Ong calls the "Asian model of pastoral care," which aims to foster "collectivist security" for the purpose of "producing citizens with the human, social, and cultural capital that will allow them to thrive in a global economy" (1999:212).[8] Hong Kong definitions of ideal citizenship, on the other hand, remain similar to those of more classically defined "neoliberal" states, in which citizens are encouraged to achieve similarly-defined levels of competence by relying primarily on individual effort and personal responsibility rather than on government cultivation. In the current trend towards neoliberalism among many Western governments, "good citizens" are expected to contribute to the provision of many "public amenities," such as "schooling, policing, welfare, and maintenance of physical infrastructure" (Hyatt 2001).

Chinese immigrants in Hong Kong are individuals who share certain similarities of language, foodways, and values with current Hong Kong permanent residents, but they have grown up as citizens in a socialist society much more focused on substantive rights than is the case in Hong Kong. The situation of mainland Chinese immigrants in Hong Kong provides a unique opportunity for comparing socialist and neoliberal approaches to the responsibilities that go along with social and cultural citizenship.

Legal responsibilities as a basis of social and cultural citizenship

As Yingchi Chu showed in her chapter on mainland Chinese television portrayals of legal cases (this volume), producers at state-owned television stations in the PRC were ambivalent about whether a rigid rule of law should always be advocated over personalistic morality. Hong Kong officials had no such ambivalence, however, as they viewed adherence to Western-style rule of law as a crucial element that distinguished Hong Kong from mainland China and enabled Hong Kong residents to partake of the prestigious cultural citizenship that came with belonging to the First World. Representatives of government organizations who I met in Hong Kong emphasized that Hong Kong "citizenship"[9] demanded that New Arrivals be "responsible" to Hong Kong's legalistic culture by eschewing mainland Chinese tendencies to personalize legal relationships. Both the Sham Shui Po Police Station and the ICAC (Independent Commission against Corruption), Hong Kong's anti-corruption organization, were featured as regular stops on the day-long Orientation Tours to various parts of Hong Kong that were held weekly and were open to all the center's New Arrival clients. Lectures given to the tour participants were never completely standardized, but the information provided, while varying in content, never changed in terms of overall message.

Representatives of both organizations sought to teach New Arrivals about Hong Kong laws, the importance of respecting these laws, the consequences of breaking these laws, and individual responsibility in knowing enough about the local legal system to protect oneself from situations that could lead to fines or prosecution. Hong Kong officials and social workers perceived the common mainland practice of gift-giving (as a means to accomplish a desired bureaucratic goal) as deviant and unlawful, and they were concerned that mainlanders would be overly dependent on such practices in Hong Kong as well. At the ICAC, skits acted out on video by actors portraying both Hong Kong locals and immigrants provided concrete scenarios in which such mainland practices were illegal in Hong Kong's more "orderly" and "law-abiding" environment. In these skits, well-intentioned mainlanders offered gifts to the authorities involved in order to 1.) help reduce a local friend's wait at a doctor office and 2.) thank local Housing Department staff members after being allotted a particularly favorable public housing unit. In both cases, their behavior is chastised by their local Hong Kong friends before any "damage" is done, and these well-meaning but poorly informed individuals are saved from prosecution. After the video had finished, however, the ICAC's representative was careful to add one additional anecdote, in which a New Arrival, who left a large "thank you" gift with a government representative and disappeared before the gift could be returned to the individual involved, was indeed reported to the authorities as having broken the law. In this case, the moderator highlighted the fact that it is the responsibility of Hong Kong residents to know, understand, and comply with all local laws. Should individuals unwittingly break the law, either through unhappy circumstance such as being tricked by locals who know better, or through ignorance, they are just as guilty under Hong Kong law as someone who knowingly commits a crime. The message at the Police Station was similar: "Hong Kong is a place of well-regulated order and principle" (C. *Heunggong haih yat go yauh kwaigwei ge deihfong*) (香港是一個有規矩的地方), and it is the responsibility of Hong Kong people to help maintain that order, through their knowledge of and compliance with local laws. In this case, knowing traffic rules and regulations (the violation of which can endanger others as well as oneself), the acceptance of police authority, and the right to perform random ID card checks were emphasized. Immigrants were told that it is the responsibility of all Hong Kong residents over the age of 15 to carry their ID cards with them at all times, thus facilitating Police efforts to find and repatriate illegal residents of Hong Kong. As the representative made clear, this responsibility supercedes any familial or individual concerns. For instance, police officials insisted that a teenager must carry his ID with him at all times, despite family members' worry that he might lose that ID and therefore have to pay the hefty fine (over US$50) to have it replaced.

Like social workers, law enforcement representatives defined citizenship in ways that focused on responsibilities rather than on rights. While both social workers and law enforcement representatives emphasized the need for Hong Kong residents to act responsibly as individuals, their concern was not focused primarily on protecting the individuals themselves. Rather, acting responsibly was deemed an important factor of overall social and community functioning and success. Citizenship meant acting responsibly towards society as a whole, and thereby contributing to the overall well-being of Hong Kong. One woman's desire to receive government support to stay at home with her child instead of working may not threaten the orderly running of society; however, if large numbers of women begin expecting or demanding such support, this would result in a significant drain on government resources and potentially undermine the confidence of working mothers who might resent the unfair advantage they perceived non-working mothers to enjoy. Likewise, understanding local legal concepts, and important differences in these concepts from practices common on the mainland, not only protected individuals from prosecution but also helps to maintain the "order" (C. *diht jeuih*, 秩序) that Hong Kong people cited as the main difference between their society and the mainland.

Social workers' attitudes toward clients' social responsibilities

Emily's concerns about her client's "irresponsible" behavior may well have been affected by the three other social workers at the center, who all voiced similar concerns to me during formal questioning about their views of their immigrant clients. In all cases, the social workers distinguished between different kinds of mainlanders: those who were well-educated, from the cities, or the more Northern areas of China, versus the mostly rural women and children from Guangdong who formed the core of the center's client base. New Arrivals whose backgrounds resembled those of the ambitious urban youth described by Vanessa Fong (this volume) and the upscale Shanghai residents described by Tianshu Pan (this volume) already had prestigious kinds of cultural citizenship that gave them the ability to secure their social rights as well as fulfill their social responsibilities. Most of the social workers' clients, however, lacked this kind of cultural citizenship and the ability to secure their social rights. Most of the center's female clients had spent at least several years in Guangdong, often in Shenzhen, where they might have migrated from other parts of China to work in factories or where their husbands might have bought apartments for them to live close enough to Hong Kong to be visited on the weekends. It was, however, the rural women from Guangdong who tended to be both the least cosmopolitan and the least educated, and this group in particular was often described by the social workers as "uncivilized" (C. *yehmaahn*).[10] In particular, what social workers objected to was that these vulnerable New Arrivals seemed more concerned about social rights than about social responsibilities. In this way, Hong Kong New Arrivals were like the "lower quarters" Shanghai residents described by Pan (this volume) and the rural children described by Wang Lu (this volume). Siu-saan, another of the center's social workers, explained what she meant by "uncivilized" in the following way:

> The way that they are "uncivilized" is [that they think]: "You gave me
> legal permission to immigrate here, so you should take complete
> responsibility for taking care of me in every way." They "blame" all of
> their problems on others. They won't think that something is their
> personal problem. It's everyone's problem.

Other types of behavioral characteristics that were associated with these
"uncivilized" clients included that they were not polite, did not understand
certain social rules such as standing in line, and had poor hygiene or personal
habits, such as not always wearing shoes. The word "quality" (*jaahtsou*)
(質素) was used frequently to describe prestigious, globally defined forms
of cultural citizenship, or immigrants' lack thereof. The term "low quality"
was used to describe less educated clients with a poor grasp of "commonly" accepted social and behavioral norms – norms that, in Hong Kong,
have been heavily influenced by access to Western-based education and
media images, as well as by British colonial government advertising.[11]

Social workers evaluated a client's progress in affirming local social and
cultural citizenship primarily in terms of the client's willingness to rely
on herself for securing her social rights, rather than "passively" relying on
government aid. Both Siu-saan and Emily, however, noted that the Hong
Kong government may contribute to attracting immigrants of "lesser quality" to Hong Kong: by providing as much aid as they do to New Arrivals,
the government may attract immigrants who come for the express purpose
of making use of such aid. According to these social workers, such policies
encourage a sense of "entitlement" among immigrants who may feel that
they deserve such aid. Although mainland officials are trying to move toward the neoliberal political economy exemplified by Hong Kong (Tianshu
Pan, this volume), most studies conducted in mainland China in the 1990s
still found that "respondents believe that either the central or the local state
should be responsible for providing the social security provisioning to which
they believe they are entitled" (Croll 1999 citing White and Shang 1995;
see also Smart and Smart 2001 and Wong and Lee 2000). New Arrivals
from the mainland may well share this view, compounded by certain expectations about other state forms of welfare which should be available in a
society as wealthy as Hong Kong. But the social workers I spoke with never
mentioned habituation to socialist practices as a possible factor in the negative qualities that they associated with their clients. Nor did they seem to
consider immigrant feelings about "entitlement" to be a cultural difference
between Hong Kong people and mainlanders. While culture was used to
explain other kinds of adjustment problems that their clients were likely
to encounter – problems such as understanding workplace norms, local
transportation, market practices, and the fast pace of everyday life – the
social workers nonetheless remained frustrated by what they perceived to be
a personality problem of many of their immigrant clients. Immigrants, on
the other hand, demonstrated their awareness of Hong Kong norms by

frequently noting one difference between the mainland and Hong Kong as the necessity of working in Hong Kong. Among my informants, not working – spending one's days relaxing with others or playing mahjong – was considered to be a normal lifestyle on the mainland, where unemployment was high and the cost of living was low enough for a woman and her children to live comfortably on remittances sent by even a relatively poor Hong Kong husband.

In most cases, the social workers qualified any negative feelings they expressed about clients by indicating that the more "considerate" mainlanders were less likely to bother the social workers or approach them to help solve problems. It became clear, however, that many of the employees at the center, and at least one social worker, felt that there was a strong distinction between the hard-working immigrants who had come in previous time periods and the current wave, who were characterized as coming in order to gain access to government resources without any intention of providing for themselves. It was Siu-saan, the social worker who had been working with immigrant clients longer than the other workers, who first voiced this viewpoint to me, noting that the immigrants she had known ten years ago had been extremely hardworking – willing to work up to three jobs at once to help support their families. She contrasted this group with the majority of immigrants she had been servicing recently, and it was her opinion that this latter group would rather not work. As Siu-saan was clearly going through a period of disillusionment, wanting a change to a different kind of client base after ten years of working with immigrants, I initially interpreted her statement about these differences in earlier and later immigrants' characteristics as exaggerated by the current discontent that she was experiencing. When questioned, however, others at the center also indicated that they shared this view – a view in turn held by many long-term Hong Kong residents. Similar to proponents of the kinds of ethnic stereotyping about immigrants prevalent in other societies, such as the US (see, e.g., Steinberg 1989), many Hong Kong residents felt that previous generations of immigrants were more hardworking, as they had to be completely responsible for themselves and did not have access to the kinds of aid that are available now. Furthermore, previous generations of immigrants were also seen as more deserving of immigration, since their lives on the mainland were considerably harder than the lives of current mainland citizens – who share the benefits of the liberalization of PRC economic and political policies and whose lifestyles on the mainland may have been more relaxed and comfortable than what they experienced in Hong Kong. Such suspicions were exacerbated by Hong Kong residents' insecurities over their own futures, given the straightened economic circumstances they had experienced since 1997. Immigrants were therefore vilified both as relying on government welfare that should be used instead to help unemployed locals and as stealing potential jobs away from locals who had lost their jobs during the long period of recession.[12] Such contradictions in local perceptions of the New Arrivals indicate that these views were based more on impressions about immigrants rather than on actual facts. Such strong public opinion of course affected the workers at the center, particularly in their interactions with clients who were seen as able but unwilling to work.

Nonetheless, when I mentioned this bias even among center workers to Elizabeth, the social worker in charge of the center, she was surprised. Although she acknowledged that many immigrants did come to Hong Kong with the intention of drawing on government resources, she was also optimistic in pointing out the hardworking nature of many more recent clients as well. Noting the importance of clients' personalities in her ability to get along well with some more than others, she distinguished between the really positive feeling that she got from working with some clients compared to the frustration that she felt in working with others. She cited the case of one long-term client, an older, widowed woman with two sons who had really "encouraged" her in her own life.

> She didn't know anything [when she came to Hong Kong]. Because before she had depended on her husband for everything. I think that her husband must have been one of those very traditional Chinese husbands. Very chauvinistic. He had to do everything himself. He made all of the decisions, and so on. So because he made all of the decisions, she didn't have to think about anything, or pay attention to anything. All she knew how to do was work in the fields, she didn't know how to do anything else. She told me that usually women who live in rural areas know how to kill chickens and ducks, but she didn't even know how to do this because her husband would help her do all of these things. And then her son got older, and he did these things. And she was illiterate. Later, her husband died, and she came to Hong Kong all by herself. She had to learn how to do everything from scratch. I feel that the way that she encouraged me is that without knowing even one word, she has slowly begun to learn [to read]. And she has also been learning English – beginning from ABC, she's now already at a Third grade level. She is really diligent. There was a period of time when she was on CSSA [Comprehensive Social Security Assistance], and she would still go and volunteer. She would spend lots of time volunteering, and she would work hard to help other people. So, you think: here's a person who didn't know anything, who continually works to improve herself. You can see that she has already improved in such a short period of time. Hong Kong is a city that is well-off, so you have to make more effort here, and here are people who will work so hard to be involved. The feeling that you get from these people is really positive. But there is another group that you see quite often, who don't have any plans to work hard to get involved with society. You can't deny that there is a group of people who come here to take resources. [They say:] "I don't know how. You teach me. You help me do it."

This kind of thing. "Give it to me. Give me money." Sometimes, with even very simple things, like filling out forms, the client will depend on the worker. And then we'll say: "Why don't I teach you how to fill it out instead of filling it out for you, because afterwards you will still have many opportunities to fill out other forms." And then you can see that the expression on their faces has changed – their attitude will be awful – they'll think: "You won't help me fill it out. You won't help me. Forget it." When you see these kinds of people, it makes you feel very frustrated.

The "model" immigrant of this anecdote was indeed just that – after being nominated by Elizabeth, she was given an official award in a public relations ceremony sponsored by the Sham Shui Po District Office, in which her hard work and efforts at adjustment into local Hong Kong life were acknowledged. In this case, her admirability stems from two particular qualities: first, that she was not a passive recipient of state welfare, but instead spent full days volunteering to help others (working in the kitchen of an old folk's home, for example) while she was depending on CSSA to pay her living expenses. Secondly, she worked hard to learn new things and "improve herself." This concept of "improving oneself" was a hallmark of Hong Kong culture that I found ubiquitous in my interactions with the local social workers and others there.

"Learning" was a big business in Hong Kong, and absolutely every employee at the center, as well as each of my other local Hong Kong contacts, were all enrolled in at least one evening class during the period of my fieldwork. In some cases, these courses were directly related to their work and were aimed at increasing their knowledge of certain aspects of social work. In other cases, languages, particularly advanced level English classes, were taken. In one case, a Hong Kong resident who tutored mainland immigrants at the center admitted that the class that he was taking – and did not enjoy – on Hong Kong popular culture was not in any way pragmatic. Yet when questioned about his motivations for taking this class, he noted the necessity of maintaining the appearance of "improving himself," which would be valued by his boss and keep him on equal footing with his coworkers, none of whom wished to "fall behind" or become outmoded by not continuing their education. Thus, this model client's openness to learning made her not just laudable for her hardworking attitude, but also ensured that she had developed certain expectations about life and learning that were considered hallmarks of Hong Kong cultural citizenship. Despite the fact that she still appeared to need help in "filling out certain forms" – as I witnessed on one occasion – her overall actions and responsible attitude continued to set her apart from other clients who were less open to the challenges that they experienced in their Hong Kong lives. Prompted by the success stories, such as that cited above, the social workers maintained a high standard of what they hoped their clients would learn, and used a variety of methods to convey key concepts to them while simultaneously trying not to be too discouraged by the "failure" of other clients to grasp these concepts. Below, I provide an in-depth look at two mutual help groups and one social work casefile. In each situation, one important aim of the social workers involved was to help increase clients' sense of social responsibility and eligibility for cultural citizenship.

Lessons in individual responsibility and cultural citizenship: the Teenage Drama Group

In running the Teenage Mutual Aid Drama Group, social worker Emily focused on teaching New Arrival teenagers skills that would qualify them for full Hong Kong cultural citizenship, as well as on teaching them the importance of social responsibilities. The group was originally intended to meet over the period of four weekends in November 2001 for just two hours each meeting; however, the high level of interest by the teenage participants and their commitment to producing a viable skit for the drama competition in which they were involved led to a total of ten meetings overall. Each meeting lasted for four hours on average, and there was almost perfect attendance at every group meeting – despite the long hours involved and heavy duties the participants faced at school and at home. This group drew greater and more enthusiastic levels of participation than any of the other groups that I encountered during the course of my fieldwork at the center. The group was comprised of ten teenagers, ranging in age from thirteen to nineteen, all of whom had to meet the center's participation requirement of having been in Hong Kong for less than one year. In most cases, the teenagers had arrived in Hong Kong some time the previous summer, in time to prepare for the academic year, and all but one spoke fluent Cantonese. The goal for the group was to compete in a Traffic and Road Safety Drama Competition for New Arrival children and teenagers, which was sponsored and funded by the Sham Shui Po Police Department. Having identified traffic safety, and violations of traffic rules, as one of the most common offenses committed by New Arrivals in the Sham Shui Po District, the Police Department hoped with this competition to elevate the level of awareness of proper traffic safety precautions among young immigrants. In addition to providing prizes, in the form of trophy cups, for the three best skits, the Police Department funds provided a hot boxed lunch and small gift for all participants as well as allowing for a budget of HK$500 (US$64) per group to help pay for props and costumes. In the case of the group in which I was involved, this HK$500 budget ended up playing a significant role in the overall content of the interaction between Emily and her clients.

Although one of Emily's aims for the drama group was to introduce her clients to some basic concepts about drama and playacting, her primary goal was to increase the participants' knowledge and awareness about communication. In particular, she hoped that they would become more comfortable and confident in expressing themselves in various situations. While "responsibility" was not openly stated as a goal to the participants, it remained an important theme in all of my discussions with Emily about the group. Following an almost "set" formula that I experienced in other mutual help groups as well, the first two sessions focused primarily on "ice breaking" games, so that the participants could begin to get to know each other, and so that they could begin to feel comfortable in their interactions with one another. In this case, the games were modeled around "acting out" expressions or other drama-related concepts, with particular attention paid to the many ways in which non-spoken communication occurs. The next two weekend meetings, as well as two additionally scheduled meetings during the week, were spent preparing for the drama competition. Two full meetings were dedicated to thinking up and deciding on possible plotlines for the skit, as well as voting on which participants would play which roles. For most of this time, I was more of an observer than a participant, as Emily and I had both noticed a tendency by the group participants to rely on me to solve problems or make required decisions. As one of her goals for the group entailed that the teenagers learn to be responsible for making their own decisions, Emily felt that it was counter-productive to include me in one of the three groups who were assigned to think up ideas for the skit. One session, lasting one full eight-hour day, was spent preparing props, and only a few hours were spent on writing and memorizing the dialogue that the various characters would say.

After much wrangling, the following plot was endorsed by all concerned. Two triad members would stand by the side of the road to hail a taxi. After the taxi driver, much to his horror, accidentally notices the extremely large knife being carried by one of the triad members, one triad member panics, kills the driver, and throws his body out of the taxi. Unfortunately for the triad members, they had forgotten that they did not know how to drive, and in trying to control the taxi, they ran over a pedestrian who happened to be crossing the street. This young, handsome victim was too busy listening to his walkman, reading a comic book, bouncing his basketball, and simultaneously trying to attract the attention of the beautiful woman across the street, so he did not notice the taxi swerving down the road towards him. After he was hit, the young man and the two triad members, who had also been injured in the crash, were taken to the hospital, where they were examined by a doctor and a nurse. Meanwhile, each patient was visited in turn by an angel and a devil, each demanding obeisance. When the two triad members refused to kowtow to the angel, their lives were effectively over, with one dying and the other becoming a human "vegetable." The student escaped with a lighter sentence – he was only paralyzed from the waist down. Finally, the whole cast reappeared on stage to announce that road safety is important. I had initially been struck by the implausibility of this creative scenario. But less than two weeks later, two bank robbers

– not triad members but illegal Chinese immigrants – were apprehended by police in a suburban Hong Kong location when they tried to escape from the scene of their crime in a taxi that they could not drive!

The lengthy process involved in proposing and agreeing on this plotline became the content through which Emily instructed her clients in the communication skills that she wanted them to learn. Emily's first struggle was an attempt to organize the group to participate as equals, contributing to the discussion in an orderly manner. After criticizing the students' inclination to shout out their ideas as loudly as possible without waiting to hear what others had to say, Emily instructed the teenagers to raise their hands when wanting to be called upon. She then endeavored to call upon each participant in turn. This practice, however, proved counterproductive to her desire to get the participants to discuss matters among themselves rather than always addressing their comments to her. Furthermore, she repeatedly stopped the participants in mid-sentence, using the pause to ask the others if they could understand what had just been said. In many cases, the other participants would confirm that the speaker had talked too quickly or quietly or incoherently, so that, indeed, the majority had not understood. Nonetheless, such instruction did not seem to have any change in the speaking manner of the criticized participants, who often continued just as they had before. Because of Emily's desire not to become overly involved, each decision made by the group took on a tortuous quality, lasting hours, until Emily would finally point out certain flaws in the students' reasoning and take enough charge to result in a completed decision. The finalization of the plot, the casting of the characters, and the process of deciding upon props and how they would be made and procured each took hours to resolve. The discussion about the props carried with it the added dimension of budgeting, as Emily had planned for the HK$500 allowance to cover not just the cost of props but also the cost of refreshments to be served at the final meeting following the competition. Although the allocation of responsibility of the procuring and making of each prop was finally decided more by Emily than by the group participants, the introduction of each new prop entailed a reminder from her about the need to plan carefully how the allowance monies would be used. Thus, the relationship between planning and responsibility became a central lesson introduced to the group participants, as this lesson was repeated yet again during the long process to decide what refreshments would be served at the final meeting. The students, of course, desired both props and foods that would have easily carried them over-budget, but as none of them had enough money to supplement the allowance provided by the police Department, Emily was adamant that all activities would remain within budget.

The following weekend, at the competition, it became apparent that the groups' efforts in joint decision-making had distracted them from producing a well-polished product. Although introducing a more creative plotline than the other skits, the actors' unpolished dialogue and shyly delivered lines did not suitably impress the judges of the competition. Although there were three prizes and only seven skits, the teenage drama group did not place, and the participants were clearly very disappointed. Afterwards, they complained to Emily that they would have "tried harder" if they had realized that there would be official prizes. Emily, however, reflected that the loss of the competition was an important lesson for the group participants, and that it was a more fitting conclusion to the group's overall content than if they had won. In fact, a few months later she admitted that the loss was the most important outcome of the group's content. To Emily's way of thinking, this loss taught participants that they should not be so self-satisfied, and therefore enable them to better learn how to cope with failure. At the time, however, the participants did not seem to make this connection, and they instead focused on the planning of the final party as a way to assuage their hurt pride. Nonetheless, and much to my dismay, not even the party refreshments were able to escape being integrated as an important "lesson" learning mechanism. Several of the kids had never eaten pizza before, and could not usually afford the HK$100 (US$13) cost of buying a large pizza at a local Dominos chain. Thus, it was a big decision to spend two-thirds of the final allowance monies budgeted for the party on a pizza as a rare treat. At that time, I was a vegetarian, and although Emily knew this, the participants did not. Despite my strident objections – after all, I said, I had eaten pizza many times – Emily forced the participants to order a vegetarian pizza, since she considered that they needed to think about my needs as well as their own. This final lesson in responsibility – the need to consider the feelings of others – was in fitting with the other means with which Emily had integrated this topic into the group's content. Individually, the group participants were held responsible to their word: if they said that they would come to the next meeting on time, they were expected to be on time and were chastised if, for any reason, they were late. As a group, they were responsible for planning their involvement in the competition and budgeting accordingly, but they were also held responsible for the fact that their failure to communicate effectively led to their loss in the competition, despite the fact that they had worked hard on the skit and its props. As an observer, I found the means with which Emily delivered her lessons on responsibility to be heavy-handed. For instance, when quizzing the participants on their anticipated arrival time the next meeting, she never seemed to consider that many of them had substantial responsibilities to their own families, such as looking after younger siblings while parents worked on the weekends. In one case, a teenage girl of fourteen was chastised for not having called to say that she would be late when she had been kept at a family gathering longer than expected. In another case, one of the thirteen year-old participants showed up each time on time, often accompanied by her 7-year-old sister and 8-year-old brother. It struck me as inconsistent that Emily never recognized these young teenagers' commitments to family responsibilities, and instead focused only on their responsibility toward group activities. In comments made to me months later, Emily acknowledged that she was happy with the group participants' overall sense of responsibility – in terms of their attendance rates and hard work, especially on the props – but that she was surprised to discover that, even after her involvement with them, some of them were not actually as "responsible" as they had seemed during the group. Many of them had failed to notify her on subsequent occasions when they did not appear for volunteer duties for which she had recruited them.

Responsibility to family: the case of Siu-ping

Social workers emphasized social responsibilities even to New Arrivals whose social rights and sense of cultural belonging were highly insecure. When I had only been at the center for a few weeks, Alexa, one of the social workers, told me about a young teenager who was part of a family casefile that she had been following. This 14-year-old girl, Siu-ping, had recently come to Hong Kong to live with her father, her stepmother, and her several step-siblings. Siu-ping's 9-year-old handicapped stepbrother was the primary client in this case, but one afternoon Alexa spent over two hours talking with the family's father, trying to give him "support." He was upset that he had lost his construction job because he had had to take time off to help his New Arrival wife and children. His wife refused to learn to use local transportation, and could not get around and take care of the children without his help. In particular, she was unable to take their handicapped son to his physical therapy appointments at a local charity hospital. Siu-ping's father was worried about money, and he was tired of trying to do everything for everyone in the family. Knowing that he was at his wit's end in trying to get by, Alexa was helping him both to apply for CSSA and to look for another job.

A few days after this two-hour interview, Alexa asked if I would be willing to provide some private English tutorial classes for Siu-ping, whose English level was particularly low – less than a local first grade level – and whom she felt also needed some symbolic token of support. Siu-ping's relationship with her stepmother was not good, her father didn't seem to take her "side" in any family disagreements, and she was often not given any money to buy lunch at school. The social worker did not know where Siu-ping's mother was, and it seemed that Siu-ping had been living with her boyfriend's family before coming to Hong Kong. Siu-ping's attendance at the Induction Program class for New Arrival children aged 6–16 was sporadic, and several times during the fall of 2001 she left home to go back to the mainland without telling anyone before she left. Sometimes she would "disappear" to the mainland after a family disagreement, and during school holidays she would regularly leave without telling her father where she was going. Throughout this time, Alexa tried to mediate between the two of them, although her attitude toward Siu-ping was significantly different from her attitude toward Siu-ping's father. Despite his need to rely, hopefully only for a short time, on CSSA, Siu-ping's father's dedication to helping his New Arrival family deal with their adjustment to Hong Kong cast him in a favorable light as being responsible in his interactions with his family members. Siu-ping, on the other hand, was viewed as acting irresponsibly towards her family – both in terms of her lack of respect for her father's position within the family and in terms of her failure to contribute to the care and well-being of her step-siblings. From Alexa's point of view, Siu-ping's marginalized position within the family did not justify the fact that she felt no need to help ease her father and stepmother's burdens in the family's adjustment to the arrival of the wife and children in Hong Kong. As a result, she remained the focus of Alexa's efforts.[13]

Alexa's attempt to arrange extra tutoring for Siu-ping was viewed as "preferential" and was not well received by other office workers, who felt that they knew of clients perhaps just as bad in English who were not getting individual attention. Quite a lively debate ensued on this subject among several center employees, during which time Alexa held her ground, and reiterated that in lieu of being able to offer Siu-ping any real long-term support, she hoped that this "gesture" would provide some sort of symbolic "support" for a young woman otherwise totally lacking in support on every level. Over the next couple of months, I met with Siu-ping four or five times, each time taking over one hour to help her learn maybe ten basic English vocabulary words, such as table, plate, orange, and bicycle. Her progress was agonizingly slow, and she constantly told me about the frustration involved with always getting a "0" on her school English assignments. She told me very little about her family, but she did say that she was very moved that Alexa had arranged this extra tutoring for her. Very quickly, however, a problem surfaced: it became apparent that Siu-ping had begun to cast me in the role of "best friend" rather than tutor – a relationship that I did not want to encourage given her youth and the extent of her serious family problems. Concerned about how to handle the situation, I turned to Alexa for help. Alexa had also been surprised by Siu-ping's rapid embracing of me into her current and future plans. She explained Siu-ping's attachment to me as indicative of the kinds of "self-centered" behavior that had led to the difficult relationship that Siu-ping continued to experience with her father and stepmother. Alexa described a number of instances when she had had to "untangle" what Siu-ping was saying and explained the necessity of guessing at a more objective account of reported family disputes to try to understand what had really gone on. Commenting that "nine times out of ten" Siu-ping's accounts of family quarrels were so completely biased as to be unreliable, Alexa considered most of Siu-ping's comments and complaints to her as untrustworthy. Noting Siu-ping's difficult family background, her history of limited contact with her father, the general unhappiness of her living situation, as well as the fact that she was a teenager and teenagers were normally very self-involved, Alexa told me that: "You could say that this behavior is natural." Nonetheless, Alexa was not prepared to pardon Siu-ping's "self-centered" behavior by relying on such excuses. Alexa very much believed that Siu-ping needed to be more responsible for her own actions and their repercussions, and their talks together frequently focused on this subject. In particular, Alexa was trying to get Siu-ping to improve her interactions with her father, whose authority as her legal guardian Siu-ping continued to ignore completely. Furthermore, Alexa began to encourage Siu-ping to become more involved as a volunteer with center activities, so that she could learn that she, too, could help others, rather than always being the recipient of others' help. In the end, Siu-ping's school schedule changed, and Alexa made use of the opportunity to end our tutorial sessions.

Shortly before I left Hong Kong, I heard from Alexa that Siu-ping had moved out of her father's house and was instead living with an uncle in another part of Hong Kong. Alexa's attempts to get Siu-ping involved in center activities had not been very successful, as she had only participated as a volunteer on one or two occasions. Likewise, her encouragement for Siu-ping to begin acting more "responsibly" towards her Hong Kong family members seemed to have failed as well. Given the mutual distrust with which Siu-ping and her Hong Kong father and step-family viewed each other, responsible, respectful behavior was apparently not possible between them.

Volunteer work as a means of enhancing social and cultural citizenship

People enjoying ample social rights and prestigious cultural citizenship are often willing to fulfill their citizenship responsibilities through volunteer work. In "The Erosion of Citizenship," Bryan Turner argues that the traditional foundations that fostered active citizen participation in the past – work, war, and reproduction – have become less viable in a modern world based on global capitalist practices (2001). Instead, he identifies the "voluntary sector" as the most important contemporary means of providing meaningful opportunities for "active citizenship" through social participation and democratic involvement at the local level (*ibid.*: 200). Although Hong Kong social workers encouraged New Arrivals to do volunteer work, some New Arrivals were leery of doing extra work that did not seem to improve their access to social rights and cultural belonging. Activities like those organized by Alexa (described below), however, drew considerable interest because they helped improve volunteers' access to the rights as well as the responsibilities of social and cultural citizenship.

The Hong Kong Department of Social Welfare launched a "volunteer movement" in 1998. With the aims of "maximizing community resources" and "enhancing a sense of social belonging," this movement tried to involve Hong Kong people "from all walks of life to participate in building society so as to develop a caring and harmonious community" (www.volunteering-hk.org). Under the sponsorship of Mrs. Betty Tung, the wife of SAR Chief Executive Tung Chee-wah, this movement was formed, in part, as a response to the economic downturn that took place following the Asian financial crisis in 1997. The concept of "volunteering" was based upon the assumption that involving individuals in volunteer activities would improve their sense of cultural belonging and social responsibility while benefiting society and relieving the state of some burden. Posters all around the city advertised this concept, which was actively promoted by various non-government organizations. Programs designed for New Arrivals by social workers at the center also frequently focused on "volunteering," which became one of the most common discourses though which the importance of responsibility was promoted to the clients at the center.

Motivated by the desire to train a core "group" of immigrants to serve as volunteers who would help to perform a variety of social work-related tasks, Alexa planned and held a "learning to volunteer" mutual help group which met over three weekends in January 2002, on both Saturdays and Sundays, for approximately two hours each time. Although clients and former clients had participated as volunteers in many of the activities and programs that I observed at the center up until that time, the social workers had expressed an interest in increasing volunteer involvement in center activities as a means of 1.) getting clients more involved in community affairs, and 2.) helping to enhance service provision to clients. New Arrivals' voluntary work in center activities was one valuable way in which social workers could continue to interact in the lives of clients who had exceeded one year of residency in Hong Kong, thus making them ineligible to participate in center programs. Furthermore, recruiting volunteers from their immigrant client base was actually one of the stipulations required by the center's Funding and Service Agreement with the Social Welfare Department, so that the workers' inability to involve sufficient numbers of clients as volunteers would jeopardize their primary funding source for the following year. Making use of the rhetoric and materials supplied by the Hong Kong-wide "volunteer movement" that had been begun in 1998, social workers gave all volunteers "log books" so that their hours of community service could be recorded. Those individuals reaching milestones of 100 or more community hours served per year were automatically recognized in a special ceremony and awarded a prize by the Social Welfare Department.

Participants in Alexa's "learning to volunteer" group were recruited primarily from the basic level English class that I had begun teaching in December 2001, and the experience of the group seemed to have been enhanced by the fact that at least half of the thirteen registered participants already knew each other from their twice weekly attendance at my class. Alexa also pointed out that perhaps their interest in English indicated personalities predisposed to an open-mindedness of expression, such that she was both pleased and surprised at the "active" participation of the majority of members in the group. Each of the first five sessions was organized along similar lines. In all classes except the first, the meeting began with a report on the previous session's "homework" assignment, followed by one or two "ice-breaking" or "getting to know each other" games. Next would come a brief component – either lecture or discussion-based – on the topic of being a volunteer and the theme of "contribution to society." The majority of each session was then spent learning about a "topical subject" related to Hong Kong life and immigrant adjustment. The two subjects emphasized in this group were housing and health care. Finally, each session concluded with a "sharing time," in which all participants were free to converse while eating the specially prepared "sweet soup dessert" which had been cooking while the earlier part of the meeting was in progress. The sixth session was meant to serve as these women's "volunteer" activity, and it involved participation in a program in which up to forty new immigrant women could come to an information session to learn more about housing and health care resources in Hong Kong. Although led by Alexa, the women (including myself) who had participated in the mutual help group were incorporated into the presentation through the performance of skits on housing and health care situations, the quizzing of clients on their understanding and retention of the talk's content, and the handing out of snacks at the end of the session. For most of the women involved, this was their first "volunteer" experience, and they found it fun and interesting enough to make them want to sign up for a five-day volunteer workshop held in conjunction with a local old folk's home one month later.

Alexa's goals for the group were multi-faceted. On the most basic level, her goals for the participating clients included learning about the local resource availability for housing and health care as well as participating as volunteers at the information session about these subjects. On a more complex level, she hoped to address the issues of communication and voluntarism with these women, so that participation in this group would represent the first step in their greater participation in community life and activities. As with any mutual help group, one main purpose of the group was to introduce a number of clients to each other in the hope that their shared meeting and experiences would allow them to further their own personal social networks, thus reducing their dependence on social workers to help them solve their problems. In this case, Alexa also hoped that they would actively share their newly gained knowledge about local resources with other friends needing such information, thus improving their self-confidence along with their demonstrated understanding of local resources. As with the example of Emily's teenage drama group discussed above, the theme of responsibility was also interwoven into the content of the group. Individuals were given "homework" assignments to report back to the class on certain subjects, took turns taking responsibility for the task of preparing a soup for each meeting, and were required to learn about new aspects of Hong Kong life while interacting with local people. The issue of "contribution" was the central theme addressed and emphasized the idea of needing to contribute actively to one's community as a matter of social responsibility.

Not only were the members of the group judged to be "active," but Alexa's structuring of group learning sessions encouraged the active involvement of group members and were well-received by the clients, who all told me that they judged the program successful, as they had all "learned something" (*hohkdou yeh*) (學過東西). To learn about health service provision and resources in the Sham Shui Po area, the group visited a public women's and children's health clinic located nearby. As part of the process of improving understanding of the types of housing options available and eligibility for applying to public housing, we also took a "fieldtrip" to the Housing Authority's Sham Shui Po office. As a group requirement during these visits, Alexa assigned certain practical "homework" questions to the group's participants, which required the women to wait for available service representatives, to ask them questions, and to report the answers back to the group. At the Housing Authority office, for example, the women had to find out: how they could check on an application in process; whether or not there were special application procedures for households with senior citizen members; whether or not only permanent residents can apply for public housing; and how the name of a child newly arrived in Hong Kong could be added to an existing application.

By defining the gathering and presentation of topic materials as a group effort, Alexa ensured her clients' involvement and interest in the discussions that were held on these topics. Complicated bureaucratic information became less "dry" with more personal involvement. But, equally as important, visits to these offices and efforts to find out the answers to particular questions at each office served to "demystify" local bureaucratic practices as well. Serving the same principle as teaching a client how to "fill out a form" rather than filling it out for her, these visits were meant to teach these women the basic protocol necessary to gain information from any Hong Kong government department or service representative. Furthermore, these exercises also required that the women practice their general communication skills with Hong Kong locals. When Amber, one of the group's immigrant participants, reported to the group the highly detailed response that she received in answer to her questions at the women's clinic, Alexa praised her for her ability to elicit information from others, and turned her "homework report" into a lesson on how to develop successful communication skills through the cultivation of a polite attitude and proper etiquette. With her communication skills, Amber seemed to have demonstrated the ability to become a cultural citizen of Hong Kong. This emphasis on improving self-expression was again practiced at the final volunteering session, in which each woman had to perform in a skit detailing some aspect of these local resources in front of a group of unfamiliar women. Unlike in the case of the teenage drama group, however, our dialogue was written for us by the social worker, Alexa.

Most of the participants from this "learning to volunteer" group were recruited for a five-day program the following month. This program was sponsored by some social work student interns working at a local home for the elderly and was jointly run by these interns and Alexa. I was initially surprised to see such a good turnout among the women from the previous group, many of whom were also working on the weekdays when this second group met. It rapidly became clear that most of the women involved viewed this additional group as a fun, social opportunity to spend time with friends. Our first two meetings were spent learning about the lives of the elderly men and women living in the home, as well as learning about common ailments and behavioral difficulties experienced by the residents of the home. Next, we planned an hour-long "party and social gathering" for the home's residents and visited the facility to become acquainted with it. The fifth meeting was the day on which the party was held. After learning about suitable activities that had been planned for the home's residents in the past, we agreed on a program that included the following elements: two games requiring very simple motor skills to be played with the group as a whole; the performance of two popular old Cantonese songs; and a snack session of dumplings with free conversation afterwards. In planning the program, the needs of the elderly were emphasized: the games allowed the residents to remain seated and did not require good sight or sudden movement; the songs were picked to appeal to people of an older generation; and the food, both dumplings and "prizes" awarded at the games, were soft and easy-to-chew. Participation by the group members was active, and the women seemed to enjoy both the planning of the party's details and their interaction with these different members of Hong Kong society who seemed clearly in need of "help" and entertainment. The day of the performance went well, and there were no surprises. Attendance for the group's meetings and final performance was high; the women were happy to spend additional free time chatting with the home's residents after the conclusion of the party; and all the center's clients (and myself) were awarded "certificates" of training to work with the elderly by the organization running the home. Thus, the "learning to volunteer" group had performed according to Alexa's hopes: the women in the group were seemingly well on their way to becoming a corps of volunteers active in participating and contributing to community involvement in different situations.

Both from comments collected by Alexa after this party, and from my conversations with the women involved, I concluded that the women's feelings about their volunteer experiences were, by and large, positive. One participant explained:

> My personality opened up, and my life became more meaningful. I was able to learn communication skills and how to get along with other people. And also learn interesting things that I had never seen or heard

before. For this, I say thank you [Miss Alexa] for giving me this opportunity to learn and hear and see more. I am very happy. Thanks again.

And Amber wrote:

> After doing this volunteer work, I feel really happy. I think that by helping other people I can hope to reach my goal of making other people happy. Helping others is really just helping oneself.

These comments and others indicated that the women felt that they learned new things, improved their communication skills, and had an opportunity to interact with local people which they valued. Amber reiterated her comments about learning and helping others, and the fact that she had been able to become "happier" through this involvement, in other conversations I had with her. Furthermore, she expressed satisfaction in learning about what it means to "volunteer," since she had always heard me say that I was "volunteering" at the center but had never been entirely sure what that meant. Another participant, Allison, was also very enthusiastic about her volunteer experience, and she was excited enough that she supplemented the "prizes" and "treats" that we had gotten for the home's residents with snacks that she bought with her own money. Coming at a time when she had just had a serious disagreement with her elderly mother-in-law – which eventually led to her and her husband's move to their own apartment – Allison found the training about dealing with the ailments and behavioral difficulties of the elderly as relevant to her own life. She added a personal interpretation to the experience that was not expressed by any of my other informants:

> I think that doing volunteer work can help me regulate my temper. My temper is usually not good – [and at my expression of surprise, she emphasized the point again:] My temper is actually not good. But I don't lose me temper when I am outside – I usually just get mad at my husband. . . . But when you are doing volunteer work, you have to take care of other people. You have to have a good temper, explaining things to other people, taking care of elderly people. Your status is like being a son or a daughter to them, [to] take care of them, give them things to eat. If you don't have a good temper, it's useless.

Focusing on the patience involved with learning and caring for others, Allison understood that this experience helped her train for the difficulties that she had been encountering in her own life. In all of these comments, it would seem that the women involved had certainly accomplished some of the goals that Alexa had initially hoped to accomplish with her mutual help group. Nevertheless, one immigrant, Cybil, was less impressed with both the message involved and the program that resulted:

Actually, I was really nervous that day because I was late. But I don't think that we really helped anyone. . . . It was such a short period of time, and there were so many elderly people. Those people who were happy didn't really need the program, and those who weren't happy won't have been changed by such a small program. Because it was a really small thing. I even sang badly. . . . I felt like I didn't really make a contribution. But I was sincere [in my participation]. If I was going to go, I didn't want to be late. I rushed to the bus stop because I was afraid that I was going to be late.

Like the other participants, Cybil picked up on Alexa's goals for the group, even using the word "contribution" spoken so often by her. Nonetheless, and unlike the others, she seems to have viewed the experience as a "token" gesture, and in recognizing that fact, she failed to derive any meaningful result from it. Her feelings were compounded by the fact that she did not even sing well, which she found particularly bothersome on the grounds that she had formerly been an amateur singer of Chinese opera. But perhaps Cybil's feelings resonated more with the overall reactions of the others than their quotes here make apparent. Within a month, Alexa was expressing her frustration to me that the women of this volunteer corps were too caught up in the busy details of their everyday lives, and that they were rarely available to participate as volunteers in other activities. As with so many of the center's clients, even these seemingly dedicated women often "disappeared" from the range of social worker involvement. Perhaps, though, armed with an increased level of local knowledge and self-awareness, these women were simply more successful than most in adjusting to the Hong Kong world around them. While other clients "disappeared" back to the mainland, most of these women were instead actively involved in their own local situations, including jobs and networking with friends. As working was viewed by Alexa and the other social workers as the primary means of "contributing" to society, the personal satisfaction and rewards from which should supercede all other commitments, Alexa could not really be too disappointed at her difficulties in organizing these women for additional volunteer activities.

Conclusion: social work interpretations of responsibility, contribution, and empowerment

The importance of "responsibility" was a central aspect of the concept of citizenship promoted by the social workers at the center, both with regards to their interactions with their clients and with regards to their decisions about their own lives and work. Siu-saan, in particular, had been heavily influenced in her own thinking by an encounter that she had with a local grassroots leader while she was still in school. At that time, she was involved in a "community development" internship, in which she and other young social workers were sent out to different grassroots organizations to help encourage participation in social and political events by individuals at the local level. This woman, whom Siu-saan described (using colloquial Cantonese) as very clever or "sharp" (*lek*), questioned her involvement in community development in a way that Siu-saan had never forgotten. As Siu-saan recalled, this leader said: "You social workers only know how to push us forward. In the end, who takes responsibility? For this behavior, for these things that we do? In the end, who bears the burden [of our actions]?" Siu-saan was so struck by the strength of this woman's argument that her personal beliefs about the roles of social workers in society changed. As a result, she has remained involved in service-provision work rather than the riskier and more demanding community development work. In fact, there was very little social work of the community development variety in Hong Kong during the period of my fieldwork. One social work professor estimated that only about 1% of government social work funding was spent on community development, the key tenet of which was based on "empowering" local individuals to act in more political (i.e., from the point of view of the government, "controversial") ways. One organization in Hong Kong, the Society for Community Organization (SoCO), is particularly known for its community development work, and for its involvement in political issues that the government would rather not address. These issues include fighting for the right of abode by illegal immigrants and advocating for increased standards of living by the "cage dwellers" – those individuals who are so poor that they live in cages rather than apartments. Although Ho Hei-wah, the head of SoCO, denies it, popular opinion has attributed SoCO's "incitement" of abode seekers to the violent protests and arson attacks that occurred in August 2000 at the Immigration Department, in which one immigration officer and one abode seeker were killed. Citing this incident as a prime example, Siu-saan cautioned that social workers needed to find socially responsible ways of interacting with their clients, and they needed to make sure that they have taught their clients what the outcomes of their actions will be. From her point of view, a "safer" way of encouraging "empowerment," for both worker and client, remained in the concept of "self-help" as a means to teach individual clients to interact in a self-confident way with the local people and situations that they encounter on a daily basis. To this end, Siu-saan was a strong supporter of the concept of "individual responsibility" as I detailed in the center casework and groups above.

In interactions between social workers and clients, the understanding of "responsibility" took on many different meanings, just as proof of an individual's sense of responsibility was indicated in many different ways. As demonstrated by the requirements of participants in the teenage drama group, individual responsibility was judged according to one's ability to plan and budget, to have thoughtful and considerate interaction with others, and to keep one's commitments. In the case of Siu-ping, responsibility to family was defined as being respectful of elders and maintaining a "traditional" hierarchy of power and command within the family, as well as by contributing to the family's overall functioning and well-being. Finally, the emphasis on volunteering and active community involvement focused on the idea of needing to "contribute" to society. Through such involvement, individuals could improve their access both to social rights and to prestigious forms of cultural citizenship by developing better communication and interaction skills and by learning about the local resources available to them. In the end, one is left with the following composite picture of the ideal Hong Kong Chinese "citizen" as someone who is self-confident and actively involved in the social world, working both for pay and for the inherent reward of cultural belonging, while also contributing to the overall stability and harmony of society as a whole.

The ideals promoted by the social workers at the center were heavily influenced by their own training in Western-based social work theories, as evidenced (at least in part) by the fact that the workers routinely used English, rather than Cantonese, when referring to key social work concepts. While Elizabeth, the social worker in charge of the center, explained that the focus on volunteering was related to the promotion of this concept by government departments, she also noted that the social workers' emphasis on "contribution" and "empowerment" was linked directly to their social work training. The importance placed on personal responsibility in understanding Hong Kong's laws and legal system by official representatives of the Police Department and the ICAC further underscores the point that other government agencies felt the need to train the newly arrived Chinese immigrants in a Westernized mindset highlighting the neoliberal emphasis on the role of individual citizens in carrying out social responsibilities. As a culturally Chinese but socioeconomically First World region, Hong Kong represented an ideal that mainland Chinese leaders as well as citizens were striving to emulate. But clashes between the demands of Hong Kong social workers and the expectations of mainland Chinese immigrants suggest that the difficulty of promoting social responsibilities among those with limited access to social rights and cultural belonging is likely to persist even if China joins the First World.

Notes

1 All names given in this paper are pseudonyms. In Hong Kong, it is common for young people in particular to refer to themselves by their English name rather than their Chinese name. Thus, I have used English pseudonyms to refer to informants who preferred to use their English name when interacting with me.

2 Since 1995, government policy in the Hong Kong Special Administration of the PRC has allowed 150 Chinese immigrants to settle in Hong Kong each day. These legal Chinese immigrants to Hong Kong are officially called "New Arrivals" by the Hong Kong government.

3 Funding and institutional support for this research were provided by NSF Grant BCS-0099244, Hong Kong University's Center of Asian Studies, and the Anthropology Department at the Chinese University of Hong Kong.

4 All of my informal interaction and interviews with the center's staff and clients took place in Cantonese. This quote, and all other quotes in this paper, are my own translations from the Cantonese. Because the education system in Hong Kong is still heavily based on English as well as Chinese instruction, Cantonese spoken in Hong Kong is peppered with English words, often inserted as nouns or verbs in the middle of an otherwise Cantonese sentence. In this quote, Emily used the English for the word "irresponsible," so I have placed quotes around this word in my translation.

5 For a discussion of Chinese educational campaigns encouraging mothers to breastfeed, see Gottschang 2001.

6 Many, but not all, of these Hong Kong husbands had themselves immigrated to Hong Kong in the 1960s, 1970s, and 1980s.

7 All quotes in this paper come from taped interviews with informants who had consented and knew they were being taped for the purpose of my research. *Per* social work ethical requirements, I never saw any of the center's casefiles, although the social workers would discuss with me the situations of their clients who were also my informants.

8 Like models that generalize about "the West," Ong's model is problematic in its sweeping claim that seeks to attribute the same state methods and goals for achieving modernization among communist, colonial, and emerging democratic regimes. Furthermore, it ignores important cases of social protest aimed at challenging these models (such as the Tiananmen uprising in 1989; see also Abelmann 1996 on South Korea) and obscures major cases of government-initiated atrocities, such as the Great Proletarian Cultural Revolution and the Great Leap Forward, which resulted in the devastation and death of millions of Chinese citizens.

9 In the formal legal terminology, there is no such thing as a Hong Kong citizen, only Chinese citizens. In the local terminology, "Hong Kong permanent resident" is used instead.

10 The local Hong Kong word for "uncivilized," *yehmaahn*, is one of many locally used words without a written form understandable in Mandarin Chinese. Therefore, I have not included the Mandarin here.

11 I understood the local Hong Kong used of this word, *jaahtsou*, or "quality" to refer to an immigrant's education level and general ability to "fit into" local Hong Kong norms of social comportment. This meaning places considerably less emphasis on the "quality of body" referred to in the mainland interpretations of this word, which link the "health of the people" with the "health of the nation" and with national health campaigns, such as the breastfeeding campaign noted above. Nonetheless, there is a clear link between the perceived poor "quality" of these immigrants and a general concern about the "quality" of the general population. (See Anagnost 1995 for more on the use of the word "quality" in the PRC.)

12 The types of welfare available to residents of Hong Kong are less comprehensive than the social security and other systems that we take for granted as part of the Western welfare state model. There is no social security in Hong Kong, but other forms of welfare available include public housing, for which one can apply if at least 50% of one's immediate family have been living in Hong Kong for seven years. Comprehensive Social Security Assistance (CSSA) provides a welfare payment to individuals or families that are unemployed, but one must have been resident in Hong Kong for one year to be eligible. Disability and old age or retirement assistance (locally called "fruit money" as the HK$700 (US$90)

per month stipend is enough to do little more than buy fruit) are available to individuals who have resided in Hong Kong between three and five years. Most government subsidized programs run for New Arrivals, such as that where I did my research, stipulate that service can only be provided to immigrants who have been in Hong Kong for less than one year.

13 A substantially different method for treating the family's problems would likely to have been employed in the United States, where a social worker working with this family would probably have pulled the whole family in for counseling (email communication with C. Geanuracos February 8, 2003).

8 Chinese youth between the margins of China and the First World

Vanessa L. Fong

This chapter examines the dilemmas of transnational Chinese youth who found themselves at the margins of both China and the West as they pursued First World citizenship.[1] Chinese citizens who also had First World citizenship had access to the opportunities associated with what Aihwa Ong called "flexible citizenship" (Ong 1999). But such opportunities came at a high price, as full First World citizenship often proved elusive, even as pursuit of it eroded the PRC citizenship that Chinese youth took for granted.

I use the term "First World" to refer not to a geographic region, but rather to an imagined global community of affluent, powerful, and prestigious people. As with any kind of citizenship, First World citizenship has social, cultural, civil, political, and legal aspects that are connected but not inseparable. While legal citizenship and physical residence play a large role in determining whether one is part of the First World or the Third World, they are not the only relevant factors. In a world of global cultural flows, interconnected political economies, and increasingly mobile people, it is possible for people to be part of the Third World even while they are living in the First World, and for people to be part of the First World even while they are living in the Third World. Economic, cultural, and social capital can be much more fluid and transnational than the physical means of production (such as machines, factories, and transportation infrastructures) that traditionally undergirded the political economy of the capitalist world system. As the significance of knowledge and information in determining global power relationships has increased, so have possibilities for individuals to develop citizenship rights and privileges that transcend the socioeconomic classifications of the countries and regions in which they reside or have legal citizenship. As Saskia Sassen argued, large cities with strong transnational linkages tend to produce denationalized elites who sometimes share greater affinities with their counterparts in the globalized cities of other countries than with the non-elite of their own countries (Sassen 2002:24).

This chapter examines the experiences of Chinese youth trying to become such denationalized elites. I draw on participant observation that I conducted between 1997 and 2004 among youth who left the People's

Republic of China (PRC) to study in Australia, the Republic of Ireland, and the United Kingdom. I use the term "Western" as a shorthand for these three countries, and "Western citizenship" as a shorthand for social, cultural, civil, political, and legal citizenship in these countries and, more broadly, in the imagined community of Western society, which in turn is part of the imagined community of the First World. I characterize Australia, Ireland, and the United Kingdom as "Western" because these countries share a language, culture, and identity commonly described as "Western," and not because of their geographic locations (airplanes departing from China fly west to go to Europe, but southeast to go to Australia). I focus on Chinese students' pursuit of "Western" citizenship because most of the Chinese students I knew ended up going to Western countries. This was partly because of the dearth of non-Western countries affluent and prestigious enough to attract Chinese students, partly because my role as an English teacher put me in contact with a disproportionate number of students who studied English and were interested in going to Western countries, and partly because most Chinese students had learned no other foreign language besides English, and wanted to go to societies where they did not have to learn yet another language. I knew a few Chinese students who pursued First World citizenship by going to non-Western First World societies like Japan and Singapore, but I did not know them well enough to include them in my research. All Chinese students were required to study a second language during high school, and those at the most prestigious schools were required to study a second language every year from primary school through college. The majority of Chinese primary school, junior high school, high school, and college students chose English as their second language because of its versatility and prestige. Most schools did not even offer other foreign languages. Students worried that choosing non-English foreign language tracks during primary school, junior high school, or high school would narrow the range of their future educational opportunities by making them ineligible for the many schools and majors that only accepted students who had previously studied English. Because of its location close to Japan, Dalian (the Chinese city where I first met many of the youth in my study) had more students offering Japanese classes and more students taking these classes than most other Chinese cities. Still, such classes and students were in the minority because Japanese was useful only for those who traveled to Japan or worked with Japanese employers, trade partners and customers, while English was useful for dealing with people from an array of Anglophone countries, and could also be used as an international lingua franca because even people from non-Anglophone societies (including Japan) were likely to have studied English. Languages other than English and Japanese were only offered at a few universities and private language schools, and studied mainly by Chinese students with specific plans and reasons for going to the countries where those languages were spoken.

While Chinese people of all ages agreed that Western citizenship was desirable, opportunities for attaining Western citizenship were most abundant for young people who had not yet finished their education, established careers, or started families, and thus had the time and flexibility to devote to the pursuit of activities that could bring them Western citizenship. PRC citizens born after the capitalist practices and low fertility rates of the First World were introduced by the economic reforms and one-child policy that began in the late 1970s and were also socialized to desire Western citizenship more strongly than older PRC citizens who had been socialized under the Maoist government, which had tried to withdraw the PRC from the capitalist world system dominated by the West.

Unlike the more disadvantaged PRC citizens described by most of the other authors in this volume, the Chinese students I studied chose their marginality. Many of them had enough education, wealth, and family connections to pave their way to comfortable positions at the center of Chinese society. Because of their high expectations, however, they were dissatisfied with the limited rights associated with PRC citizenship, and chose to move to the margins of Chinese society in order to pursue the superior rights associated with First World citizenship. They spent years studying abroad, trying to prolong their sojourns whenever possible, and in some cases moving from one First World society to another in the pursuit of even better opportunities. The Chinese youth I knew delighted in their acquisition of new rights, but they also paid a price for their pursuit of flexible citizenship. Many felt torn between the responsibilities associated with their Chinese and First World citizenships. They wanted to maintain full citizenship in the PRC, but their desire for First World citizenship made them leery of permanent residence in the PRC. They wanted to attain full First World citizenship, but their loyalty to China made them wary of strategies such as seeking political asylum or marriage to a Western citizen. Their indecision ensured that they remained marginal not only in their homeland, but also in the West. While a life of double marginality conferred freedom and opportunity, it also entailed insecurity, conflict, and unfulfilled desires.

Research settings and methods

My focus is on the experiences of several hundred transnational Chinese youth I met over the course of my research in the PRC, Australia, the United Kingdom, and the Republic of Ireland. I spent 28 months between 1997 and 2004 examining the effects of near-universal only-child status on the subjectivities, experiences, and aspirations of teenagers in Dalian, a large coastal city in northeastern China.[2] Between 1998 and 2000, I worked in Dalian as an unpaid English conversation teacher at a vocational high school, a junior high school, and a non-keypoint college prep high school in exchange for the opportunity to survey students and observe their classes and other activities. Held during periods that were normally used for study hall, the English conversation classes I offered consisted of English language games and lively discussions of whatever topics the students wanted to discuss. I visited some homerooms (*banji*) once a week, some once a month, and some once a year. I also spent several days each month sitting in homerooms, observing students' activities throughout the day. Each homeroom consisted of 40–60 students who sat at their desks during the bulk of the school day, while different teachers came in to teach different subjects.

The first people I got to know in Dalian were teachers, students, and administrators at the schools where I taught, and random staff members, businesspeople, and fellow customers I met at shops, markets, malls, parks, restaurants, bus stops, post offices, internet cafes, and photocopying service centers. After these initial contacts introduced me to their friends, relatives, and acquaintances as a "Chinese American doctoral student," I received many invitations to go to teenagers' homes to tutor them in English or provide information about how to go abroad. During the bulk of my fieldwork, I lived with a junior high school student I tutored, his factory worker father, and his mother, who invited me to live with her family after several long conversations at the small shop where she worked as a salesclerk after retiring from her factory. I also lived with eight other families for periods ranging from a few days to a month.

Over the course of my fieldwork, I was invited to the homes of 107 young people, usually to provide tutoring or advice about how they might get opportunities to study or work abroad. Because of time constraints, however, I lost touch with most of them after one or several visits. I maintained long-term friendships only with the 31 families that developed the strongest rapport with me. The rapport that transformed members of these families from acquaintances into friends was based on intersubjective factors (such as trust, emotional compatibility, and a shared sense of humor) that did not seem to correlate with quantifiable variables like income, occupational status, or educational attainment. Thus, the sample of 31 families that I ended up befriending was about as socioeconomically diverse as my original sample of 107 families. I visited these 31 families on a regular basis, and still keep in touch with them by telephone and e-mail. All but two of them were single-child nuclear or stem families. Most of their children were teenagers when I first met them, though the youngest was 10 and the oldest was 28.

Almost all of the young people I met in the PRC told me at some point or other that they wanted to work and study in First World societies. Unlike the Maoist government, the post-Mao Chinese government did little to discourage its citizens from going abroad, and some state-owned schools and work units even provided funds for top students and employees to visit or study abroad. Graduates of top Chinese universities could get fellowships and jobs in the First World by applying directly to foreign companies and universities. Most other would-be emigrants, however, had to rely on private companies of varying degrees of legality that sprang up during the 1990s to meet the demand for opportunities to go abroad. In exchange for fees ranging from 10,000 to 100,000 yuan (US$1,209–US$12,092),[3] these companies provided work, study, and immigration opportunities in the First World or in countries that might serve as springboards to the First World, and did the paperwork and other kinds of work necessary to convert these opportunities into visas for those able to pay for them. A visa to go abroad was seen as a hard-won opportunity to become part of the Western elite with the legal and economic wherewithal to move frequently and easily across national borders. Obtaining a visa required immense time, energy, and economic and social capital. The financial burden was especially great for parents of students who could not earn enough to pay for their own tuition and living expenses while abroad. Teachers and alumni of the schools I studied told me that only about 5–10 students out of each homeroom of 40–60 students eventually went abroad.

While most of the people I met in the PRC lacked the cultural and financial capital necessary for obtaining visas to First World societies, a small proportion of them did manage to go abroad. Most of those who went abroad had finished high school but not college in China, though some had finished college and a few had not even completed high school. Most had significantly more wealth and/or more prestigious academic credentials than the vast majority of PRC citizens, though I also knew a few academically average students from relatively poor families who had managed to convince a large number of friends and relatives to loan them enough money to enable them to go abroad. Five of the 33 children of the 31 families that I have kept in continual touch with since my initial fieldwork in 1997–2000 with have gone abroad at the time of this writing. In addition, 14 of these 31 families had at least one member who could introduce me to at least one friend, relative, spouse, boyfriend, girlfriend, co-worker, or friend or relative of a friend or relative who was either studying abroad or was in the process of trying to get opportunities to study abroad. I also renewed contact with six of the young adults who I had met during my initial fieldwork in the PRC, but who had lost touch with me after I returned to the United States and they went to other First World countries. Among the youth I knew through all of these social networks in Dalian City, 17 are studying abroad, including 12 who are currently in Australia, the United Kingdom, or the Republic of Ireland. These three countries were the most popular destinations for the youth I knew from my research in China. In 2003 and 2004, I conducted research in these three countries, living with students that I had met in the PRC, and getting to know hundreds of their roommates, classmates, and co-workers, most of whom had also recently left China to study abroad. All names in this chapter are pseudonyms, except for those of published authors I cite and those of public figures I never met.

The pursuit of First World citizenship

PRC leaders promulgated the one-child policy in 1979 in order to produce a generation with consumption and education levels similar to those enjoyed by its counterparts in the First World (Fong 2004). Having only one child encouraged parents to concentrate all their resources on providing that child with the best that money could buy. Consequently, those born under the one-child policy often had the high expectations, consumption patterns, and educational attainment characteristic of First World citizens. As Anagnost observed, "The child's body becomes the repository of expended value, presumably justified by its heightened 'quality,' which compensates for the loss of more reproduction" (Anagnost 1997:124). Frequently told by their parents and national leaders that they were the generation with the education, resources, and ambition to bring their families and country into the First World, many Chinese youth I knew spoke as if they themselves were already cultural citizens of the First World, but just unfortunate enough to lack civil, political, and social citizenship in a First World society. While they hoped that this problem would be resolved by the transformation of China into a First World society, they were highly pessimistic about the likelihood of such a transformation occurring within their lifetime. Therefore, many of them wanted to gain the First World citizenship they saw as their birthright by learning First World languages, working for First World employers, and eventually migrating to a First World society, which they hoped would make them part of the transnational elite.

In Benedict Anderson's (1991) view, nationalism developed worldwide once people were able to see themselves as part of an "imagined community" thanks to the print media, a shared language, and most significantly the educational "pilgrimages" that ambitious young people made to national centers. In describing how the Communist Chinese state encouraged its people to imagine themselves as part of the same transnational "Confucian" community as people in the rest of East and Southeast Asia, Aihwa Ong suggested that Anderson's idea of "imagined communities" could also apply to "imaginaries ... brought together by the reconfigurations of global capitalism" (1997:172). Arjun Appadurai argued that mass migration and media are breaking down national boundaries in unprecedented ways (1996). Expanding on these ideas, I address how Chinese youth imagine themselves as social and cultural citizens not only of a transnational "Confucian" community, but also of an even larger, more powerful community of the First World. Some Chinese youth even managed to turn this imagination into reality by winning recognition from First World societies in the form of First World college degrees, employment, and residency rights. Most of the Chinese youth I knew, however, were trapped in the liminal zones between their citizenship dreams and the realities of their marginality.

Anderson noted (1991:54), "There was, to be sure, always a double aspect to the choreography of the great religious pilgrimages: a vast horde of illiterate vernacular-speakers provided the dense, physical reality of the ceremonial passage; while a small segment of literate bilingual adepts drawn from each vernacular community performed the unifying rites, interpreting to their respective followings the meaning of their collective motion." So it was in Dalian, as in other cities in China and the rest of the developing world, from where a small English-speaking elite was drawn for study or work abroad, and for interpreting and exalting an unattainable but easily imagined community of modernity for envious, yearning local communities. Many Chinese youth I knew wanted to become part of that elite. They claimed that pilgrimages to First World societies would not only help them acquire superior social rights and expanded cultural citizenship, but also facilitate efforts to make China part of the First World – a goal central to the responsibilities associated with their Chinese social and cultural citizenship. Ideally, First World citizenship would add to rather than replace their Chinese citizenship. First World citizenship was actually the best way to acquire the kind of ideal Chinese citizenship enjoyed by the upper-quarters residents described by Tianshu Pan (this volume). Many Chinese youth told me that, after they gained full First World citizenship, they would channel First World cultural and economic capital into China by working in transnational businesses and organizations that would help to transform China into a First World society. Some even told me that they hoped to follow in the footsteps of the many influential Chinese political leaders of the 20th century (including Deng Xiaoping, Sun Yat-sen, and Zhou Enlai) who had studied abroad and returned to modernize China from high positions within the Chinese state. These Chinese youth dreamed that their pursuit of First World citizenship would eventually transform them into ideal citizens not only of the First World, but also of China.

What the Chinese youth I knew wanted most was not legal, civil, and political citizenship in a First World society, but rather the prestige, geographic mobility, and high standard of living enjoyed by those who had First World citizenship. Aihwa Ong defined cultural citizenship as "a dual process of self-making and being-made. . . . in shifting fields of power that include the nation-state and the wider world" (Ong and Nonini 1997:738). Building on Ong's definition, I argue that cultural citizenship processes can transcend national boundaries, as individuals are made and make themselves in the context not only of the societies in which they lived and held civil/political citizenship, but also in the context of the capitalist world system. Part of the power of the capitalist world system's neoliberal ideology derives from its claim that anyone who acquired the discipline, skills, and affluence of the First World could become social and cultural citizens of the First World (regardless of where they lived or what was written on their passports). At the same time, even those with First World legal citizenship and residency could be denied First World social and cultural citizenship, as was the case for many of the impoverished Asian refugees Ong studied in the United States (1996; 2003). The civil and political citizenship associated with permanent residency or naturalization documents from First World societies was useful, but not necessary or sufficient, for the attainment of First World social rights and cultural belonging. Those unable or unwilling to trade their Chinese passports for passports issued by First World societies could still become social and cultural citizens of the First World by attaining prestigious careers that would provide them with incomes comparable to those received by professionals and businesspeople in First World societies. Regardless of whether they lived in China or abroad and whether they had Chinese or foreign passports, those who had such careers would command the respect of Chinese and foreigners alike, cross national borders with ease, and enjoy a high standard of living. This kind of social and cultural citizenship was the most difficult as well as the most desirable kind of citizenship to attain, as it was not guaranteed even for those who had attained legal, civil, and political citizenship in a First World society.

Many Chinese youth told me of their strong desire for First World incomes, which could be both a means to and indicator of First World social and cultural citizenship. They often lamented about how much lower PRC incomes were than the incomes available in the First World. The United States federal government's official 1999 poverty line for an American family of three was US$13,880.[4] Yet, according to information collected by China's National Bureau of Statistics from PRC work units, the average 1999 annual salary in the PRC was 8,346 yuan (US$1,008).[5] According to a representative sample survey[6] conducted in PRC cities by China's National Bureau of Statistics in 1999, the average annual per capita income was 5,889 yuan (US$711) for all respondents, 12,148 yuan (US$1,467) for the wealthiest ten percent of respondents, and 2,647 yuan (US$320) for the poorest ten percent of respondents.[7] Of course, the cost of basic necessities such as food and housing was much lower in the PRC than in the First World, and few urban PRC citizens were actually at risk of the starvation and homelessness that would befall someone who earned an average PRC salary while living in a First World country. Yet many luxury goods and services available in the PRC (such as plane tickets, automobiles, electronics, household appliances, clothing with First World brand names, lodging in world-class hotels, and meals at restaurants run by First World corporations) cost at least as much in the PRC as they did in the First World.

First World citizens were more likely than PRC citizens to become part of the super-elite. "There's such a difference between developed and developing countries," junior high student Chen Peng lamented to me in 1998, as we watched a television feature on Internet companies in the U.S. "Why doesn't China have internet entrepreneurs who get rich overnight?"

Moreover, even relatively disadvantaged First World citizens were seen as more advantaged than most PRC citizens. As high school student Chen Junhua told me in 2002, when I asked him why he wanted to go abroad, "My cousin in Ireland is a dishwasher, which is the worst job you can get, but he still made over €1,000 [US$1,000] a month, and he had enough money to buy a car just a few months after he started working in Ireland. If I get a really good job in China, as a white collar office worker, I might make 1,000 yuan [US$121] a month, but you can't buy anything with 1,000 yuan." While the gap between PRC and First World purchasing power had not been so disturbing as under the autarkic, isolationist policies of the Maoist government (1949–1976), it was painfully compelling in the increasingly globalized environment of the post-Mao era in which the Chinese youth I knew were socialized.

In addition to yearning for luxury goods that could only be purchased with First World level incomes, the Chinese youth I knew also yearned for the prestige associated with First World consumption patterns. Commodities and brand names produced by companies from the First World were perceived to be of higher quality than those produced by PRC companies, and even those that were not of higher quality basked in the halo effect of those that were. PRC businesses tried to enhance their appeal by emphasizing the foreign connections (real or fictitious) of their products by putting the flags, maps, place names, and historical figures of developed countries on their signs and advertisements and on the products themselves. Some wealthy people bought brands from the First World rather than brands from the PRC whenever possible, even though foreign brands were more expensive than PRC brands. In 2002, College student Liu Qingmei told me that she periodically went with her friends to Pizza Hut even though she did not like the taste of pizza and felt uncomfortable that each time they went, they spent as much as they would spend for a week's worth of meals at Chinese restaurants. When I asked why she kept going to Pizza Hut even though she did not like the food or the prices, she replied, "I like the environment. There are many wealthy people and foreigners, and when I'm there, it feels like I'm abroad."

Because First World incomes were many times higher than incomes from similar work in the PRC, those who returned from working in the First World were extremely wealthy by PRC standards, as were those who received remittances from family members working in the First World. Even PRC citizens who worked in at least partially foreign-owned companies or in fields such as shipping, trade, travel, translation, and tourism had much higher salaries than their counterparts working for PRC employers who did not deal with the First World. Though legal citizens of the First World who feared illegal immigration made it tremendously difficult for average PRC citizens to get visas to enter First World countries for tourism, business, work, or study, such visas were readily granted to PRC citizens with First World level incomes, records of previous travel to First World societies, and First World friends, relatives, and colleagues who could issue them invitations. Many of the young PRC citizens I knew aimed to gain First World social and cultural citizenship by doing business with people from the First World, or by securing work that offered First World incomes, whether in the PRC or in the First World. "I want to work for a foreign company, or go abroad," high school student Xiong Bo told me in 2000. "There's no future in Chinese work units. They have no money, so they can't pay a good salary even if you work very hard for them. Besides, after China joins the WTO [World Trade Organization], all the Chinese work units will go bankrupt, because their technology and management methods are not as advanced as those abroad, and they won't be able to compete."

Parents were eager to send their children to First World societies. Though most parents I knew in the PRC felt great love and protectiveness toward their only children, their desire to keep their only children close by was often overridden by their desire to help their children gain First World citizenship by going abroad. "I don't want my son to have a life like mine," high school student Long Wende's father told me in 1999. "I have a good job in an office, a white-collar job, and yet I'm always thinking of how to save money. You just can't make a lot of money in a Chinese work unit. I want him to be just like foreigners, and be able to have whatever he wants, and not have to worry about money." Long Wende's parents hoped to send him abroad for college. They had been sending him to expensive private English classes since he was a toddler, and they often bought him English language tapes, books, and movies on Video Compact Discs (VCDs). "I want him to go abroad to study, and stay there if he can get a good job," Long Wende's mother told me. "Or, at the very worst, he can just get a college degree abroad, and let the foreign enterprises fight over him when he comes back to China. In those enterprises, he can make at least 4,000 yuan [US$483] a month for doing the same work as people in Chinese work units who make 1,000 yuan [US$121] a month."

Images of affluence exerted a halo effect on all aspects of the First World. Kalman Applbaum observed that, in their effort to create new markets for their products, transnational corporations are "grounded in a classifying framework in which local people's life situations (demographic characteristics, mentality, and political environment) are evaluated, classified, and incorporated into the Western hierarchy of values for the purposes of making sales" to people worldwide who "can be reached and appealed to with the message of the objective superiority of Company X's products, 'brought to you by' the civilization that made them possible" (Applbaum 2000:275). The Chinese youth I knew accepted this hierarchy and lamented that life in China fell woefully short by its standards.

Dilemmas of citizenship at the margins of Chinese and Western societies

In his reflections on the complexities of citizenship for transnational people, David Harvey wrote that "A diaspora of Chinese business entrepreneurs (armed with a whole set of values drawn from their own civilization's history) operates capitalistically (armed with universalizing Western concepts about wealth, power, and technology) and globally in a world of scattered but tightly bound ethnically distinct Chinese communities. Forming enclaves often isolated from the habits and laws of the host country, these communities provide pools of captive and compliant labor for Chinese entrepreneurs, giving the latter a certain competitive advantage" (Harvey 2000:80). While the transnational entrepreneurs managed to secure First World cultural and social citizenship, their transnational laborers were trapped between the margins of their Chinese homeland and the margins of their adopted First World societies. The Chinese youth I knew dreamed of joining the transnational business entrepreneurs as ideal citizens of the First World as well as of China, but most ended up more like the captive and compliant laborers.

Study abroad was considered most appropriate for young, single, childless high school or college graduates. PRC citizens who were not in this category had great difficulty persuading their families and foreign embassy officials that they were suitable for study abroad. Most of the Chinese youth I knew who studied abroad first left China between the ages of 16 and 25. The process of applying for student visas and admission to First World schools often took several years, during which many applicants put their lives on hold, avoiding dating, marriage, opportunities for further education in China, and jobs that required long-term contracts. To obtain student visas, PRC citizens had to prove to First World embassy officers that they had enough funds to pay for education and living expenses in the First World, enough education and language proficiency to be able to attend college immediately or after a few years of language school in the host country, and no intention of trying to gain permanent residence in the host country. Because few PRC citizens could meet these requirements, visa applications are often rejected. It was common for Chinese youth to pay large fees for Chinese study abroad agencies to connect them with Western schools and obtain paperwork that could facilitate their visa applications.

Nearly all the Chinese youth I met through my academic career in the United States had enough funding (through scholarships, loans, and research or teaching assistantships) from their universities to cover tuition and living expenses. The United States only granted visas to Chinese youth like those I met in the United States: exceptionally talented graduates of China's top schools who had been accepted into American universities with large financial aid packages, extraordinary professionals with job offers from American employers who claimed that no qualified employees could be found in the United States, or extremely wealthy people with enough savings to enable them to live, study, or do business comfortably in the United States. Most of them eventually found elite professional work in the United States or China, and became full citizens of the United States and the First World, while maintaining varying degrees of Chinese social, cultural, and sometimes legal, civil, and political citizenship. In many ways, they were the ideal to which the Chinese youth at the center of my research aspired. But this ideal was extraordinarily difficult to attain. Few of the Chinese youth I met in Australia, China, the Republic of Ireland, and the United Kingdom had even attended college, much less graduated from prestigious universities, while they were in China. It was common for these Chinese youth to attend English language schools when they first entered a Western society, trying to gain enough English language proficiency to win admission to a Western college. Few managed to secure scholarships or white collar work while abroad. Those who did not have unusually wealthy parents could not attend college until they managed to earn and save enough money to pay the high college tuitions Western countries charged those who lacked legal citizenship. Most of them ended up spending far more time and money in language schools than they had intended, because of the difficulty of saving enough money and/or acquiring enough English language proficiency while spending most of their time working for minimum wage at menial jobs.

Many Chinese youth studying abroad told me that they were ambivalent about their goals. They were torn between wanting to settle permanently in the First World, wanting to earn enough money from part-time (or illegal full-time) work while studying in the First World to start lucrative businesses in China, and wanting to earn First World college degrees that could help them win prestigious, high-paying jobs after returning to China. Most hoped to accomplish all of these goals, and become part of the transnational elite with flexible citizenship. It was common, however, for these goals to be mutually contradictory. Spending too much time working and too little money on education could hinder efforts to earn a Western degree that could enable one to get a prestigious, high-paying job in China or the West. Spending too much time and money on education could hinder efforts to accumulate enough savings to start a business after returning to China. Permanent immigration often required strategies such as petitioning for political asylum, marrying a citizen of the host country, or bearing a child in the host country; such strategies sometimes conflicted with the social, cultural, and political responsibilities of Chinese citizenship, and could take time away from work and study as well as hinder future efforts to return to China. The Chinese youth I knew paid a high price for their ambivalence, as it caused them to linger between the margins of their homeland and the margins of the societies in which they sojourned. Though they hoped to deploy their flexible citizenship strategically to enjoy the best of all worlds, it was more common for them to drift between worlds. Like the minority students Lin Yi studied in China, the transnational Chinese youth I studied abroad feared that they would not be able to pursue superior citizenship statuses without losing the inferior but personally valued citizenship statuses they held while growing up.

Some Chinese youth who went abroad had parents who were cadres in state organs or enterprises. These youth could easily have followed in their parents' footsteps, but they chose to move themselves to the margins of

Chinese society in preparation for their pilgrimages to the First World. While in the PRC, they avoided political meetings, politics courses, and the rigorous application process to join the Chinese Communist Party because they felt such things were a waste of time that could be better used in the pursuit of their transnational ambitions. In many cases, they refrained from pursuing further education or jobs that required long-term contracts while they waited (sometimes for years) for a visa to study in a First World society. In the meantime, they immersed themselves in English language studies and tried to learn as much as they could about First World societies. Their parents usually encouraged their transnational ambitions, while expressing ambivalence about the apparent lack of patriotism that accompanied such ambitions.

This ambivalence was apparent when I had dinner in 2002 at the home of Song Lianlian, a Communist Party member and low-level cadre in a bureau of Dalian City's government, and her 16-year-old son Hu Chengjun. When we talked about the 1997 return of Hong Kong from British to Chinese rule, he expressed skepticism about the benefits for Hong Kong. "Hong Kong is too good, so it's not worth it for them," he said. "Our government is poor and corrupt. I wish England had colonized all of China, and not just Hong Kong. Then we'd be as good as Hong Kong."

"How can you say that?" Song Lianlian protested. "That's slave mentality! Don't say that at school, or you'll get into fights. I haven't taught you well. We should love our country." Song Lianlian later told me that she found Hu Chengjun's statements disturbing, but that it was partly her own fault for telling him all his life that she planned to send him to college in the United Kingdom. Though she considered herself highly patriotic and often tried to temper Hu Chengjun's complaints about China, she had also inundated him with English language tutors, movies, and reading materials to prepare him for his future sojourn abroad. She told me that she believed this approach caused Hu Chengjun to "worship foreigners" and speak "as if he were an Englishman and not Chinese." She worried that his attitude would get in him in trouble with more patriotic teachers and classmates. His disdain for the Chinese state and admiration of the United Kingdom was unusual even by the standards of others his age, most of whom praised First World societies and complained about China but also condemned colonialism and strongly supported the PRC's claims to disputed or colonized territories like Hong Kong, Taiwan, and Macao. Song Lianlian also worried that her son would be disappointed once he actually went to the United Kingdom, because it could not possibly be as wonderful as he imagined it would be.

It was common for young people preparing to leave China to develop passionate obsessions with the supposed virtues of the societies they intended to join, as well as cynical attitudes about China. This tended to arouse the anger of others around them, who called it a "Chinese tragedy" that so many Chinese youth wanted to go abroad. As Rachel Murphy (this volume) and Yingchi Chu pointed out (this volume), Chinese ideas of legal, civil, and political citizenship were much more strongly focused on the responsibility to remain loyal and obedient to the Chinese state than on the legal, civil, and political rights of the individual. Most of the transnational Chinese youth I knew saw this concept of citizenship as an unfair deal, but still took their patriotic responsibility very seriously and felt uncomfortable when others accused them of betraying it. Some who were trying to get visas to go abroad emphasized to their friends and family members that they intended to return, but they were often met with cynicism and disbelief. "I want to go abroad and learn the most advanced science, and come back to make China strong and prosperous" college student Liu Ling told her friend in 2000, while the three of us were conversing about reasons for going abroad. "You're just blowing hot air," Liu Ling's friend scoffed. "I'd better say goodbye to you forever at the airport, because once you're living the good life abroad, you'll never want to come back."

Liu Ling left to take English language classes (and eventually attend college, she hoped) in the United Kingdom in 2002, but still has not returned to China, even for a visit. Like many other Chinese students abroad, Liu Ling feared that visits home would be prohibitively expensive and disruptive. She told me that a trip to China would not only set her back financially due to the high price of the plane ticket, but also jeopardize her job as a server at a fast food restaurant, since she was not sure if her employer would be willing to take her back if she quit to visit China during summer vacation. She still insisted, however, that she hoped to return to China after completing a college degree in the United Kingdom. "But I don't know if I can get good work in China," she added.

Like most Chinese youth studying abroad, Liu Ling defined good work as a career which would pay her as much as she could earn in the First World. In China, this kind of work was usually reserved for high officials in the Chinese government, professors at a few elite universities, owners of large businesses, and high-level employees of transnational companies and organizations who had college degrees as well as legal residency or citizenship statuses in First World societies. Such work was so rare that it was only available to a small, unusually talented, wealthy, or well-connected minority of the already elite minority that went abroad. Study abroad could help others get better work in China than they would have gotten without going abroad, but the incomes from such work could still be much lower than what they could earn from even the lowest-paid jobs in the First World. Even ordinary middle-class work in China would be out of reach for those who went abroad without first getting college degrees in China, but lacked the money and English language skills to get college degrees in the First World. "We want to return to our country, but we can't," 20-year-old Yang Yi told me in 2003 when I visited him in Australia, where he was taking English language classes in the hope of eventually enrolling at a university. "If we go back and don't get good jobs, we could work all our lives and not earn as much as what our parents already spent to send us here. Our old classmates will have finished college, but we'll just be high school graduates. Maybe we wouldn't even be able to get into a Chinese university."

Even as their absence from China eroded their Chinese social and cultural citizenship, most of the PRC citizens at the center of my research found themselves unable to move beyond the margins of the Western societies they lived in. Like the rural migrant students studied by Lu Wang (this volume) and the mainland New Arrivals studied by Nicole Newendorp (this volume), Chinese students in Australia, Ireland, and the United Kingdom were stigmatized by their outsider status. As non-citizens in these Western societies, they lacked access to many of the social welfare benefits (such as public housing, poverty relief stipends, and free or subsidized education) enjoyed by citizens, and faced constraints not faced by citizens. Chinese students complained bitterly about how the education and welfare benefits of wealthy First World countries' citizens was subsidized by tuition money and taxes from students from poor countries like China. Chinese youth on student visas had to pay taxes and limit their work hours to those allowed by their student visas, or work extra hours illegally for employers who felt free to exploit them. They had to stay enrolled in language schools and meet school attendance quotas to avoid deportation. In many cases, limited English proficiency, fear of threats to their visa status, and lack of understanding about the legal system prevented them from taking advantage of even the limited legal protections and social welfare benefits that were available to them. Recognizing that most Chinese youth lacked the knowledge and political and financial security to file complaints or lawsuits, landlords and employers sometimes cheated them of money or discriminated against them in illegal ways. Many Chinese students told me that landlords had illegally evicted them, raised their rents, refused to make repairs or improve poor housing conditions, or kept their rental deposits, and that employers had ignored laws that guaranteed workers minimum wages, working conditions, and overtime, but also that challenging such landlords and employers through the legal system was too difficult to be worth the risk, expense, and stress. Some Chinese youths in the Republic of Ireland told me that Irish children had thrown stones at them, causing them to plan their routes with an eye towards avoiding areas with large concentrations of such children. It was difficult for Chinese youths to get white-collar work because they lacked the English proficiency required for such work. Even Chinese youths with high English proficiency faced significant discrimination and had difficulty competing with natives for white-collar jobs. I knew several PRC citizens who had earned graduate degrees in Western countries who were nevertheless working as cooks, waiters, or store clerks in those countries. Though most Chinese youths studying abroad came from elite Chinese families, they often lived in poverty in Western countries, rooming in crowded conditions with other Chinese youths in impoverished, high-crime urban neighborhoods or in inconveniently located suburban neighborhoods that added high transportation costs and long commute times to their already overburdened budgets and schedules. Many complained about hunger. This was not only due to lack of money to buy food, but also due to their lack of appetite for the inexpensive Western foods they could afford, and to their lack of time to shop or cook due to transportation limitations and long school and work hours.

Marriage to a Western citizen was one means of securing social/cultural as well as civil/political citizenship in a Western society, but pursuit of such marriage was fraught with risk. Because Western as well as Chinese gender ideologies deemed it more acceptable for lower-status women to date or marry higher-status men than vice-versa, almost all the PRC citizens I knew or heard of who dated or married Western citizens were women. While PRC citizens who dated non-PRC citizens of Chinese descent faced no more approbation than lower-status PRC citizens who dated more elite PRC citizens, PRC citizens who dated across ethnic lines risked unpleasant reputational and practical consequences.

The idea of marriage between Chinese and non-Chinese was not necessarily stigmatized. During my research in China, I sometimes heard female (and, more rarely, male) PRC citizens in China as well as abroad talking about wanting to marry foreigners, and they were not always reproached by other PRC citizens for such talk. Some PRC citizens asked me to introduce Americans who might be interested in marrying them, their children, their relatives, or their friends. I also heard some PRC citizens speak with approval and admiration of successful marriages between Chinese women and non-Chinese men that they knew or had heard of. Mark "Dashan" Rowswell, a white Canadian famed throughout China for his televised comedy acts and English lessons, even made a cameo appearance with his Chinese wife and their child, along with other young Chinese celebrity couples, in a nationally televised performance of a song about family reunions in the Spring Festival variety show of 1999 (Che Xing 1999). The performance implied that Rowswell and his wife were just another one of many admirable, culturally Chinese couples visiting their parents (symbolized by two elderly Chinese couples). Most of the PRC citizens I knew in China and abroad considered marriage between Chinese and non-Chinese acceptable as long as it followed the same cultural scripts that urban Chinese youth were supposed to follow when marrying each other. These scripts required that spouse-seeking be the primary purpose of dating, that premarital chastity be maintained (particularly by women, but also to a lesser extent by men), that the age and socioeconomic differences between husband and wife not be too great, that there would be enough personal compatibility between spouses to enable a companionate marriage, and that both spouses would be able to maintain ties to their natal families and fulfill their filial obligations. The problem faced by PRC citizens I knew or heard of who pursued marriage with non-Chinese, however, was that such pursuits could easily deviate from Chinese cultural scripts, and could also easily be misinterpreted as deviating from those scripts even when they did not.

Chinese women were suspected by their fellow PRC citizens of compromising their chastity to attract non-Chinese men, who were presumed to be more likely to demand premarital sex than Chinese men. I often heard Western and Chinese men and women criticize what they perceived as loveless, mercenary romances between Western men seeking a young, submissive sexual partner and Chinese women seeking Western citizenship, particularly in cases where the men were much older than the women. As Nicole Constable (2003) and Karen Kelsky (2001) observed, negative stereotypes about romances between Asian women and Western men were common both in the West and in Asia, portraying the Western man in such a romance as a shallow playboy, patriarchal oppressor, or besotted dupe, and his Chinese female partner as a promiscuous mistress, submissive victim, or calculating manipulator. Like Constable and Kelsky, I found that many individuals in such romances belied the stereotypes. Even these individuals, however, sometimes experienced shame, guilt, and ostracism because of the stereotypes and those who believed in them. I also knew of cases that seemed to reflect some of the cultural and sexual tensions at the heart of the stereotypes. While Chinese stereotypes of non-Chinese men's casual attitudes towards sex were exaggerated, they also reflected awareness of the risks faced by Chinese women trying to use romance as a strategy for securing Western citizenship. The language barrier was a significant obstacle to successful relationships. Cultural differences and gender-based double standards also heightened opportunities for conflict and misunderstandings. Because of Western cultural norms that de-emphasized the importance of chastity (particularly for men) and because of their relatively secure position as citizens of their own societies, Western men were more likely to view dating, sex, and romance as enjoyable for their own sake, and not necessarily as a means to marriage. They were also more likely to disdain the idea of marriage as an instrumental means to advantages like citizenship. Chinese women, on the other hand, were more likely to see marriage as the primary (and often the only) reason for dating – a perspective that reflected not only their strong desire to secure citizenship through marriage, but also ideas about the importance of women's chastity that were key components of Chinese standards of social and cultural citizenship and, to a lesser extent, a part of Western constructions of gender relations as well. Chinese women were also more likely to be comfortable with the idea of marriage as a means to socioeconomic advantages, due to a Chinese cultural model of marriage that stressed social and economic factors over emotional ones. As 23-year-old Lin Yuan told me in 2000 while she was dating a Canadian man in China, "Of course I want to go to Canada, and that's part of why I like him, but it's not the only reason. When I was looking for a match, I was just like anyone else, looking for someone who had good conditions and who I also liked. My Ma married my Pa because his parents were poor farmers, so he could protect her [from political persecution due to her parents' classification as landlords] during the Cultural Revolution. Now people all say they want to marry people with good jobs and good educations. So why is it different if I want to marry a Canadian?"

Lin Yuan was devastated when her Canadian boyfriend broke up with her, claiming that he was not ready for marriage. Not only had her romance failed to gain her Western citizenship, it had also caused other PRC citizens to suspect her of violating standards of patriotism and chastity associated with Chinese social and cultural citizenship. Though she had not discussed her sex life with me, some of her acquaintances told me that they had heard that she had sex with her Canadian boyfriend, that many people assumed that she unpatriotically preferred Western men over Chinese men, and that Chinese men would now be cautious about marrying her because they would fear that she was promiscuous and would run off with a foreigner at the first opportunity. While I had doubts about how Lin Yuan's acquaintances could have known about her sex life, it was clear that her romance with a non-Chinese had damaged her reputation. Moreover, because romances with non-Chinese were often seen as detrimental to the responsibilities of Chinese social and cultural citizenship, the gossip about Lin Yuan seemed even harsher than gossip about Chinese women who had premarital sex with Chinese men.

Many PRC citizens I met in China and abroad spoke with disdain about PRC women who spent a lot of time in bars and cafes in China that catered to foreigners, and even likened such behavior to prostitution. Several PRC citizens told me about Chinese female acquaintances who had been arrested in Chinese hotels after spending the night in hotels with their non-Chinese boyfriends, and about how Chinese strangers hurled insults and stones at Chinese women and non-Chinese men who walked hand in hand down Chinese streets. Many Chinese youth I met in Western countries also seemed to condemn Chinese women who dated non-Chinese men. In 2003, when I lived in a house in the United Kingdom with seven men and women in their 20s who had recently arrived from China, I found that 25-year-old Hu Yan seemed to be disliked by many of her housemates, who said she was "strange," had "problems," "doesn't respect herself," and "thinks she's better than us." Hu Yan told me that her housemates' disdain toward her resulted from a combination of prejudice against non-Chinese and envy at the advantages she gained by dating non-Chinese British citizens. "Chinese people are envious," Hu Yan explained to me. "If you're lucky, Chinese people say 'why are you so lucky when you're no better than me?' They say I'll have a bad result if I keep dating foreigners, but how do they know? They're just envious."

Even romances between Chinese and non-Chinese that did lead to marriage were suspect. There were no such marriages among the Chinese youth I studied, but I did hear them gossip, often with disapproval, about such marriages among others in their social networks. Gossipers seemed at least partly motivated by the envy Hu Yan complained about, as they implied that women who used marriage as a shortcut to Western citizenship were less deserving of than those (like the gossipers themselves) who were trying to earn Western citizenship through academic and professional achievement. Their gossip also focused on the presumed mercenary nature of marriages between Chinese women and Western men. While Chinese people were more likely than Westerners to consider the pursuit of social and economic advantages an acceptable consideration in romance, many Chinese people I knew were still disdainful of romances that seemed based purely on the exchange of youth and beauty for practical advantages, without any regard for interpersonal compatibility. Romances between Chinese women and much older Western men were often placed in this category by people in the couple's Chinese and Western social networks.

There was also a nationalistic component to Chinese disapproval of romances between Chinese women and Western men. Some PRC citizens who expressed such disapproval told me that Chinese women who dated Western men insulted Chinese national pride by disdaining Chinese men. This idea seemed based partly on Chinese discourses of nationalism that associated Western imperialism with the emasculation of Chinese men (Brownell and Wasserstrom 2002; Louie 2002; Zhong Xueping 1994), and partly on the persisting significance of virilocal, patrilineal, androcentric Chinese kinship models that equated marriage with the bride's abandonment of her natal kin and absorption into her husband's lineage (Cohen 1976; Greenhalgh 1985; Sangren 1984; Watson and Ebrey 1986; Watson 1996). Though they were increasingly irrelevant among families in urban China that could live in close proximity to the parents of the wife as well as of the husband (Davis 1989; Davis and Harrell 1990; Fong 2002, 2004), such kinship models persisted in the Chinese countryside, partly because village exogamy, long distances between villages, and a lack of vehicles and public transportation meant that married daughters tended to live too far away to maintain close relationships with their natal families. Some Chinese women studying abroad told me that they would face a similar problem if they married Westerners. Geographic distance was a factor that could make it difficult for PRC citizens who married Westerners to maintain ties with their parents and motherland. Marrying a Westerner could entail a commitment to spend the rest of one's life in a Western country, with only occasional visits to China. Despite their desire for Western citizenship, many Chinese women were not ready to give up the option of settling permanently in China. Because of the problems that could result from romances with non-Chinese men, most Chinese women I knew avoided such romances. As 23-year-old Du Juan told me in Ireland in 2003, "I want to stay in Ireland, but I don't want to marry an Irishman. I want to marry a Chinese man even in Ireland, because I am Chinese and will always be Chinese."

Unlike in the United States, children born in Australia or the United Kingdom to non-citizen parents were not granted legal citizenship. Prior to 2003, Chinese youth could expand their access to Irish social and cultural citizenship by giving birth in the Republic of Ireland, which granted legal citizenship to every child born in its territory and granted non-citizen parents of legal citizens the right to live in Ireland. On January 23, 2003, however, the Irish Supreme Court ruled that non-citizen parents of Irish citizens did not have the right to stay in Ireland; on June 11, 2004, Irish voters overwhelmingly approved a referendum to insert a clause into the Irish Constitution that limited Irish citizenship to those who at the time of birth had at least one parent who was an Irish citizen or was entitled to be an Irish citizen. When I lived with Chinese youths studying in the Republic of Ireland in June–July 2003, I met some PRC citizens who had become pregnant or given birth in Ireland. In some cases, pregnancies were initially accidents that became permanent because abortion for non-medical, non-rape reasons was illegal in the Republic of Ireland, it was difficult for PRC citizens leave the Republic of Ireland on short notice because unplanned return visits to China could jeopardize their finances, jobs, schooling, and visa status in Ireland, and PRC citizens needed to go through complicated visa applications to enter nearby countries where abortion was legal. In other cases, pregnancies had been planned, and the desire to acquire Irish citizenship for the children and possibly the parents were among the factors that led to the planned pregnancies. In all these cases, parents and expecting parents were alarmed at the impending contraction of the citizenship rights they had hoped to acquire for themselves and their child.

An even more controversial means to legal citizenship in a Western society entailed applying for political asylum. This approach involved a difficult, uncertain, time-consuming, and expensive legal process during which the applicant tried to prove to a Western government that he or she would face political persecution upon return to China. Participation in the 1989 demonstrations against the PRC government or in the Falungong meditation cult banned by the PRC government seemed to be the most readily recognized by Western governments as legitimate reasons for needing political asylum, since participants in these movements were relatively few and could sometimes have their participation confirmed by other participants who had already been granted political asylum. Some PRC citizens have tried to apply for political asylum because they had criticized the Chinese government or had given birth to more than one child, in violation of the one-child policy, but such applications were rarely successful, since Western government officials were fearful of granting political asylum for actions that could be performed by a large proportion of the Chinese population. None of the Chinese youths I knew told me that they had applied for political asylum, though some told me about distant acquaintances who had. The Chinese youths I knew and others in their social circles were too young to have participated in the 1989 demonstrations, so most of the political asylum applicants I heard about were members of Falungong. Because all the Chinese students I knew wanted to maintain at least some aspects of their PRC citizenship, they were wary of associating with Falungong members or others who took public stances against the Chinese government. Gaining Western citizenship as a political refugee carried a high price, as it could prevent one from returning to China even for visits, and could be seen as a betrayal of the responsibilities of Chinese social/cultural as well as legal/civil/political citizenship. Some PRC citizens I spoke with in Western societies who were critical of the Chinese government were also critical of other Chinese youths who were applying for asylum. As Meng Jiangbo, a 24-year-old Chinese student in Ireland, told me in 2003, "I do have criticisms of the Chinese government, but I think applying for political asylum is too much. There are people who exaggerate just because they want to stay in Ireland, but they are betraying their own country. No matter how much your mother beats you, she is still your mother and you can't abandon her."

Securing a white-collar job in the West was the ideal way to gain Western citizenship while hanging on to Chinese citizenship. In addition to providing the income and prestige necessary for becoming a social/cultural citizen of the West, a white collar career in a Western society could make one eligible for permanent residency, and eventually legal, civil, and political citizenship, in that society. This path to Western citizenship entailed far fewer sacrifices of Chinese citizenship than strategies like marriage to a Westerner or the pursuit of political asylum. Frequent travel to or even residency in China could even be part of the job if one worked for (or owned) a Western company that did business in China. Yet only the highest-achieving and wealthiest Chinese students managed to secure white-collar work in the First World.

Conclusion: the price of flexible citizenship

Though all the Chinese students I knew hoped to attain some aspect of Western citizenship by studying abroad, most were not willing to take measures that could close off the possibility of returning to live as permanent residents of China. They told me that they wanted to return to China for a variety of reasons, including patriotism, a belief that they would be able to get more prestigious jobs in China than they could get abroad, a belief that they would have greater purchasing power in China than abroad, even if their income in China might be lower, a preference for lifestyles in China over lifestyles abroad, and a desire to be close to their friends, relatives, and especially parents (most of whom were too old or poorly educated to ever gain any kind of citizenship in the West). Yet they found their Chinese social/cultural citizenship as well as their Chinese legal/civil/political citizenship slipping away as they prolonged their quest for Western citizenship. The insidiousness of this process was illustrated by the narrative of He Jianpeng, a 35-year-old who at the age of 21 had left a college instructor job in China to study English in Australia, where he became a cook and eventually a small business owner. He told me in 2004 that, despite his hard-won Australian legal, civil, political, and social/cultural citizenship, he often felt "more miserable than the rural migrants in Chinese cities, because at least they could speak the same language as the people around them." When I asked him if he would make the same decision to go abroad if he could do it over again, he responded:

No, I would have stayed in China. I had a good job and my life would have been quite good. I experienced too much bitterness here. When Chinese people ask me whether they should go abroad, I tell them not to do it. It's good to visit other countries, but you shouldn't spend half your life in one country and the other half in another. I spent most of my youth eating bitterness. For my first five years in Australia, I kept trying to improve my situation. I wanted to return to my country, but couldn't, because it would make me and my family lose face. I needed to get money before going back. After three months in Australia, I had no money left. I stayed at home, eating instant noodles, staying under the covers trying not to move, because moving would use up more energy and cause me to be hungry again. I went to someone from my hometown and asked to borrow 50 [Australian] dollars so I could eat, promised to repay him as soon as I got a job with more hours. After five years, though, when my situation was finally stable enough to let me return to my country, I was no longer used to it. It had changed so much, I could no longer cross the street. There were so many cars and motorcycles. The air was dirty, and I couldn't get used to it. I couldn't sleep at night, because there were too many people talking. While abroad, I kept thinking of the snacks from street vendors in China, and how delicious they were, but when I went back to China, I saw that the snacks were covered with exhaust fumes from cars and motorcycles on the street, and dishes were washed in dirty water, so I didn't dare eat them. In Australia, I learned to say "can I have the hamburger?" to the waitress, and then "thank you" when she gave me a hamburger. In China, when I did that, the waitress thought I was strange, I must be crazy or I must have just gotten out of prison or come from elsewhere and so must be easily cheated. I can't even be a businessman in China, because I don't have the connections anymore, and you need connections to do any business in China. So now I can't return. If you're in China, don't go out; if you've come out, you can't return.

He Jianpeng was seen by other recent arrivals from the PRC as a model of the flexible citizenship they strove for, but even he was pained by the citizenship tradeoffs he had to make. Don Nonini observed that "Chinese transnationalists seek to elude the localizations imposed on them by nation-state regimes by, above all, moving between national spaces, playing off one nation-state regime against another, seeking tactical advantage" (Nonini and Ong 1997:23). This strategy could potentially open up a brave new world of opportunities unavailable to those who just had PRC citizenship. But the transnational Chinese youth I knew paid a high price for their pursuit of flexible citizenship. Even as they struggled for access to the best of all worlds, they found themselves adrift between the margins of the PRC and the First World.

Notes

1 The research, writing, and revision process for this chapter was funded by a Beinecke Brothers Memorial Fellowship, an Andrew W. Mellon Grant for Predissertation Research, a National Science Foundation Graduate Research Fellowship, a grant from the Weatherhead Center at Harvard University, an Eliot Dissertation Completion Fellowship from Harvard University, a postdoctoral fellowship at the Population Studies Center of the University of Michigan at Ann Arbor, a grant from the Mellon Demography Fund, a grant from the Wenner-Gren Foundation for Anthropological Research, a visiting fellowship from the Center for Research in the Arts, Social Sciences, and Humanities at Cambridge University, a grant from the Harvard Graduate School of Education, and a fellowship from the Spencer Foundation and National Academy of Education.
2 I spent June–August, 1997, August 1998–May 2000, June–July, 2002, and April–May, 2004 in China. I lived in urban Dalian during most of this time, though I also made brief visits to Beijing, Guangzhou, Hong Kong, Shanghai, Shenyang, Tianjin, and several rural villages near urban Dalian.
3 Throughout this paper, I convert Chinese yuan to U.S. dollars at the rate of 8.28 yuan = 1 U.S. dollar when discussing incomes and expenses. This was the approximate currency conversion rate prevalent between 1995 and 2004 (Goldstein 2004; Guojia Tongji Ju [National Bureau of Statistics] 1998:940; Guojia Tongji Ju [National Bureau of Statistics] 2000:885; Guojia Tongji Ju [National Bureau of Statistics] 2001:895). The conversions I present are rough estimates that do not account for inflation or daily fluctuations in exchange rates. All monetary figures have been rounded off to the nearest whole number.
4 (Office of the Federal Register 1999:13428–13430).
5 (Guojia Tongji Ju [National Bureau of Statistics] 2001:135).
6 $N = 36,000$.
7 (Guojia Tongji Ju [National Bureau of Statistics] 2001:313, 315, 319).

Bibliography

Abelmann, Nancy. 1996. *Echoes of the Past, Epics of Dissent: A South Korean Social Movement*. Berkeley, CA: University of California Press.

Alpermann, Björn. 2001. 'The Post-Election Administration of Chinese Villages', *The China Journal* (46): 45–67.

Anagnost, Ann. 1997. *National Past-times: Narratives, Representation and Power in Modern China*. Durham, NC: Duke University Press.

Anagnost, Ann. 1995. 'A Surfeit of Bodies: Population and the Rationality of the State in Post-Mao China', in *Conceiving the New World Order: The Global Politics of Reproduction*, eds Faye D. Ginsburg and Rayna Rapp. Berkeley, CA: University of California Press, pp. 22–41.

Anderson, Benedict. 1991. *Imagined Communities: Reflections on the Origin and Spread of Nationalism*. Revised Edition. London: Verso.

Appadurai, Arjun. 1996. *Modernity at Large: Cultural Dimensions of Globalization*. Minneapolis, MN: Minnesota University Press.

Appardurai, Arjun. 1988. 'Putting Hierarchy in Its Place', *Cultural Anthropology* 3 (1): 36–49.

Applbaum, Kalman. 2000. 'Crossing Borders: Globalization as Myth and Charter in American Transnational Consumer Marketing', *American Ethnologist* 27 (2): 257–282.

Applbaum, Kalman. 1996. 'The Endurance of Neighborhood Organizations in a Japanese Commuter City', *Urban Anthropology* 25 (1): 1–39.

Bahro, Rudolf. 1978. *The Alternatives in Eastern Europe*. London: Verso.

Bakken, Børge. 2000. *The Exemplary Society*. Oxford: Oxford University Press.

Barbalet, J.M. 1988. *Citizenship: Rights, Struggle, and Class Inequality*. Minneapolis, MN: University of Minnesota Press.

Barker, Rodney. 2001. *Legitimating Identities: the Self-Representation of Rulers and Subjects*. Cambridge: Cambridge University Press.

Beijing Committee for Minmeng Party. 2000. 'Recommendations on Improving Education of Migrant Children', *Internal Report 2*.

Bendix, Reinhard. 1964. *Nation-Building and Citizenship*. New York: John Wiley & Sons.

Bestor, Theodore C. 1989. *Neighborhood Tokyo*. Stanford, CA: Stanford University Press.

Blecher, Marc and Vivienne Shue. 2001. 'Into Leather: State-led Development and the Private Sector in Xinji', *The China Quarterly* 166: 368–393.

Blum, Susan D. 2002. 'Rural China and the WTO', *Journal of Contemporary China* 11 (32): 459–472.

Borneman, John. 1997. *Settling Accounts: Violence, Justice, and Accountability in Postsocialist Europe*. Princeton, NJ: Princeton University Press.

Bourdieu, Pierre. 1999. 'Rethinking the State: Genesis and Structure of the Bureaucratic Field', in *State/Culture: State-Formation after the Cultural Turn*. Ithaca, NY: Cornell University Press, pp. 53–75.

Brownell, Susan and Jeffrey N. Wasserstrom, eds. 2002. *Chinese Femininities/ Chinese Masculinities*. Berkeley, CA: University of California Press.

Caldeira, Teresa. 2000. *City of Walls: Crime, Segregation, and Citizenship in São Paulo*. Berkeley, CA: University of California Press.

Cao Jinqing. 2004. *China Along the Yellow River* (translated by Nicky Harmann). London: Routledge.

Che Xing. 1999. *Chang Huijia Kankan [Visit Home Often]*. Hebei: Hebei Sheng Juyuan [Hebei Province Theater].

Chow, Nelson. 1997. 'China', in *International Handbook on Social Work Theory and Practice*, eds Nazneen Mayadas, Thomas Watts, and Doreen Elliot. Westport, CT: Greenwood Press.

Cohen, Myron L. 1993. 'Cultural and Political Inventions in Modern China: The Case of the Chinese "Peasant"', *Daedalus* 122 (1–2): 151–170.

Cohen, Myron L. 1976. *House United, House Divided: The Chinese Family in Taiwan*. New York: Columbia University Press.

Constable, Nicole. 2003. *Romance on a Global Stage: Pen Pals, Virtual Ethnography, and 'Mail Order' Marriages*. Berkeley, CA: University of California Press.

Constable, Nicole. 1999. 'At Home but Not at Home: Filipina Naratives of Ambivalent Returns', *Cultural Anthropology* 14 (2): 203–228.

Cornwall, Abdrea and John Gaventa. 2000. 'From Users and Choosers to Makers and Shapers', *IDS Bulletin* 31 (4).

Croll, Elisabeth. 1999. 'Social Welfare Reform: Trends and Tensions', *China Quarterly* 159: 684–699.

Dahrendorf, Rolf. 1994. 'Citizenship and Beyond: The Social Dynamics of an Idea', in *Citizenship: Critical Concepts*, eds Bryan S. Turner and Peter Hamilton, Vol. 2. London: Routledge, pp. 292–308.

Davidson, Alastair. 1999. 'Never the Twain Shall Meet? Europe, Asia and the Citizen', in *Globalization and Citizenship in the Asia-Pacific*, eds Alastair Davidson and Kathleen Weekley. London: Macmillan, pp. 221–242.

Davin, Delia. 1999. *Internal Migration in Contemporary China*. London: Macmillan.

Davis, Deborah. 1989. 'My Mother's House', in *Unofficial China: Popular Culture and Thought in the People's Republic*, eds E. Perry Link, Richard Madsen and Paul Pickowicz. Boulder, CO: Westview Press, pp. 88–100.

Davis, Deborah and Stevan Harrell, eds. 1990. *Family Strategies in Post-Mao China*. Berkeley, CA: University of California Press.

de Certeau, Michel. 1984. *The Practice of Everyday Life*, Berkeley, CA: University of California Press.

Delanty, Gerard. 2000. *Citizenship in a Global Age: Society, Culture, Politics*. Buckingham: Open University Press.

Delman, Jorgen. 1993. *Agricultural Extension in Renshou County, China: A Case Study of Bureaucratic Intervention and Agricultural Innovation and Change*. Hamburg: Institut fur Asienkunde.

Development Research Centre of the State Council. 2000. 'Marginalized Basic Education – preliminary investigation of schools for children of migrants', in *Beijing. Internal references*, No. 49, General No. 1227.

Devereux, Stephen and Sarah Cook. 2000. 'Does Social Policy Meet Social Needs?', *IDS Bulletin* 31 (4).

Douglas, Mary. 1966. *Purity and Danger: An Analysis of the Concepts of Pollution and Taboo*. London: Routledge and Kegan Paul.

Dower, Nigel and John Williams, eds. 2002. *Global Citizenship: A Critical Reader*. Edinburgh: Edinburgh University Press.

Duan Chenrong. 2000. 'Importance must be given to the education of children of migrants', research report.

Duan Lihua and Zhou Min. 1999. Study on the issues around education of migrant children, *Contemporary Primary and Secondary School Education* (*xiandan zhongxiaoxue Jiaoyu*), No. 2.

Edin, Maria. 2000. *Market Forces and Communist Power: Local Political Institutions and Economic Development in China*. Uppsala: Uppsala University Press.

Escobar, Arturo. 1995. *Encountering Development: The Making and Unmaking of the Third World*. Princeton, NJ: Princeton University Press.

Falk, Richard. 2002. 'An Emergent Matrix of Citizenship', in *Global Citizenship: A Critical Reader*, eds Nigel Dower and John Williams. Edinburgh: Edinburgh University Press, pp. 15–29.

Fei, Xiaotong. 1989. 'Zhonghua Minzu de Duoyuan Yiti Geju (Configuration of Plurality and Unity of the Chinese Nation)', in *Zhonghua Minzu Duoyuan Yiti Geju* (Configuration of Plurality and Unity of Chinese Nation), eds Fei Xiaotong, Gubao, Chen Liankai and Jia Jingyan. Beijing: Zhongyang Minzu Xueyuan Chubanshe (Central Nationalities Institute Press), pp. 1–36.

Feng Yuan. 2000. 'Children of casual workers also have dreams of receiving education', *China Women's News*, (1 November), p. 5.

Follesdal, Andreas. 2002. 'Citizenship: European and Global', in *Global Citizenship: A Critical Reader*, eds Nigel Dower and John Williams. Edinburgh: University Press, pp. 71–83.

Fong, Vanessa L. 2002. 'China's One-Child Policy and the Empowerment of Urban Daughters', *American Anthropologist* 104 (4): 1098–1109.

Fong, Vanessa. 2004. *Only Hope: Coming of Age under China's One-Child Policy*. Palo Alto, CA: Stanford University Press.

Foucault, Michel. 1991. 'Governmentality', in *The Foucault Effect: Studies in Governmentality*, eds Graham Burchell, Colin Gordon and Peter Miller. Chicago, IL: University of Chicago Press, pp. 87–104.

Foucault, Michel. 1980. *Power/Knowledge*. New York: Pantheon Books.

Foucault, Michel. 1977. *Discipline and Punish: The Birth of the Prison*. New York: Pantheon Books.

Gibson, Margaret A. 1988. *Accommodation without Assimilation: Sikh Immigrants in an American High School*. Ithaca, NY: Cornell University Press.

Gladney, Dru C. 1999. 'Making Muslims in China: Education, Islamicization and Representation', in *China's National Minority Education: Culture, Schooling, and Development*, ed. Gerard A. Postiglione. New York and London: Falmer Press, pp. 55–94.

Goldfarb, Brian. 2002. *Visual Pedagogy*. Durham, NC: Duke University Press.

Goldman, Merle and Elizabeth J. Perry, eds. 2002. *Changing Meanings of Citizenship in Modern China*. Cambridge, MA: Harvard University Press.

Goldman, Merle and Elizabeth Perry. 2002. 'Introduction: Political Citizenship in Modern China', in *Changing Meanings of Citizenship in Modern China*, eds Merle Goldman and Elizabeth Perry. Cambridge, MA: Harvard University Press, pp. 1–22.

Goldstein, Melvyn C. 1998. 'Introduction', in *Buddhism in Contemporary Tibet: Religious Revival and Cultural Identity*, eds Melvyn C. Goldstein and Matthew T. Kapstein. Berkeley, CA: University of California Press, pp. 1–14.

Goldstein, Morris. 2004. Adjusting China's Exchange Rate Policies, Dalian, China. International Monetary Fund Seminar on China's Foreign Exchange System.

Gottschang, Suzanne. 2001. 'The Consuming Mother: Infant Feeding and the Feminine Body in Urban China', in *China Urban: Ethnographies of Urban China*, eds Nancy Chen, Constance Clark, Suzanne Gottschang, and Lyn Jeffrey. Durham, NC: Duke University Press.

Government of Kaiyuan District. 2000. 'Making efforts on solving the problems in the education of migrant children', research report.

Greenhalgh, Susan. 1985. 'Sexual Stratification: The Other Side of "Growth with Equity"', *Population and Development Review* 11: 265–314.

GRPB and GTRSKT (Guowuyuan Renkou Pucha Bangongshi, Guojia Tongjiju Renkou he Shehui Keji Tongjisi (Population Census Office under the State Council and Department of Population, Social, Science and Technology Statistics, National Bureau of Statistics of China)). 2002. *Zhongguo 2000 Nian Renkou Pucha Ziliao (Tabulation on the 2000 Population Census of the People's Republic of China)*. Beijing: Zhongguo Tongji Chubanshe (China Statistics Press).

Guojia Tongji Ju [National Bureau of Statistics]. 1998. *Zhongguo Tongji Nianjian [China Statistical Yearbook], 1998*. Beijing: Zhongguo Tongji Chubanshe [China Statistics Press].

Guojia Tongji Ju. 2000. *Zhongguo Tongji Nianjian [China Statistical Yearbook], 2000*. Beijing: Zhongguo Tongji Chubanshe [China Statistics Press].

Guojia Tongji Ju. 2001. *Zhongguo Tongji Nianjian [China Statistical Yearbook], 2001*. Beijing: Zhongguo Tongji Chubanshe [China Statistics Press].

Guowuyuan (The State Council). 2002. 'Guowuyuan Zuochu Guanyu Shenhua Gaige Jiakuai Fazhan Minzu Jiaoyu de Jueding (The State Council Passes Resolution to Deepen Reform and Expedite Developing Minority Education)', *Zhongguo Jiaoyu Bao (China Education Daily)*, 20 August.

Gupta, Akhil. 1998. *Postcolonial Developments: Agriculture in the Making of Modern India*. Durham, NC: Duke University Press.

Gupta, A. 1995. 'Blurred Boundaries – the Discourse of Corruption, the Culture of Politics, and the Imagined State', *American Ethnologist* 22 (2): 375–402.

Habermas, Jürgen. 1994. 'Citizenship and National Identity: Some Reflections on the Future of Europe', in *Citizenship: Critical Concepts*, eds Bryan S. Turner and Peter Hamilton, Vol. 2. London: Routledge, pp. 341–358.

Hansen, Thomas Blom and Finn Stepputat, eds. 2002. *States of Imagination: Ethnographic Explorations of the Post-Colonial State*. Durham, NC: Duke University Press.

Hansen, Thomas Blom and Finn Stepputat. 2002. 'Introduction: States of Imagination', in Thomas Blom Hansen and Finn Stepputat, *States of Imagination:*

Ethnographic Explorations of the Post-Colonial State. Durham, NC: Duke University Press.

Hao, Tiechuang. 2001. 'Dezhi he fazhi shuangguang qixia (Working along both lines of governing country by morality and by law)', in *Fazhi yu dezhi (Governing the Nation by Law and by Morality,* ed. Shanghai Yanhuang Wenhua Yanjiu Hui. 2002. Shanghai: Zhongguo jiancha chuban she, pp. 13–18.

Harrell, Stephen. 1995. 'Introduction: Civilizing Projects and the Reaction to Them', in *Cultural Encounters on China's Ethnic Frontiers,* ed. Stephen Harrell, Seattle, WA: University of Washington Press, pp. 3–36.

Harrison, Henrietta. 2000. *The Making of the Republican Citizen.* London: Oxford University Press.

Harvey, David. 2000. *Spaces of Hope.* Berkeley, CA: University of California Press.

Heater, Derek. 1990. *Citizenship: The Civic Ideal in World History, Politics and Education.* London and New York: Longman.

Herzfeld, Michael. 1997. *Cultural Intimacy: Social Poetics in the Nation-State.* New York and London: Routledge.

Holston, James, ed. 1999. *Cities and Citizenship.* Durham, NC: Duke University Press.

Holston, James and Arjun Appadurai. 1999. 'Introduction: Cities and Citizenship', in *Cities and Citizenship,* ed. James Holston. Durham, NC: Duke University Press.

Honig, Emily. 1992. *Creating Chinese Ethnicity: Subei People in Shanghai, 1850–1980.* New Haven, CT: Yale University Press.

Honig, Emily. 1986. *Sisters and Strangers: Women in Shanghai Cotton Mills* (1919–1949). Stanford, CA: Stanford University Press.

Hooper, Beverley. 2000. 'Globalisation and Resistance in Post-Mao China: The Case of Foreign Consumer Products', *Asian Studies Review* 24 (4): 439–470.

Hu, Angang and Wen, Jun. 2002. 'Shehui Fazhan Youxian: Xibu Minzu Diqu Xin de Zhuigan Zhanlue (Social Development as the Priority: the New Catch-up Strategy in Western Minority Regions)', in *Minzu Zhengce Yanjiu Wencong (1) (Collection of Studies of Minority Policies (1)),* eds Tie Mu'er and Liu Wanqing. Beijing: Minzu Chubanshe (Ethnic Publishing House), pp. 181–203.

Hu Hongzheng and Peng Yun. 2000. 'Not one less', *China Women's News* (1 November), p. 5.

Hyatt, Susan. 2001. 'From Citizen to Volunteer: Neoliberal Governance and the Erasure of Poverty', in *The New Poverty Studies: The Ethnography of Power, Politics, and Impoverished People in the United States,* eds Judith Goode and Jeff Maskovsky. New York: New York University Press.

HZT. 2003a. 2002 Nian Huangnan Zhou Guomin Jingji he Shehui Fazhan Tongji Gongbao (2002 Statistical Communique of National Economy and Social Development in Huangnan Prefecture), in *Huangnan Bao (Huangnan Newspaper),* 15 March.

HZT. (Huangnan Zhou Tongjiju (Huangnan Prefectural Bureau of Statistics)). 2003b. *Huangnan Zangzu Zizhizhou 2002 Nian Guomin Jingji Zhuyao Tongji Zhibiao (Major Statistical Indexes of National Economy in Huangnan Tibetan Autonomous Prefecture 2002),* Huangnan (Qinghai): Huangnan Zhou Tongjiju.

HZT. 2002. *Huangnan Tongji Nianjian (Huangnan Statistical Yearbook) 1999–2001.* Huangnan (Qinghai): Huangnan Zangzu Zizhizhou Tongjiju.

HZT. 1999. *Huangnan Zangzu Zizhizhou Tongji Nianjian (Huangnan Tibetan Autonomous Prefecture Statistical Yearbook) 1978–1998*. Huangnan (Qinghai): Huangnan Zangzu Zizhizhou Tongjiju.

HZZBW (Huangnan Zangzu Zizhizhouzhi Bianzuan Weiyuanhui (The Compiling Committee of Huangnan Tibetan Autonomous Prefecture Annals)). 1999. *Huangnan Zhou Zhi (Huangnan Prefecture Annals)*. Lanzhou: Gansu Renmin Chubanshe (Gansu People Press).

JBB and GMB (Jiaoyu Bu Bangongting, Guojia Minwei Bangongting (General Office of the Ministry of Education, General Office of the State Nationalities Affairs Commission). 1999. 'Guanyu zai Quanguo Zhongxiaoxue Kaizhan Minzu Tuanjie Jiaoyu de Tongzhi (Circular on Developing Educational Activity of Ethnic Unity in Primary and High Schools Nationwide)' (document online). Accessed 26 February 2003. http://www.chin9vedu.net/fagai/99-3_18.htm.

Jiang, Xiangyu. 2001. Shilun yifa zhiguo yu yide zhiguo bingzhong de jige wenti (Several Questions on the Importance of both Governing the Country by law and by Morality). In *Fazhi yu dezhi (Governing the Nation by Law and by Morality)*, ed. Shanghai Yanhuang Wenhua Yanjiu Hui. 2002. Shanghai: Zhongguo jiancha chuban she, pp. 241–50.

Jiang, Zemin. 1992. 'Jiaqiang Ge Minzu Da Tuanjie, Wei Jianshe You Zhongguo Tese de Shehuizhuyi Xieshou Qianjin (Enhance Ethnic Unity, Go Forward Hand in Hand to Build the Socialism with Chinese Characteristics)', in *Zhongguo Gongchandang Guanyu Minzu Wenti de Jiben Guandian he Zhengce (The CCP's Basic Viewpoints and Policies on the Ethnic Question)*, ed. Guojia Minzu Shiwu Weiyuanhui (The State Nationalities Affairs Commission), 2002. Beijing: Minzu Chubanshe (Ethnic Publishing House), pp. 277–294.

Jiaoyu Bu (Ministry of Education). 1983. *Guanyu Zhengque Chuli Shaoshuminzu Diqu Zongjiao Ganrao Xuexiao Jiaoyu Wenti de Yijian (Suggestions on Properly Tackle the Question that Religion Interfere with School Education in Minority Nationality Areas)* (document online). Accessed 3 February 2003. http://www.e56.com.cn/minzu/Nation_Policy/Policy_detail.asp?Nation_Policy_ID=271.

Jiaoyu Bu. 2002. *Guanyu Guanche Shishi 'Zhonghua Renmin Gongheguo Minzu Quyu Zizhifa' Youguan Qingkuang de Huibao (A Report of Implementing 'Law on Minority Region Autonomy of PRC')* (document online). Accessed 15 February 2003. http://www.moe.edu.cn/minority/jianghua/3.htm.

Ji Dangsheng and Zhou Qin. 1995. *State of Mobility of Chinese Population and Management*. Beijing: China Population Press.

Johnson, V., E. Ivan-Smith, G. Gordon, P. Pridmore and P. Scott. 1998. *Stepping Forward, Children and Young People's Participation in the Development Process*. London: Intermediate Technology Publications Ltd.

Kabeer, Naila. 2000. 'Social Exclusion, Poverty and Discrimination: Towards an Analytical Framework', *IDS Bulletin* 31 (4).

Ka Ho Mok. 1997. 'Privatization or marketization: educational development in post-Mao China', in *Tradition, Modernity and Post Modernity in Comparative Education*, eds Vandra Masemann and Anthony Welch. Dordrecht: Kluwer Academic Publishers.

Kam Wing Chan. 1999. 'Internal migration in China: A dualistic approach', in *Internal and International Migration, Chinese Perspective*, eds Frank N. Pieke and Hein Mallee. Richmond, Surrey: Curzon Press.

Kang, Yan. 2001. *Deciphering Shanghai (jiedu shanghai)*. Shanghai: Shanghai People's Publishing House.

Keane, Michael. 2001. 'Redefining Chinese Citizenship', *Economy and Society* 30 (1): 1–17.

Keith M. Lewin and Angela Little with Wang Lu. 1996. 'Access, equity and efficiency, perspectives on the Chinese school system', *China Research Monograph* (6), British Council.

Keith M. Lewin and Wang Ying Jie. 1994. *Implementing Basic education in China: Progress and Prospects in Rich, Poor and National Minority Areas*, IIEP, UNESCO.

Kelsky, Karen. 2001. *Women on the Verge: Japanese Women, Western Dreams*. Durham, NC: Duke University Press.

Kung, Hans. 2002. 'A Global Ethic for a New Global Order', in *Global Citizenship: A Critical Reader*, eds Nigel Dower and John Williams. Edinburgh: Edinburgh University Press, pp. 133–145.

Ku, Hok Bun. 2003. *Moral Politics in a South Chinese Village*. Lanham: Rowman and Littlefield.

Kymlicka, Will and Wayne Norman. 2000. *Citizenship in Diverse Societies*. Oxford: Oxford University Press.

Liang Kan. 2003. 'The Rise of Mao and his Cultural Legacy: The Yan'an Rectification Movement', *Journal of Contemporary China* 12 (34) (February): 225–228.

Li, Buyun and Wu, Yuzhang. 1999. 'The Concept of Citizenship in the People's Republic of China', in *Globalization and Citizenship in the Asia-Pacific*, eds Alastair Davidson and Kathleen Weekley. New York: Macmillan Press, pp. 157–168.

Li, Dezhu. 2000. 'Dangdai Shijie Minzu Wenti de Jiben Tedian he Fazhan Qushi (Basic Features and Development Trends of the Ethnic Question of the Contemporary World), *Minzu Tuanjie (Ethnic Unity)*, 9 and 10 (document online). Accessed 18 February 2003. http://www.56china.com.cn/mztj/9/yi9M2.htm.

Li, Dezhu. 2002. *Zai Quanguo Diwuci Minzujiaoyu Gongzuo Huiyi Shang Zongjie de jianghua (A Summary in the Fifth National Working Conference of Minority Education)* (document online). Accessed 22 February 2003. http://www.moe.edu.cn/minority/jianghua/1.htm.

Li, Peidong. 2001. 'Dezhi gongneng lungang (An Outline for the Function of Governing the Country by Morality)', in *Fazhi yu dezhi (Governing the Nation by Law and by Morality)*, ed. Shanghai Yanhuang Wenhua Yanjiu Hui. 2002. Shanghai: Zhongguo jiancha chuban she, pp. 163–168.

Li Peilin. 1999. 'Economic Transition, Social Transformation and Social Policy Options', in *China: Public Policy Options Towards 21st Century*, ed. Liu Rong-Cang. Social Science Press.

Li, Ruihuan. 2002. 'Daixuyan: Yao Zhongshi Minzu Zongjiao Wenti (We Should Take the Ethnic and Religious Question Seriously)', in *Zhongguo Gongchandang Guanyu Minzu Wenti de Jiben Guandian he Zhengce (The CCP's Basic Viewpoints and Policies on the Ethnic Question)*, ed. Guojia Minzu Shiwu Weiyuanhui (The State Nationalities Affairs Commission). Beijing: Minzu Chubanshe (Ethnic Publishing House), pp. 1–7.

Lishi (Yiwu Jiaoyu Kecheng Biaozhun Shiyan Jiaokeshu), Qi Nianji Shangce (Compulsory Education Curriculum Standard Experimental Textbooks: History for Grade Seven vol. 1). 2001. Beijing: Beijing Shifan Daxue Chubanshe (Beijing Normal University Press).

Li Zhang. 2002. 'Spatiality and Urban Citizenship in Late Socialist China', *Public Culture* 14 (2): 311–334.

Liu Bin. 1999. 'Major Reform is Needed if Investment in Compulsory Education is Guaranteed', *People's Education* No. 5.

Liu Guicai. 2000. 'Analysis of the Reasons and Trends Behind the Recent Fall in Grain Prices in China', *Chinese Rural Economy* 4: 44–48. (in Chinese).

Liu, Huishu. 2002. 'Lun Zhongguo Lujia daode sixiang yu dezhi (A Thought on Confucian Morality and Governing the Country by Morality)', in *Fazhi yu dezhi (Governing the Nation by Law and by Morality)*, ed. Shanghai Yanhuang Wenhua Yanjiu Hui. 2002. Shanghai: Zhongguo jiancha chuban she, pp. 203–210.

Liu Rongcang. 1999. 'The Transformation of China's Economic System and the Redefining of Public Policy', in *China: Options of Public Policy Towards 21st Century*, ed. Liu Rongcang. Social Sciences Press.

Litzinger, Ralph A. 2000. *Other Chinas: The Yao and the Politics of National Belonging*. Durham, NC: Duke University Press.

Louie, Kam. 2002. *Theorising Chinese Masculinity: Society and Gender in China*. Cambridge: Cambridge University Press.

Lu Hanchao. 1999. *Beyond the Neon Lights: Everyday Shanghai in the Early Twentieth Century*. Berkeley, CA: University of California Press.

Lyotard, Jean-Francois. 1988. *The Differend: Phrases in Dispute*. Manchester: Manchester University Press.

Ma, Rong. 2001. *Minzu he Shehui Fazhan (Ethnicity and Social Development)*. Beijing: Minzu Chubanshe (Ethnic Publishing House).

Mackerras, Colin. 1999. 'Religion and the Education of China's Minorities', in *China's National Minority Education: Culture, Schooling, and Development*, ed. Gerard A. Postiglione. New York and London: Falmer Press, pp. 23–54.

Marshall, Thomas Humphrey. 1950. *Citizenship and Social Class*. Cambridge: Cambridge University Press.

Martin, Will. 2001. 'Implications of Reform and WTO Accession for China's Agricultural Policies', *Economics of Transition* 9 (3): 717–742.

Meisner, Maurice. 1977. *Mao's China and After*, New York: The Free Press.

Mi Hong and Ding Yu. 1998. 'Study of the Characteristics of education of migrant children and management strategies', *Southern Population (nanfang renkou)* No. 4.

Ministry of Education. 1998. 'Temporary Methods for education of Migrant Children', *People's Education* 5.

Ministry of Education. 2000. *National Report: Education for All in China*.

Minogue, Kenneth. 1995. 'Two Concepts of Citizenship', in *Citizenship East and West*, eds A. Liebich and Daniel Warner. London: Kegan Paul, pp. 9–22.

Migdal, Joel S. 2001. *State in Society*. Cambridge: Cambridge University Press.

Mishra, Ramesh. 1981. *Society and Social Policy*. London: Macmillan.

Mueggler, Erik. 1998. 'The Poetics of Grief and the Price of Hemp in Southwest China', *Journal of Asian Studies* 57 (4): 979–1008.

Munro, Donald J. 1977. *The Concept of Man in Contemporary China*. Ann Arbor, MI: University of Michigan Press.

Murphy, Rachel. 2004. 'Turning Peasants into Modern Citizens: Population Quality Discourse, Demographic Transition and Primary Education', *China Quarterly* 177 (March): 1–20.

Murphy, Rachel. 2002. *How Migrant Labor Is Changing Rural China*. Cambridge: Cambridge University Press.

Nonini, Donald M. and Aihwa Ong. 1997. 'Introduction: Chinese Transnationalism as an Alternative Modernity', in *Ungrounded Empires: The Cultural Politics of Modern Chinese Transnationalism*, eds Aihwa Ong and Donald Macon Nonini. New York and London: Routledge.

Office of Census of Migrants of Beijing. 1998. *Data of Census of Beijing Migrants of 1997*. Beijing: China Commercial Press.

Office of the Federal Register. 1999. *The Federal Register* 64 (52).

Oi, Jean. 1999. *Rural China Takes Off: Institutional Foundations of Economic Reform*, Berkeley, CA: University of California Press.

Oi, Jean. 1992. 'Fiscal Reform and the Economic Foundations of Local State Corporatism in China', *World Politics* 45: 99–126.

Ong, Aiwah. 2003. *Buddha Is Hiding: Refugees, Citizenship, the New America*. Berkeley, CA: University of California Press.

Ong, Aihwa. 2002. 'Globalization and New Strategies of Ruling in Developing Countries', *Études rurales* 163–164 (July–December): 233–248.

Ong, Aiwah. 1999. *Flexible Citizenship: The Cultural Logics of Transnationality*. Durham, NC: Duke University Press.

Ong, Aiwah. 1997. 'Chinese Modernities: Narratives of Nation and of Capitalism', in *Ungrounded Empires: The Cultural Politics of Modern Chinese Transnationalism*, eds Aihwa Ong and Donald Macon Nonini. New York: Routledge, pp. 171–202.

Ong, Aihwa. 1996. 'Cultural Citizenship as Subject-Making: Immigrants Negotiate Racial and Cultural Boundaries in the United States', *Current Anthropology* 37 (5): 737–762.

Ong, Aihwa and Donald Macon Nonini. 1997. *Ungrounded Empires: The Cultural Politics of Modern Chinese Transnationalism*. New York and London: Routledge.

Orlove, Benjamin S. 1997. *The Allure of the Foreign: Imported Goods in Post-Colonial Latin America*. Ann Arbor, MI: University of Michigan Press.

Peng, Yali. 1996. 'The Politics of Tobacco: Relations Between Farmers and Local Governments in China's Southwest', *The China Journal* 36: 67–82.

Perry, Elizabeth J. 2002. 'From Paris to the Paris of the East – and Back: Workers as Citizens in Modern Shanghai', in *Changing Meanings of Citizenship in Modern China*, eds Merle Goldman and Elizabeth J. Perry. Cambridge, MA and London: Harvard University Press, pp.133–158.

People's Daily, Editorial, 1 Feb 2001.

Perry, Elizabeth J. and Mark Selden. 2000. *Chinese Society: Change, Conflict, and Resistance*. London: Routledge.

Pigg, Stacy Leigh. 1992. 'Inventing Social Categories through Place: Social Representations and Development in Nepal', *Comparative Studies in Society and History* 34 (3) (July): 491–513.

Postiglione, Gerard A. 1999. 'Introduction: State Schooling and Ethnicity in China', in *China's National Minority Education: Culture, Schooling, and Development*, ed. Gerard A. Postiglione. New York and London: Falmer, pp. 3–19.

Postiglione, Gerard A., Zhu Zhiyong and Ben Jiao. 2004. 'From Ethnic Segregation to Impact Integration: State Schooling and Identity Construction for Rural Tibetans', *Asian Ethnicity* 5 (2): 195–217.

Potter, Pitman B. 2003. 'Belief in Control: Regulation of Religion in China', *The China Quarterly* 174: 317–337.

Preston, Rosemary. 1987. 'Education and Migration in Highland Ecuador', *Comparative Education* 23 (2).

Qin Qingwu and Chen Zepu. 2000. 'Debating Strategic Readjustment for the Economic Readjustment of Rural China', *Chinese Rural Economy* 9: 19–23. (in Chinese).

Radcliffe, Sarah A. 2002. 'Imagining the State as Space: Territoriality and the Formation of the State in Ecuador', in *States of Imagination: Ethnographic Explorations of the Post-Colonial State*. Durham, NC: Duke University Press, pp. 123–148.

Ran Tao. 2004. 'Reclaiming the slopes and China's grain for green program', unpublished paper, Contemporary Chinese Studies Programme, Oxford University.

Renmin Ribao Shelun (People's Daily Editorial): 'Jinmi Tuanjie Xinjiao Qunzhong, Gongtong Zhiliyu Jianshe You Zhongguo Tese Shehui Zhuyi de Weida Shiye (Closely Unite Religious People, Jointly Devote to the Great Cause of Building the Socialism with Chinese Characteristics)', *Renmin Ribao (People's Daily)*, 13 December 2001.

Richardson, Robin and Angela Wood. 2000. *Inclusive School and Society*. Stoke-on-Trent: Trentham Books Limited.

Rose, Nikolas. 1996. 'Identity, Genealogy, History', in *Questions of Cultural Identity*, eds Stuart Hall and Paul du Gay. London: Sage, pp. 128–150.

Sangren, P. Steven. 1984. 'Traditional Chinese Corporations: Beyond Kinship', *Journal of Asian studies* 43 (3): 391–415.

Sassen, Saskia. 2002. 'Introduction: Locating Cities on Global Circuits', in *Global Networks, Linked Cities*, ed. Saskia Sassen. New York: Routledge, pp. 1–38.

Sautman, Barry. 1999. 'Expanding Access to Higher Education for China's National Minorities: Policies of Preferential Admissions', in *China's National Minority Education: Culture, Schooling and Development*, ed. Gerard A. Postiglione. London: Falmer Press, pp. 173–210.

Scott, James C. 1999. *Seeing Like a State: How Certain Schemes to Improve the Human Condition Have Failed*. New Haven, CT: Yale University Press.

Scott, James. 1985. *Weapons of the Weak: Everyday Forms of Resistance*. New Haven, CT: Yale University Press.

Scott, James. 1976. *The Moral Economy of the Peasant*. New Haven, CT: Yale University Press, 1976.

Schein, Louisa. 2000. *Minority Rules: The Miao and the Feminine in China's Cultural Politics*. Durham, NC: Duke University Press.

Shafir, Gershon and Yoav Peled. 2002. *Being Israeli: The Dynamics of Multiple Citizenship*. Cambridge: Cambridge University Press.

Shafir, Gershon, ed. 1998. *The Citizenship Debates: A Reader*. Minneapolis, MN: University of Minnesota Press.

Shanghai Yanhuang Wenhua Yanjiu Hui, ed. 2002. *Fazhi yu dezhi (Governing the Nation by Law and by Morality*. Shanghai: Zhongguo jiancha chuban she.

Shen, Hong. 1995. 'Zhongguo Lishi Shang Shaoshu Minzu Renkou de Bianyuanhua – Shaoshu Minzu Pinkun de Lishi Toushi (Marginalization of the Minority Population in the Chinese History – An Historical Perspective of the Poverty of the Minority Population)', *Xibei Minzu Xueyuan Xuebao (Zhexue Shehui Kexue Ban) (Journal of Northwest Minorities Institute (Philosophy and Social Sciences))*, Vol. 2, pp. 53–60.

Shen Zhi and Li Tao eds. 1996. *The Shanghai Labor History (shanghai laogong shi)*. Shanghai: The Shanghai Academy of Social Sciences Press.

Shi, Ning and Wang, Jie, eds. 2002. *Zhongguo gongmin suzhi xunlian 100 lie* (100 examples for Training Chinese Citizens in Quality). Beijing: New World Press.

Shue, Vivienne. 1988. *The Reach of the State: Sketches of the Chinese Body Politic.* Stanford, CA: Stanford University Press.

Smart, Alan. 2003. 'Sharp Edges, Fuzzy Categories and Transborder Networks: Managing and Housing New Arrivals in Hong Kong', *Ethnic and Racial Studies* 26 (2): 218–233.

Smart, Alan and Josephine Smart. 2001. 'Local Citizenship: Welfare Reform, Urban/Rural Status, and Exclusion in China', *Environment and Planning A* 33: 1853–1869.

Smith, Christopher J. 2000. 'The Floating Population in China's Cities: A New Ethnic Underclass?', in *China's Economic Growth The Impact on Regions, Migrants and the Environment*, ed. Terry Cannon. London: Macmillan Press Ltd.

Smith, Rogers M. 1999. *Civic Ideals: Conflicting Visions of Citizenship in U.S. History*. New Haven, CT: Yale University Press.

Solinger, Dorothy. 1999. *Contesting Citizenship in Urban China: Peasant Migrants, the State, and the Logic of the Market*. Berkeley, CA: University of California Press.

Steinberg, Stephen. 1989. *The Ethnic Myth: Race, Ethnicity, and Class in America.* Boston, MA: Beacon Press.

Steinmetz, George. 1999. 'Introduction: Culture and the State', in *State/Culture: State Formation After the Cultural Turn*. Ithaca, NY: Cornell University Press.

Tang, Ming. 2003. 'Zhongguo Xian Jieduan Minzu Maodun de Jingji Yuanyin Fenxi (An Analysis of Economic Causes of Ethnic Conflicts in the Present Stage of China)', in *Zhongguo de Minzu Guanxi he Minzu Fazhan (Ethnic Relations and Ethnic Development in China)*, eds Yu Zhen and Dawa Cairen. Beijing: Minzu Chubanshe (Ethnic Publishing House), pp. 1–38.

Teng Xing et al. 1997. 'Zai Jing Zhong Qingnian Xuezhe Tan Minzu Jiaoyu (Middle-aged and Young Scholars in Bejing Talking About Minority Education)', *Minzu Jiaoyu Yanjiu* (Research of Minority Education), 1 (document online). Accessed on 17 October 2004. http://www.cbe21.com/zhuanti/minzujy/minzujydd/0010.htm.

Teng, Xing and Wang, Jun. 2001. 20 *Shiji Zhongguo Shaoshu Minzu yu Jiaoyu (Chinese Ethnic Minorities and Education in 20 Century)*. Beijing: Minzu Chubanshe (Ethnic Publishing House).

Thøgersen, Stig. 2003. 'Parasites or Civilisers: The Legitimacy of the Chinese Communist Party in Rural Areas', *China: An International Journal* 1 (2) (September): 200–223.

The Economist. 2000. 'China – Misery Behind the Migration', November 18–24, pp. 106–107.

The State Council. 1997. 'Regulations of Social Sector Schools', *People's Education* 9.

Thompson, Neil. 2003. *Promoting Equality, Challenging Discrimination and Oppression*. Basingstoke: Palgrave Macmillan.

Tilly, Charles. 1999. 'Epilogue: Now Where', in *State/Culture: State Formation after the Cultural Turn*, ed. George Steinmetz. Ithaca, NY: Cornell University Press, pp. 407–420.

Torpey, John C. 2000. *The Invention of the Passport: Surveillance, Citizenship and the State*. Cambridge: Cambridge University Press.

Triantafillou, Peter. 2001. 'Governing Agricultural Progress: A Genealogy of the Politics of Pest Control in Malaysia', *Comparative Studies in Society and History* 43 (1): 193–221.

Turner, Bryan. 2001. 'The Erosion of Citizenship', *British Journal of Sociology* 52 (2): 198–209.

Turner, Bryan S. 2000. 'Liberal Citizenship and Cosmopolitan Virtue', in *Citizenship and Democracy in a Global Era*, ed. Andrew Vandenberg. London: Macmillan, pp. 18–32.

Turner, Bryan S. 1994. 'Outline of a Theory of Human Rights', in *Citizenship: Critical Concepts*, eds Bryan S. Turner and Peter Hamilton, Vol. 2. London: Routledge, pp. 461–82.

Turner, Bryan. 1986. *Citizenship and Capitalism*. London: Allen and Unwin.

Turner, Bryan S. and Peter Hamilton, eds. (1994). *Citizenship: Critical Concepts*, Vol. 2. London: Routledge.

TXBW (Tongren Xian Zhi Bianzuan Weiyuanhui (The Compiling Committee of Tongren County Annals)). 2001. *Tongren Xian Zhi (Tongren County Annals)*. Xi'an: Sanqin Chubanshe (Sanqin Press).

Unger, Jonathan. 2002. *The Transformation of Rural China*. Armonk, NY: ME Sharpe.

Veit, Bader. 1997. *Citizenship and Exclusion*, New York: St. Martin's Press, Inc.

Verdery, Katherine. 1996. *What was Socialism, and What Comes Next?* Princeton, NJ: Princeton University Press.

Walder, Andrew G. 1986. *Communist Neo-traditionalism: Work and Authority in Chinese Industry*. Berkeley, CA: University of California Press.

Wang Fei-Ling. 1998. 'Floaters, moonlighters, and the underemployed: a national labor market with Chinese characteristics', *Journal of Contemporary China* 7 (19): 459–475.

Wang Liqun, et al. 1995. *Migrants in Shanghai in the 1990s*. Shanghai: East China Normal University Press.

Wang Lu and Sarah Cook. 2000. 'Interpreting entitlement: local level implementation of China's urban relief program', Social policy research workshop, Shanghai, (July).

Wang Luolin. 1999. 'Preface', in *China: Options of Public Policy Towards 21st Century*, ed. Liu Rongcang. Social Sciences Press.

Wang, Geliu and Chen, Jianyue. 2001. *Minzu Quyu Zizhi Zhidu de Fazhan (Development of the Self-Autonomy System of Ethnic Minority Regions)*. Beijing: Minzu Chubanshe (Ethnic Publishing House).

Wasserstrom, Jeffrey N. 2002. 'Questioning the Modernity of the Model Settlement: Citizenship and Exclusion in Old Shanghai', in Merle Goldman and Elizabeth J. Perry eds *Changing Meanings of Citizenship in Modern China*. Cambridge, MA: Harvard University Press, pp. 110–132.

Watson, James L. 1997. *Golden Arches East: Macdonald's in East Asia*. Stanford, CA: Stanford University Press.

Watson, James L. ed. 1984. *Class and Social Stratification in Post-Revolution China*. London and New York: Cambridge University Press.

Watson, James L. and Patricia Ebrey, eds. 1986. *Kinship Organization in Late Imperial China, 1000–1940*. Berkeley, CA: University of California Press.

Watson, Rubie S. 1996. 'Chinese Bridal Laments: The Claims of a Dutiful Daughter', in *Harmony and Counterpoint: Ritual Music in Chinese Context*, eds Bell Yung, Evelyn Sakakida Rawski and Rubie S. Watson. Stanford, CA: Stanford University Press, pp. 107–129.

Watson, Rubie S., ed. 1994. *Memory, History, and Opposition under State Socialism*. Sante Fe, NM: School of American Research Press.

Wei, Yongzheng. 2001. 'Falü he daode de qubie he lianxi (Distinction and Connections between Law and Morality)', in *Fazhi yu dezhi* (*Governing the Nation by Law and by Morality*), ed. Shanghai Yanhuang Wenhua Yanjiu Hui 2002. Shanghai: Zhongguo jiancha chuban she, pp. 118–121.

Whyte, Hayden. 1987. *The Content of the Form: Narrative, Discourse and Historical Representation*. Baltimore, MD: Johns Hopkins University Press.

Wolf, Eric. 1982. *Europe and the People without History*. Berkeley, CA: University of California Press.

Wolf, Margery. 1972. *Women and the Family in Rural Taiwan*. Stanford, CA: Stanford University Press.

Wolf, Margery. 1985. *Revolution Postponed: Women in Contemporary China*. Stanford, CA: Stanford University Press.

Wong, Christine P.W. 1992. 'Fiscal Reform and Local Industrialisation: The Problems of Sequencing Reform in Post-Mao China', *Modern China* 18: 197–227.

Wong, C.K. and N.S.P. Lee. 2000. 'Popular Belief in State Intervention for Social Protection in China', *Journal of Social Policy* 29: 109–116.

Wu, Bin. 2003. *Sustainable Development in Rural China: Farmer Innovation and Self-Organization in Marginal Areas*. London: RoutledgeCurzon.

Xiang Biao. 1997. 'From *Hukou* Holder Based System to Tax-Payer Based System: Suggestions on Reform of Primary Education System in China' seminar on 'Education of Migrant Children and Policy Responses', Beijing Education Research Center, Education Bureau of Beijing Municipal Government.

Xiang Biao. 1998. 'Education of Migrant Children and Urban Community Management', seminar on 'Education of the Migrant Children in Beijing', China Youth Politics College, Beijing.

Xiang Xianming. 1997. 'Compulsory Education: Concepts, Dimensions and Perspectives in the Context of Demographic Change of Space', *Shanghai Higher Education Studies* No. 6.

Xiao Wentao. 1997. 'Study on Poverty Issues in Social Transition Period in China', *Sociology Research* 5.

Xie, Beijian. 2001. 'Daode, falü yu fanzui (Morality, Law and Crime)', in *Fazhi yu dezhi* (*Governing the Nation by Law and by Morality*), ed. Shanghai Yanhuang Wenhua Yanjiu Hui: 2002. Shanghai: Zhongguo jiancha chuban she. *Xinhua Editorial Daily*, 13 Feb 2001, pp. 169–177.

Xie Weihe. 1997. 'Solving the Education Problems Migrants' Children and Promoting the Reform of Education and Social Development', *Shanghai Higher Education Studies* No. 6.

Xin Liu. 2000. *In One's Own Shadow: An Ethnographic Account of the Condition of Post-reform Rural China*. Berkeley, CA: University of California Press.

Yang Jian and Wu Huaguo. 2000. 'The Jiangxi Provincial Party Secretary Shu Huiguo Discusses the Intervening Problems that Need to be Overcome in Restructuring Agricultural Production', *Liaowang* (Outlook) 17: 64–65. (in Chinese).

Yang Yunyan. 1996. 'The State of Informal Migration in China since the Reform and Open door policy – Analysis based on population census data', *China Social Science* No. 6.

Yin, Li, ed. 2001a. *Jinri shuofa (Legal Report)* [episodes 1999–2000]. Vols 1–4. Beijing: Zhongguo Renmin Public Security University Press.

Yin, Li, ed. 2001b. *Jinri shuofa (Legal Report)* [Episodes 2001]. Vols 1–12. Beijing: Zhongguo Renmin Public Security University Press.

You, Junyi. 2001. 'Xuexi Jiang Zemin tongzhi dezhi sixiang, jianchi fade jiehe de zhiguo zhidao (Study Jiang Zemin's Governing the country by morality, and insist the combination of governing the country by morality and law)', in *Fazhi yu dezhi (Governing the Nation by Law and by Morality)*, ed. Shanghai Yanhuang Wenhua Yanjiu Hui: 2002. Shanghai: Zhongguo jiancha chuban she, pp. 18–35.

Young, Iris Marion. 1998. 'Polity and Group Difference: A Critique of the Ideal of Universal Citizenship', in *The Citizenship Debates: A Reader*, ed. Gershon Shafir. Minneapolis, MN: University of Minnesota Press, pp. 263–290.

Young, Iris Marion. 1990. *Justice and the Politics of Difference*. New Jersey: Princeton University Press.

Yu, Guomin. 2002. *Jiesi chuanmei bianju: Laizi Zhongguo chuanmeiye diyi xianchang de baogao (Deconstructing Media)*. Guangzhou: Nanfang chuban she.

Yuan, Yansheng. 2000. *Speech on the Situation and Development of Tobacco in Rivercounty* (17 page transcript), Rivercounty Tobacco Company, Jiangxi Province, China, 17 November.

Zhang, Li. 2001. *Strangers in the City: Reconfigurations of Space, Power, and Social Networks within China's Floating Population*. Stanford, CA: Stanford University Press.

Zhang Shenhua, et al. 1998. *Current State and Prospects of Shanghai Migrants*. Shanghai: East China Normal University Press.

Zhao Shukai. 2000a. 'Where are their desks? – Study on compulsory education of migrant children in big cities,' in *The selected research report of DRC of the State Council*, eds Ma Hong and Wang Mengkui. Beijing: China Development Press.

Zhao Shukai. 2000b. 'Marginalized Basic Education: Preliminary Study of Migrant Schools in Beijing', *Research Reports of the Development and Research Center, the State Council*, No. 49 (General No. 1227).

Zheng, Dachen. 2002. *Dianshi meiti cehua (TV Media Scheming)*. Beijing: China Broadcasting Publishing. Zhongguo Guojia Tongjiju (National Bureau of Statistics in China). 2000. *Di Wuci Renkou Pucha: Chengxiang Renkou Fenbu (The Fifth Census: Urban and Rural Population Distribution))* (data online). Accessed 20 September 2003. www.stats.gov.cn/detail?record=2&channelid=52984.

Zhou Hao. 2000. 'Research Report on Population Migration and Children', *Save the Children Foundation*, Beijing Office.

Zhou Yongping. 1998. 'Analysis of the State of Schooling for the school age children of migrants in Beijing', *Journal of China Youth Political Academy* No. 2.

Zhongguo Lishi (Jiunian Yiwu Jiaoyu Sannianzhi Chuji Zhongxue Jiaokeshu) Disi Ce (Nine-years' Compulsory Education Three-years' System Junior High School Textbooks: History of China vol. 4). 1995. Beijing: Renmin Jiaoyu Chubanshe (Peoples' Education Press).

ZJXS (Zhongguo Jindai Xiandai Shi, Quanrizhi Putong Gaoji Zhongxue Jiaokeshu *(Full-Time Regular High School Textbooks: Modern and Contemporary History of China))*, vol. 2. 2000. Beijing: Renmin Jiaoyu Chubanshe (Peoples' Education Press).

Zhong Xueping. 1994. 'Male Suffering and Male Desire: The Politics of Reading Half of Man Is Woman by Zhang Xianliang', in *Engendering China: Women, Culture, and the State*, eds Christina Gilmartin, Gail Hershatter, Lisa Rofel and Tyrene White. Cambridge, MA: Harvard University Press, pp. 175–194.

Zhou, Enlai. 1957. 'Guanyu Wo Guo Minzu Zhengce de Jige Wenti (On Several Questions of Our Country's Ethnic Policy)', in *Zhongguo Gongchandang Guanyu Minzu Wenti de Jiben Guandian he Zhengce (The CCP's Basic Viewpoints and Policies on the Ethnic Question)*, ed. Guojia Minzu Shiwu Weiyuanhui (The State Nationalities Affairs Committee), 2002. Beijing: Minzu Chubanshe (Ethnic Publishing House), pp. 233–260.

Zuo Xuejin. 1997. 'China's Fiscal Decentralisation and the Financing of Local Services in Poor Townships', *IDS Bulletin* 28 (1): 80–91.

Index

Agricultural Bureau 16
agricultural diversification 22, 25
AIDS 84
alternative citizenship practices 22
Anagnost, A. 156
Anderson, B. 99, 156–7
Appadurai, A. 156; and Holston, J. 126
Australia 152, 155, 162, 170, 172

Bader, V. 30
Baqiu Township 19
barefoot doctors 107
Bay Bridge: ethnographic examination Shanghai 96–121; gentrification 116–20; granny cadres 103–5; managing the debris of socialism 102–3; textile sisters 110
Beijing: migrant education 31, 32–3; private migrants schools 36–9; rural migrants 28–9, 30, 31
birth planning 18; quotas 14
bound foot police 103–5
Buddhism 55
Bureau of Medicine Inspection 78, 79
bureaucratism 108

cadres 97; citizenship education 13–17; dispositional and technical training 9–25; government control 109; granny 103–5; residential committee 115; three stresses (sanjiang) campaign 13
Chiang, K-S. 91
Chief Officer 120
China Central TV 69, 70, 72
Chinese Citizenship Morality Handbook 93

Chinese Civil Affairs Ministry 102
Chinese Communist Party (CCP) 75, 92, 93, 94, 106, 163
Chinese language education 49
Chinese state 1, 3, 7, 9; as guarantor of rights 21
Chu, Y. 2, 3, 102, 113, 127, 164
Cities and Citizenship (Holston and Appadurai) 126
citizen dilemmas: return to China 164–5
citizenship: showcasing 116–20
citizenship classifications 4
citizenship cultivation: Shanghai 96–101
citizenship dilemmas: margins of societies 160–71
citizenship education: cadres 13–17; farmers 17–23; rural China 9–25; television 70; television documentaries 68–75; three stresses (sanjiang) campaign 13–17
citizenship practices 8
citizenship rights 7
City People's Commune 109
civil law 72
Civil War (1947–9) 100
civilized community: acknowledgement as 117
collectivist security 127
college entrance examinations 51, 56, 61
common morality 89
Communist ideology 70
Communist Land Reform (1945–50) 100
community affairs: Hong Kong 141
community affairs management centre 111

compensation 77
computing 56
Confucian models 5
Confucianism 44, 89, 90, 91
Constable, N. 167
consumer rights 77
contribution: social responsibility 142–3; social work interpretations 146–8
cultivation 19
cultivation of citizenship 96–121
cultural citizenship 2, 42, 130, 158; First World 110; Hong Kong 133; and the poor 105–10; Shanghainese 97; term 126; Tibetan 3
cultural majority 1
Cultural Revolution 168

Dahrendorf, R. 87, 88, 89
Dalian 152, 153, 157
democratic life groups 13
demography 52
Deng, X. 91, 157
District Gazette 101
District Government 106, 107, 119
District Officials: global cultural citizenship 110–13
District Police Station 104
divorce 85
Duan, C. 39

economy: transformation 7
education: and upward mobility 48–50; urban China 27–40
empowerment: social work interpretations 146–8
entrepreneurial activities 112
Erosion of Citizenship (Turner) 140
ethnic citizenship: and Chinese citizenship 41–64; Han/Tibetan citizenship dilemmas 58–63
ethnic minorities: three backwardnesses 43
European citizenship 88

farmers: citizenship education 17–23; dispositional and technical training 9–25
filial obligations 166
filial piety 85
First World citizenship 97; pursuit 156–60
First World societies 6
fiscal decentralization 10

fiscal system 24
flexible citizenship: price 171–3
Fong, V. 2, 129
Foucault, M. 6
French Concession 98, 100, 101
French Revolution 88
Fudan University 111

Gansu 53
gated community 120
Gibson, M.A. 41
global cultural citizenship: District Officials 110–13
globalization 7
Goldman, M.: and Perry, E.J. 126
gongmin (citizens) 90
government mediation 94
granny cadres 103–5, 115
Great Cultural Revolution 55
Guangdong 129
guomin (nationals) 90
Gupta, A. 10

Han 3
Hao, T. 92
Harvey, D. 160
Holston, J.: and Appadurai, A. 126
Hong Kong 1, 11, 89, 163; accepted social and behavioral norms 130; Chinese immigrants 123–48; community affairs 141; concept of improving oneself 133; cultural citizenship and individual responsibility 134–8; family responsibility 138–40; ID cards 128; individual responsibility 134–8; lesser quality immigrants 130; New Arrivals 129; Orientation Tours 127; public housing 143; responsibility to family 138–40; social and cultural citizenship 124, 127; Social Welfare Department 141; social workers and clients' social responsibilities 129–34; social workers and cultural citizenship 123–48; teaching responsibility 123–48; Teenage Mutual Aid Drama Group 134–8; volunteer work 140–6
Hong Kong Departure of Social Welfare 140
household registration (*hukou*) 3, 27, 29, 30
Hu-Wen leadership 25

Huangnan Tibetan autonomous
  prefecture: education and upward
  mobility 48–50; Huangnan High
  School 52, 53, 57, 62; Huangnan
  Minority Senior High 52, 55, 58, 61;
  minority education policy 41–64;
  ordinary and minority school system
  50–5; overview 44–7; social mobility
  opportunities 47–8; students' school
  preferences 55–63

impersonal professionalism 113
Independent Commission against
  Corruption (ICAC) 127, 128, 148
individual responsibility 147
industrialization 107
International Settlement: Shanghai 98
International Women's Day 104
Ireland 152, 155, 158, 163, 169

Japan 152
Jiang, Z. 13, 93, 94, 110
Jiangxi Province 25, 114
jiedu fei: migrant students 31

Kelsky, K. 167

Land Reform 106
Latin America 116
Law Promotion Day 72
legal citizenship 1, 4, 31, 170
legal concepts: local 129
legal consciousness 73, 81
legal culture 73
Legal Report: background 69–73;
  case studies 73–81; and Chinese
  citizenship conceptualizations 87–94;
  Chinese legal culture 73; citizenship
  education via television documentary
  68–95; corruption cases 83;
  documentary style 83–4; female
  crimes and gender difference 80–1;
  narrative formula 86; narrative
  structure 82–7; *Ocean Accident*
  73–7; *Origin of Fake Medicine*
  77–9; representative events/acts/
  agents 84–6; SARS epidemic 72;
  thematics and audience report 86;
  use of interviews 83
legal responsibilities: social and
  cultural citizenship 127–9
legal system 2
Lei, F. 91
Li, B.: and Wu, Y. 89

liberalization: China 131
Lin, Y. 2, 4
local officials 96
Longwu Township 46–7
lower quarters: gentrifying 116–20
lower and upper quarters: Shanghai
  97–101
Lu, H. 99
Luwan District 105–8

Macau 89
manual dexterity 52
Mao, Z. 69, 72, 94, 99, 107, 108
Maoist socialism 109
market economy 9, 85
marriage: to Western citizen 166–9
marriage choice: freedom 106
Marshall, T.H. 126
migrant children: marginality 27–40
migration: marginality of migrant
  children 27–40
Model Communities: Shanghai 115,
  116, 117, 120
modernity 7, 23
moral education 92
mother tongue: importance to Tibetan
  students 56, 58
Murphy, R. 2, 3, 5, 8, 30, 59, 68, 102,
  163
Muslim students 50

nation-state: Chinese view 90
National Bureau of Statistics 158
National Park: Shenzhen 82
nationalism 89
nationality 88
neighborhood committee 112
neighborhood council 113
neighborhood organizations 105;
  professionalization 116
neoliberal transition: rural China
  10–12
neoliberalism 13
New Arrivals: Hong Kong 124, 125,
  127, 129, 138, 165
New China 99
Newendorp, N. 6, 11, 63, 113
Ningjing Fishing Company 74
Nonini, D.N. 172–3; and Ong, A. 157

Ong, A. 6, 124; and Nonini, D.N. 157
open village elections (*haixuan*) 16
Organization Bureau 13, 15, 20
Orientation Tours: Hong Kong 127

Pan, T. 68, 129
Party-state monopoly 13
Party-state policies 12
pastoral care: Asian model 127
patriarchal culture 81
patriotism 163, 171
Pearl River Delta 30
People's Daily 92
Perry, E.J.: and Goldman, M. 126
pharmaceutical market 78
political asylum: Western society
    170–1
political citizenship 161, 164
political education 17
political jargon 113
political propaganda 69
poor: and social and cultural
    citizenship 105–10
private migrant schools 35–9
professionalization programs:
    neighborhood organisation 96,
    110–16
public opinion: and media 79
purchasing power: gap with First
    World 159

Qingdao Ocean Affairs Court 74,
    76
Qinghai Province 44, 45

Redbud Pavilion 118
renmin (people) 90, 91
Renmin Ribao Shelun 42
responsibilities 9; citizenship 126–7
responsibility 135, 136; family
    138–40; social work interpretations
    146–8; teaching 123–48
rights 9
Rivercounty: citizenship education in
    rural China 9–25
Rivercounty Film Company 18
Rivercounty Party Secretary 14, 15
Rivercounty Vocational College 9, 13
robbery 82
Rongcheng Court 75, 76
Rowswell, M. 166
rulers and citizens: relationship 90
rural China: citizenship education
    9–25; neoliberal transition and rigid
    bureaucracy 10–12; social contract
    11

SARS epidemic 72
Sassen, S. 151

Science and Technology Bureau
    Rivercounty 16
scientific cultivation 18
Shaghainese dialect 97
Sham Shui Po district: Hong Kong
    125, 134, 143
Sham Shui Po District Office 133
Shandong 20
Shanghai 4; citizenship cultivation
    96–121; lower and upper quarters
    97–101; Model Communities
    115, 116, 117, 120; showcasing
    citizenship 116–20
Shenzhen 84, 129
Sichuan 53
Singapore 152
small government: and big society
    118
social citizenship 2, 41; and declining
    social rights 113–16; and the poor
    105–10
social contract 11
social and cultural citizenship: legal
    responsibilities 127–9; volunteer
    work 140–6
social mobility 41
social morality 8
social responsibility 143; contribution
    142–3
social rights 24
social transformations 4
social welfare 126
Social Welfare Department: Hong
    Kong 141
social work theories: Western-based
    148
social workers 115; Chinese
    immigrants to Hong Kong 123–48;
    and Hong Kong social and cultural
    citizenship 123–48
Socialist Education Movement 13
socialist legal system 91
socialist morality 93
socialist planning era 12
Society for Community Organization
    (SoCo) 147
socio-economic mobility 58, 62
socioeconomic entitlements 22
Solinger, D. 6
special agricultural taxes: rural China
    10, 12
State Council 91
state enterprises: structural reform
    102

Story of Qiuju (Zhang) 69, 71, 87, 90
Street Office 99, 102, 104, 105, 113, 117
street officers: social and cultural citizenship 105–10, 112, 116, 119
Subei people 98, 101
substantive rights 126–7
Sun, Y-s. 157
suzhi 21, 22

Taiwan 89
technical education 19
Teenage Mutual Aid Drama Group: Hong Kong 134–8
textile sisters 110
three stresses (*sanjiang*) campaign 13–17; education 14–15; inspection teams 14; pedagogy 15, 17
Tibet 8
Tibetan Buddhism 44
Tibetan minority education 41–64; academic outcomes 61; and cultural backwardness 59; discrimination 60; ethnic culture courses 56; ethno-religious customs 56–7; higher education 61; Huangnan Tibetan autonomous prefecture 41–64; importance of mother tongue 56; importance of mother tongue and culture 56, 58, 63–4; ordinary and minority school system comparison 50–5; parental dilemma and school choice 53–5, 60–1, 62, 63; students' preferences 55–8, 61, 62–3; and upward mobility 48–50
Tibetan minority education: higher education 53, 55, 61; importance of mother tongue and culture 53, 58, 61
Tibetology 48
top-down government 12
top-down pedagogy 10
Traffic and Road Safety Drama Competition 134
transnational Chinese youth: childrens' citizenship 170; dilemmas of citizenship 160–71; margins of First World and China 151–73; marriage to Western citizen 166–9, 171; obtaining visas 155; price of flexible citizenship 171–3; pursuit of First World citizenship 156–60; research setting and methods 153–5

Treaty of Westphalia (1648) 88
Tung, C-w. 141
Turner, B. 140

unemployment 108
United Kingdom (UK) 152, 155, 163, 164, 168, 170
United States of America (USA) 157, 161, 170; universities 161
universities: desire to study abroad 161, 162; USA 161
upper and lower quarters: Shanghai 97–101
upward mobility 7
urban Chinese educational system: additional migrant fees 31–3; and migrant children 27–40; migrant children enrollment obstacles 31–3; private migrant schools 35–9; public school discrimination 34–5
urban citizenship 27, 30, 40
urbanization 102

Video Compact Discs (VCDs) 160
Volkswagen Town 118, 120
voluntarism 152
voluntary associations: community-based 119
volunteer work: learning to volunteer mutual help group 141, 144; social and cultural citizenship 140–6

Wang, L. 2, 3, 4, 5, 21, 63
Wei, Y. 92
Western citizenship: desirability 153
Western global citizenship 95
Western imperialism 89
Women's Federation 105, 109
workers' villages 118
World Trade Organization (WTO) 11, 85, 160
Wu, Y.: and Li, B. 89

Xiamen: migrant education 29, 30, 34; private migrants schools 36–9
Xiamen Education Bureau 27
xiaokang (comfortable standard of living) 11, 16, 18, 20
Xu, K. 110

Yin, L. 71
You, J. 92
Yunnan 53

zan zhu fei: migrant students 32
Zang yuwen (Tibetan language and
    literature) 52
ze xiao fei: migrant students 32
Zhang, L. 3–4

Zhang, Y. 68, 87, 90
Zhao, L. 76–7
Zheng, D. 69
Zhou, E. 157
Zhu, R. 110